JAMES A. SANDOS

Converting California

INDIANS AND FRANCISCANS
IN THE MISSIONS

Yale University Press
New Haven &
London

Published with assistance from the Annie Burr Lewis Fund.

Set in Sabon type by Keystone Typesetting, Inc.
Printed in the United States of America by Sheridan Books.

LC Control Number: 2003070398
ISBN: 0-300-10100-7

A catalogue record for this book is available from the British Library.

The paper in this book meets the guidelines for permanence and durability of the Committee on Production Guidelines for Book Longevity of the Council on Library Resources.

10 9 8 7 6 5 4 3 2 1

For Woodrow W. Borah and Sherburne F. Cook

Contents

Acknowledgments

I began working seriously on the California missions in 1984, making the number of intellectual debts to people and repositories far too lengthy to list. I will be selective and ask that anyone not mentioned grant me what may pass for forgiveness. The National Endowment for the Humanities awarded me a Columbian Quincentenary Fellowship (FB-28160-91) permitting me to devote the 1991–1992 academic year to full-time research. Dean Nancy Carrick at the University of Redlands made possible my taking a six-month leave to accept a modest fellowship at the Henry E. Huntington Library in 1999–2000, where I wrote three chapters of this book. She supported my sabbatical request for 2001–2002 to complete it. Without the encouragement I have received in time and money I could never have brought this work to term. Nor could I have completed it without the support of my colleagues in the history department, who graciously dealt with the inconveniences my departures caused.

Over the course of the past two decades I have benefited greatly from ongoing conversations — marked by disagreement as much as agreement — with two people of decidedly different persuasions. Edward D. Castillo (Cahuilla/Luiseño), director of Native American Studies at Sonoma State University, is the first descendant of California mission Indians to subject that historical experience to scholarly criticism. The late Francis F. Guest, O.F.M. (Order of

Friars Minor) spent much of his career trying to justify theologically Franciscan activity in California. I have learned from them both.

Although I began this project twenty years ago, it has its deep background in my graduate work at the University of California at Berkeley. In the early 1970s Woodrow W. Borah, who would become my dissertation director, was involved in an active collaboration with Sherburne F. Cook, and some of Borah's graduate students were involved in aspects of completing finishing details for some of their projects. These included the third volume of their *Essays in Population History,* which addressed the California missions, and later, after his death, the compilation of Cook's essays that became *The Conflict between the California Indians and White Civilization.* The charmingly witty Eric Van Young worked on the former, and the clever Harry E. Cross, with whom I shared a house, labored on the latter. House chat was full of the missions, and on Friday afternoons fellow graduate student José Cuello and I would meet at a local pub and talk for hours about Herbert Eugene Bolton and the Borderlands. Those were heady times indeed.

David Weber through his William P. Clements Center for Southwest Studies at Southern Methodist University has revived study of the Borderlands, something for which all of us in the field are deeply grateful. In a project that David engineered and Ross Frank and Frank de la Téja (affectionately dubbed "los dos Franks") implemented, scholars from Spain, Mexico, and the United States gathered to address the theme of "Social Control on Spain's North American Frontiers: Choice, Persuasion, and Coercion," from 2000 to 2002. I was invited to contribute the essay on Alta California, and my fellow contributors will see the debt that I owe them reflected in my first chapter. Weber's critical reading of this manuscript forced me to clarify arguments and sharpen my prose. It is a much better read because of his attentions.

I will also take this opportunity to say that the recent death of Martin Ridge is a tremendous loss for the community of scholars of the American West and, indeed, for his family, his students, and his readers. He is an exemplar of the highest standards of the history guild. All of us will miss him.

I have tackled several diverse projects since I left graduate school, and when I returned to the California missions my goals were modest. Yet as time continued I could see how much more needed to be done. At one point, however, I considered giving it up. My wife, Tish Sandos, urged me to continue and bring this effort to resolution. I thank her. The staffs of the Bancroft Library, the Huntington Library, the Armacost Library, the Santa Barbara Mission Archive-Library, and the California Historical Society all contributed materials I used in this work. I thank Iris Engstrand for the use of her photographs from the Museo Naval in Madrid and for securing the permission for their use.

Anthony Kirk, Ph.D., who served as my illustrations editor, created captions that complement and enhance my text. Bill Nelson provided the maps, which I think clearly indicate the diversity of the Indian world in which the Franciscans tried to operate.

I conclude by raising a *copita* of *slivovitz* (Woodrow's preferred late afternoon spirit) to Woodrow Borah and Sherburne Cook, distinguished scholars, collaborators, friends, and curmudgeons. And I say to you maestros in the old way, ¡a Dios!

Introduction

"Why yet another book on the California missions?" my colleagues have asked. "Don't we already know all that we need to know?" My reply has been in two parts. Writing about the California missions over the past century has been dominated by two schools of thought: the pro- and anti-Franciscan. David Weber has called the pro-mission school of writing "Christophilic Triumphalist";[1] self-sacrificing priests of the Christian God selflessly devote themselves to bringing spiritual truth and moral uplift to benighted savages.[2] Its opposite has emerged over the past fifty years; missionaries are monsters who committed genocide against native peoples in the name of religion.[3] I have called this latter school "Christophilic Nihilist" or more accurately, "Christophobic Nihilist."[4] Such polarization has prevented any detached analysis of a complex historical phenomenon. Another development has been the emergence both in history and in anthropology of a group of scholars who generally seek to avoid the treatment of religion and have devoted themselves to studies of mission material culture.[5]

In writing about California, the Christophilic Triumphalists and Christophobic Nihilists, as well as the more recent material culture studies, generally have overlooked a significant realm of human historical activity — conversion. With the exception of Francis Guest, a Franciscan studying California,[6] and Ramón Gutiérrez, analyzing New Mexico,[7] scholars have paid scant attention to Franciscan theology and ritual in their missionary enterprise. Triumphalists have criticized the lack of attention to the religious endeavor as evidence of a scholarly bias prompted by anti-Catholicism or by ignorance of the workings of a major institution in the Western world with a two-thousand-year-old history. Triumphalists, however, have offered only an unqualified defense of priestly actions while assuming Indian passivity in the face of Western civilization's "uplift." Nihilists and material culturalists, stressing deeper appreciation of Indian contributions and resistance to the missionaries, have done little to explain the Franciscan side of the interaction. All have taken at face value the specifically Californian priestly calculus that the receipt of the sacrament of Baptism by a pagan, or non-Christian Indian — the act that made the pagan a mission neophyte — automatically made that neophyte a convert.

In other parts of the Spanish empire in the eighteenth century, even as California was being evangelized, missionaries including Franciscans pursued a different course regarding Baptism. Influenced by Enlightenment thinking and crown policy of allowing Indians, in David Weber's words, "to live autonomously beyond the bounds of empire," Spanish missionaries gave their adult catechumens — those studying in preparation for Baptism — periods of instruction lasting up to a year before administering the sacrament.[8] In California, however, the situation was different.

Serra felt impelled to bring Indians to Christ in anticipation of his God's imminent return. In anticipating his assignment to this new mission field he felt obliged to respond to what he described as the call of many thousands of pagan Indians in California for "holy Baptism."[9] These pagans, or gentiles as the Franciscans called them, Serra thought should be instructed quickly and baptized, making them neophytes. By church convention in the New World, abbreviated catechization could be justified in evangelizing a new territory by three circumstances, all of which prevailed in California. If Indians were ill and at the point of death then they could be baptized with family consent. While missionaries were still learning the indigenous languages, various means of communicating the basic ideas of Christianity by sign and symbol would suffice to ready them to receive the sacrament quickly. And perhaps most important from the plan envisioned by Serra, if Indians were to be reduced or congregated (*reducción* or *congregación*) — that is, required to live at the new mission and contribute their labor to its construction — then a brief period of instruction before Baptism was permitted. The bulk of instruction then would come *after* Baptism.[10]

In Alta California (upper, or new, California to distinguish it from Baja, lower, or old California) only lack of religious manpower would permit gentile Indians to live "beyond the bounds of empire." Three years after founding mission San Juan Capistrano, Serra criticized its missionaries for having baptized only 125 Indians. They had proceeded more slowly than satisfied Serra because they invoked the long-standing Franciscan requirements to baptize only the number of Indians the mission could feed. Serra regarded the missionaries' behavior as too cautious and administered a corrective. In his eight-day visit Serra helped them baptize 26 gentiles and departed, telling the missionaries not to stop until they had reached 200.[11] Obviously, the instruction period had been brief. Serra similarly criticized the priests at Santa Clara and San Francisco for using the excuse of lack of food to prevent "accomplishing wonders by way of conversions and baptisms."[12]

In one five-year period Serra and his fellow priests had baptized 2,500 Indians, an average of 500 a year, or more than one a day. In the first five years of evangelization the majority of those baptized had been children; thereafter adults became more significant.[13] And Serra regarded the newly baptized as Christians, as converts.[14] So did his colleagues.[15] Not surprisingly, then, most scholars writing subsequently about the Franciscan enterprise in California, regardless of their viewpoint, have tended to consider baptism as the equivalent of conversion by using the term *convert* synonymously with *neophyte.*[16]

"Baptism equals conversion" is a conventional Christian view that in this case is erroneous. It assumes that both Christians and pagans understood from the outset what conversion entailed, but that assumption seems unwarranted by the evidence. Christianity is a missionary religion with an exclusive claim to truth. When one converts to it, one renounces all other beliefs as false. California Indians lived in a world where truth was multiple. Accepting the ritual of Baptism after eight to thirty days of rote recitation of Christian prayers did not mean Indians expelled other beliefs from their hearts and heads.[17] In the case of one major California Indian group, the Chumash, conversion was a process of some indeterminate length, begun by, rather than concluded by, Baptism.[18] A closer equivalent of the term *neophyte* is *baptized Indian* rather than *Indian convert.*

By equating Baptism with conversion, however, the Franciscans left themselves no alternative but to regard subsequent Indian behavior that violated the Christian standards as sinful. Franciscans mistook evidence of Indian resistance to the mission rule and lack of conversion not for what it was — a failure to adopt Christianity in the ways the priests intended — but for what it was not — evidence of Indian moral turpitude and limited mental ability. In the tension over time between Indian receipt of Baptism and conversion, if conversion happened at all, lies a new story about the California missions. By reexamining the sources, taking into account both Indian and Franciscan worldviews, a new synthesis and interpretation can be achieved.

One way to understand Indian activity in the missions has been through ethnohistory. Ethnohistory combines ethnography — the detailed study of a particular group or tribe — with history, in this case to reveal Indians as actors in the narrative they shared with whites. A corresponding approach to the missionaries would combine theology — the detailed study of one religious group's relationship to their god — with history to demonstrate Franciscans as religiously inspired actors in the past they shared with Indians.[19] A missionary writing to the governor of California regarding difficulties with the Indians in his mission San Francisco, wrote, "I love them very much, because they have caused me great sorrow . . . and ultimately my shattered health. In return and with good will I dedicate what little health I have left and shall expend it to help them." To a modern reader the language could be construed to be that of a masochist; the priest loved the Indians because they hurt him. A nineteenth-century transcriber working for the first modern historian of California, Hubert Howe Bancroft, found the sentence sufficiently troubling to change it. He replaced *porque* (because) with *aunque* (although) completely altering the priest's meaning but making it acceptable to Bancroft's readers. To understand the padre like the governor did, we must understand the theological and christological context of his words.[20] Fervent Franciscans wanted to feel the sufferings of the crucified Christ. For this missionary, working among the Indians of mission San Francisco had helped him to achieve that empathetic co-suffering with his God. He loved the Indians for helping him to be a better Christian. His love also meant that he wanted to control Indian behavior and remold it to fit his Christian expectations. This combination of theology and history I call "theohistory" to complement ethnohistory.

An example of this approach can be found in my analysis of an episode at the founding of mission San Gabriel, which Franciscans regarded as miraculous. On August 6, 1771, two years after the first mission had been founded at San Diego, an expedition of two Franciscans accompanied by ten soldiers and muleteers with a pack-train, stopped along the banks of the Santa Ana River to determine a suitable mission site. The priests, who had arrived together in California five months earlier, were Pedro Cambón, a Spaniard, three years older than his companion and subordinate Ángel Fernández Somera, a native of the province of Michoacán in New Spain. While the Spanish force was exploring, a large group of armed Gabrielino Indians suddenly appeared and approached them shouting threateningly. The priests, fearing an imminent attack, brought out a banner and unfurled its painting to the approaching Indians. The painting depicted the Virgin Mary as Our Lady of Sorrows with swords piercing her heart, the mother who endures the sufferings of her son who was also the Son of God. At the sight of this image, according to Franciscan lore, the Indians threw down their weapons. Their two leaders rushed forward and placed at her feet the beads they had been wearing around their necks and made the priests know that they wished to be at peace with them. These leaders then called together Indians from nearby villages who came in ever increasing numbers of men, women, and children to place various seeds before the image of Our Lady of Sorrows. Mary had conquered peacefully the Indians of San Gabriel.[21]

From an ethnohistoric perspective, this Christian miracle has an Indian explanation. In Gabrielino religious tradition, a virgin gave birth to a child called *Mactutu,* meaning the Son of God who was persecuted by his enemies but promised them that he would rise again three days after his death.[22] The ability of the Franciscans to communicate the story of their image of Our Lady of Sorrows to the Gabrielino resonated with their own Indian religious beliefs—augmented, however, by a visual representation in color. Such a religious affinity provided a potential bond between priests and pagans, and a month later Indians and Spaniards together founded mission San Gabriel on September 8, 1771.

There was another bond between Franciscans and Gabrielinos. Padre Fernández Somera was a native of Michoacán, making him either partially or fully Tarascan Indian; the Gabrielino, therefore, could recognize themselves in him. From the perspective of theohistory, Fernández Somera represented the example of a native clergyman from New Spain, a phenomenon that had developed over the preceding two centuries of Spanish colonization. Cultivation of a native clergy had been seen as an asset in converting new Indians to Christianity because it suggested to pagans that they could, in time, become equal to their Spanish religious teachers. In California, however, Fernández Somera proved unique. Within a year of this incident Father President Junípero Serra, leader of the Franciscans, sent Fernández Somera back to Mexico City for unspecified reasons.[23] Serra decided in 1772 that Indians would remain visibly subordinate to their spiritual fathers, the missionaries. The example of Indian equality with priests, then, would not be part of California's Spanish mission story under Serra.[24]

Theohistory along with ethnohistory reveals a more complex past. It offers a balanced picture of both sides of the frontier of Indian-Spanish contact from the founding of the first mission, San Diego de Alcalá in 1769, to the period when missions lost control of neophytes and land—secularization—about 1836. This combination of theohistory and ethnohistory is intended to put Gods, both Indian and Christian, at the core of this fundamentally religious struggle.[25] Studying Franciscan conversion strategies and Indian responses to them permits reconsideration and reevaluation of the role of ritual, punishment, confession, and other sacraments, along with total immersion of Indians into the mission system, in a missionary attempt to transform Indians into new Catholic-Spanish people.

In the first seven chapters I treat the material chronologically from 1769 to 1836. In the remaining chapters I explore select themes. Following the overview, which addresses the issue of social control, in Chapter 1, Chapters 2 through 7 cover new as well as familiar topics within the contexts framed by combining theohistory and ethnohistory. Serra's medieval worldview and his imprint on the mission system are described in a new way, as are the coping strategies of the Indians whose lives he sought to change. The underappreciated role of venereal disease within the epidemiological struggle in which missionization occurred is highlighted and its impact on the native population described in Chapter 8, and the disease's heretofore unappreciated impact on Indian women is analyzed. Within evangelization priests desired something from their choristers that Indians could turn to their advantage — the individual ability to replicate European sound in song. Mission music, then, as an agent in conversion becomes an important new topic, treated in Chapter 9. Chapter 10 reexamines Indian resistance by detailing Indian strategies for coping with the missions and disclosing Indian options beyond resistance or death. In addition to the violent uprisings, the day-to-day forms of resistance are studied, whether they were adopting sloppy work habits, inscribing graffiti on the church walls, poisoning the priest's soup, or circulating rumors. The culture created by Franciscans and Indians together shows the limits and the accomplishments of missionization.

The summary of the investigation in Chapter 11 concludes by addressing the question: Were the California missions a success? Several perspectives must be considered in the answer, including those of Franciscans, Spanish and Mexican secular officials and settlers, and Indians. The efforts to canonize Junípero Serra, founder of the California missions, raise new questions. Did Franciscans abuse Indians? Did Franciscans commit genocide against them? Were the missions positive models of how a dominant culture should treat a weaker one? Or were they negative examples of what to avoid? More fundamentally, is the question of success or failure the wrong one? Or is it more pertinent to ask how the shared Indian-Franciscan past depicted in this study differs from the mythologized or demonized past commemorated by the "Christophilic Triumphalists" and the "Christophobic Nihilists?"

In this study I use well-established names and terms for Indians so that the general reader can more easily follow the text. These are followed by the more specialized usage:

Datura cult — ʔ*antap*, the Chumash word for *Datura meteloides*
Diegueño — Kumeyaay, formerly Ipai-Tipai
Gabrielino — Kumi·vit
Juaneño — part of the Luiseño
Luiseño — includes Juaneño

California's Missions as Instruments of Social Control

Issues of social control affected all levels of the new Spanish society initiated into what proved to be Spain's last colony in North America, Alta California, in 1769. Both Crown and Cross agreed that Indians as prospective new members of this society would need to be disciplined. But the Crown and the Cross also recognized the need to control Spain's military and clerical elites as well as Alta California's soldiers and settlers of mixed blood. Into the coastal area containing perhaps 65,000 Indians at contact in 1769, the Spanish enterprise introduced a new population of 150. By the end of Spanish rule in 1820 the white and mixed-blood population, the *gente de razón,* counted only 3,400, while the Indian people in the missions, declining largely from European diseases inadvertently introduced, numbered less than 22,000. Just prior to secularization under Mexican governance in 1832, the gente de razón were still fewer than 4,000 and the Indians down to 17,000. During the Spanish era the Franciscans founded twenty missions to congregate and convert the Indians. In the process they occupied a coastal strip that began at San Diego in the south and extended 700 miles north to San Rafael. Under Mexican rule that sought to limit and ultimately disestablish the enterprise, Franciscans could found only one new mission and extended settlement north of San Rafael just to present-day Sonoma. Wherever possible Franciscans sought flatland with a good water source to allow irrigated farming. Mission influence

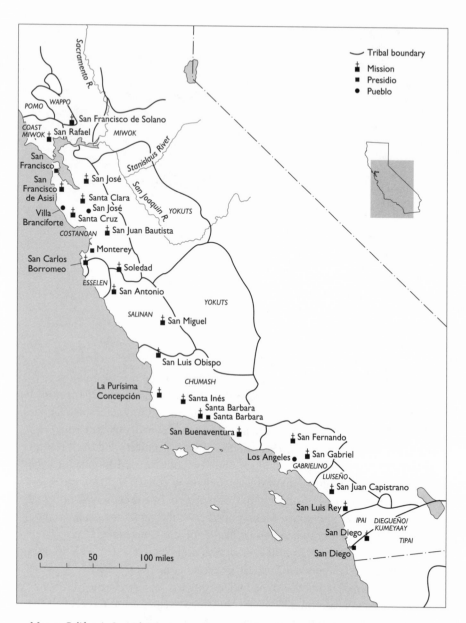

Map 1. California Spanish/Mexican settlements in the mission zone, circa 1823.

extended inland in a meandering pattern to the ridge of the coastal range in the north and center and in the south to the base of the mountains, distances varying between 50 and 150 miles.[1]

Seventeenth-century missionaries had led the effort to extend Spain's dominion over new peoples and territories in a policy based largely upon persuasion rather than military conquest. By the last third of the eighteenth century, however, especially under the impress of the Enlightenment-inspired Bourbon Reforms, the military became dominant in the campaign to subjugate Indians. The regulations of 1772 issued by King Carlos III codified military superiority over the clergy in colonial frontier matters and remained in effect throughout the rest of Spanish rule.[2]

Three years earlier in 1769, however, the Crown had resorted to the older, superseded policy when it chose to occupy Alta California. Perceiving a need to thwart Russian advancement down the California coast the king, through his representative in New Spain, took drastic action. Lacking sufficient numbers of soldiers and settlers to effect a military conquest, a combined force of missionaries and soldiers set out from Baja California to take control of Alta California without colonizing it. This was called the Sacred Expedition, to signify the religious purpose that concealed the political and territorial motivation behind it. The king gave the lead hand to Junípero Serra, first father president of the missions, and the Franciscans. The king had unknowingly given power over California to a man with a medieval worldview, the antithesis and enemy of the Enlightenment thinking that simultaneously supported the Crown while unleashing the forces that would ultimately undo it.

Serra, a Mallorcan missionary with twenty years' experience preaching and administering in New Spain, brought to his task a profound sense of religious determination reinforced by a personal piety that led him to asceticism. Culturally Serra rode the wave of the past, subjecting Indians to strictly enforced religious controls the way peasants had been treated in medieval times. The Crown's abrupt and anomalous backward turn from the path of reform in this instance proved a continuous source of friction between the Sword and the Cross, especially with the military officers who moved from province to province in the northern frontier, enjoyed their power and pride of place, and were reluctant or unwilling to subordinate their authority to the unique situation in Alta California.

Social control at all levels of society merits consideration — social control over soldiers and settlers, men and women, administrators and missionaries along with the Indians they sought to colonize. Social control was achieved not simply by imposing legal constrictions. Social behavior was influenced by moral precepts and by psychological manipulation. Two cases from 1785 — an

Indian conspiracy to oust the Spanish and a new Spanish code of conduct for soldier treatment of Indians—illustrate the limits of social control. Both instances involved Don Pedro Fages and the Franciscans. Serra had succeeded in removing Fages, a member of the Sacred Expedition, from his earlier post as commander of the *presidios* (forts) in 1774. Fages' subsequent distinguished military record, however, won him the governorship and he returned to California a decade later with a more gracious demeanor toward the priests while still insisting on military values in determining colonial rule. The Serra-Fages rivalry reflected the ongoing tension between military/civil and religious authority in the colonial enterprise.

If Fages could not get along with the father president of the California missions, he nevertheless cultivated good relations with several of Serra's subordinates. Chief among them stood Francisco Palóu, Serra's second in command, who was also Serra's former student, religious companion, fellow apostolic missionary, confessor, and longtime friend. After Serra's death, Palóu wrote to his superior that Fages "gave a fine example to those neophytes (baptized Indians) and soldiers. With his conduct and presence much was accomplished. May God reward him for it!"[3] Fages and the Catalán troops he commanded caused no scandal with Indian women, a major accomplishment in the friar's eyes.

Less than eighteen months into his governorship, Fages dealt with the threat of an Indian uprising that raised again the issues of colonial control over subject people. In October 1785, the corporal of the mission guard discovered a plot by eight Gabrielino villages to overthrow mission San Gabriel and expel the Spanish. A powerful shaman had prophesied that when the war party entered the mission complex it would find the armed guard dead, leaving the unarmed priests vulnerable to the warriors who would only need to deal with them and the confused corporal. Once the warriors had removed the remaining Spaniards, she prophesied, they would free the neophytes, divide the spoils of cattle and goods, and return to the old ways. When the Indians penetrated the mission compound to effect their plan, however, instead of finding the prophecies fulfilled they were seized. Four ringleaders were identified, including Nicolás José, a mission neophyte, and three gentiles (unbaptized Indians). All three came from different villages. Two were men, one of whom Fages later accused of using warlock spells or charms against the neophytes; the other was a woman, Toypurina, known for her wisdom, who had come unarmed to exhort the warriors to action. Toypurina, from Jachivit *ranchería* where her brother was headman, had been given beads by Nicolás José to invite people from the surrounding rancherías to join the plot.[4] A high-status Gabrielino woman—as indicated by her personal reputation, her brother's position, and the neophyte's willingness to pay her in the currency of gentiles — Toypurina was obviously the shaman who had claimed to be able to kill the guard at a distance. Her contribution would have allowed the Gabrielinos to restore their pre-Spanish world.

At the trial, over which Fages presided, Nicolás José complained about the priestly prohibition against native dances, something particularly disturbing to him, because he wished to perform a mourning dance for his recently deceased son and could not do so. Nicolás José had been at the mission for about ten years and had been involved in an earlier plot against the priests. He had participated in the worlds of the mission and of his Gabrielino culture and found himself in late 1785 forced to choose between them. He chose to try to restore his Indian world by ousting the Spanish.

Toypurina's interrogation revealed that she, a gentile, was offended by the presence of the priests and of all those at the mission because they occupied her tribal land. Toypurina resented not just the Spanish but also those Indians who had entered the mission and adopted its ways. Fages, at the sentencing, expressed disgust and amazement that warriors had allowed themselves to be dominated by this woman. Nicolás José was sentenced to perpetual banishment at the San Diego presidio, the southernmost military outpost; Toypurina was exiled to Monterey, the northernmost presidio. Fages sent a clear message that such Indian conspiracies to return to the pre–Sacred Expedition status quo would be dealt with severely.

Following the trial Toypurina made a series of choices crucial to her future. She accepted baptism, the outward sign of conversion, adopted the Christian name Regina Josefa, and married a presidio soldier, Manuel Montero, a Spaniard from Puebla.[5] She subsequently bore him four children, then died from European-introduced disease ten years after the plot against San Gabriel.[6] Was Toypurina a victim of colonial domination or was she an insurgent resisting as far as she could the imposition of Christian European culture? Did Toypurina lose or gain in this experience, and what does her example, and that of Nicolás José, indicate about the social control of Indians?

Those who view Toypurina as a model of feminist resistance emphasize her behavior before and during her trial; those who view her case as the triumph of civilization over darkness through the vehicle of religion emphasize her life following baptism. But there is at least one other perspective. The aftermath of the trial meant not only that Toypurina's plan and those of the others had failed but also that she had made enemies among the neophytes by her condemnation of them. She had made enemies among the gentiles because her power had failed and her prophecies were unfulfilled. Even if she could do so, which she could not, remaining in her homeland would be personally dangerous. By accepting the outward sign of the Christian religion she could begin her life anew. Removal to a new land without enemies offered survival and a fresh start. Marriage to a presidial soldier gave her some status in the nascent Hispanic community. The mixed-blood marriage she entered, between herself as a native and the soldier as newcomer and eventual settler, was a model highly desired by the priests but rarely replicated. Hers was one of only two such marriages recorded at missions San Carlos, Santa Clara, and San Juan Bautista in the decade following the San Gabriel plot.[7]

In accepting the Spanish system she saved herself to live a life different from the one she had known. Superficially, she would seem to have been conquered by colonial ideas of social control. For the Franciscans in California, the acceptance of baptism by a pagan Indian represented another body counted in the "spiritual conquest" of the province. The priests wanted baptism to signify conversion, meaning that the preexisting religious belief system of the Indians had been expelled from their hearts and minds in favor of the one truth taught by the missionary. Yet everywhere they saw instances where this had not been the case — as in the example of Nicolás José, who had been Christianized for a decade but still practiced his native religion. The priests saw in his behavior not the failure of baptism to convert but rather the failure of the Indian to live up to his newly adopted standards. Indians were guilty of backsliding, and they fell into behavior that priests identified as sin. The priestly desire that baptism equal conversion was an error as evidenced by their own cradle-to-grave care for their Indian charges. Conversion was a process of some indeterminate length initiated, rather than completed, by baptism.[8]

For Toypurina, then, accepting baptism was a way to begin the process that a social psychologist describes as "protective ingratiation." It is a strategy by which a subordinate assumes the behavior the superior wants in order to minimize or avoid further interference in the subordinate's life.[9] If she converted at all — and Spanish language acquisition among a host of other variables influenced that outcome — Toypurina doubtlessly had not done so at the time of baptism. As a shaman she was a student of power and a seeker of it. In the new order Toypurina seems to have decided that by going along she could get along within the system. Certainly the priests taught California Indians patriarchy, and her husband had been reared under its influence, but in the intimacy of her marriage patriarchy's impact upon Toypurina's life is hard to know. Since she had resisted as a gentile in her Christian life she may well have continued a less visible resistance. Despite the appearances of acceptance of Christian life there is no reason to think that the boundaries of social control as applied to Indians and to Indian women had defeated her. She had negotiated another course of action. Such behavior by California Indians, and by

Indians elsewhere, whether shaman or layperson, is often difficult to comprehend. As defined, Indians must defend Indianness, usually some cultural essentialism, against the onslaught of externally induced cultural change; Indian failure to do so then becomes the secular equivalent of backsliding. Yet instances abound of Indians seemingly changing patterns in their lives in order to continue them, a pragmatic survival option that permitted them to closet the behavior of yesterday in favor of living tomorrow. Toypurina's case illustrates the ambiguities inherent in social control. To some degree behavior can be modified, but securing the assent of mind and heart is difficult to determine.

After sentencing the plotters against mission San Gabriel, Fages turned his attention to prescribing a new code of conduct toward Indians. He addressed the new issue of gentile presence in mission communities, while simultaneously reinforcing existing standards of behavior toward native peoples. Fages had been among those admonished by Governor Gaspar de Portolá in the founding of the colony in 1769, and Portolá's instructions were those of Inspector General José de Gálvez. In unequivocal terms Gálvez told the governor to ensure that "the soldiers and muleteers of his company observe a most exact discipline." The governor must make them understand "as an inviolable regulation the need for treating the Indians well and he shall punish them as for an irremissible crime any molestations or violence toward the native women for, besides being offenses against God which they would commit by such excesses, they could also endanger the success of the expedition."[10] Fages and his Catalonian Volunteers took these admonitions to heart as Palóu's description of them confirms. But the Catalonians, numbering about twenty-five, constituted only a small portion of the soldiers in California, a number that exceeded 200 only late in the colonial era. The remaining soldiers were recruited from the lowest class, and their behavior proved very difficult to control. Sexual abuse of Indian women, including rape, became a serious problem. Priests and officers protested it, but disciplining soldiers with public floggings, banishment, or death became a serious problem for the military. Officers feared that such actions would make Spanish rule appear weak and encourage Indian resistance. Even incarceration, the customary punishment, could leave military posts more lightly staffed. In the 1790 enumeration, for example, two of the six soldiers assigned to mission San Gabriel were in prison for sexual crimes against or with Indian women. The social control of soldiers, especially with women Indians, proved a difficult challenge for Spanish authority. But it would be incorrect to assert, as one historian has done, that the Spanish condoned an informal policy of allowing the rape of Indian women in order to control Indian society.[11] As Gálvez had noted from the beginning of Spanish settlement, instead of conquering native society, Spanish rape of indigenous women would provoke native resistance and thwart imperial goals of social control.

The central object of social control was the Indian. Mission Indians — neophytes — constituted the core of the colony. They were the work force upon which all else was built. Creating that human base was the task of the Franciscans, who sought to persuade gardeners and hunter-gatherers to abandon coastal plains and forests to become sedentary farmers and pastoralists in a new life at the missions. Those who remained in their native state, the gentiles, offered an alternative to mission ways and a refuge for mission runaways. Consequently, tensions developed between neophytes and gentiles. Over time the gentile villages nearest the missions declined as their members succumbed either to disease or to priestly blandishments, and priests had to move farther inland to find recruits.

Inside the mission compound priests had extraordinary power. By 1773, Serra had secured a viceregal decree recognizing that baptized Indians and those being catechized were under the protection of the priests, meaning that Franciscans had the power over mission Indians of conservator to ward or patriarchal father to his children. Priests employed the immersion system of conversion by taking complete control of their wards' lives from cradle to grave. Franciscans directed their charges in the ways of religion and work; two activities united by the European sense of time embodied in the sundial and translated into measured activity by the bell. Everything had its appropriate daily time — breakfast, religious instruction, participation in the daily Mass, morning work, noontime prayer and meal, afternoon work, choir practice for some and catechism for others, dinner, evening activities, bed. At bedtime unmarried Indian women over seven years of age were locked down in a single dormitory (*monjerío*) under the supervision of an elderly Indian woman and released only at morning. At some missions the boys were also sequestered. Both practices derived from the Franciscan views that sex happened only at night and that Indian girls, like their European superiors, must save their chastity until marriage in order to bring honor to their husbands.

In the new Spanish material culture, which also incorporated some earlier Indian practices, Indian women ground corn, prepared meals, supervised children, wove woolen thread on looms, helped with grain threshing, and hauled wood and water. In religious culture women, like men, were to learn beyond the catechism in the daily experience of the Mass. The Mass was participatory for Indians as they prayed aloud, sang responses, and listened to or were part of Indian choirs joining together with Franciscan priests in the symbolic re-creation of the Last Supper of Christ.

Figure 1. The mission compound of San Carlos Borromeo in 1794, as depicted in an engraving based on a drawing by John Sykes, a young master's mate on George Vancouver's 'round the world expedition. The earliest published image of a California mission, it shows the stone walls of the seventh and present-day church rising on the far side of the courtyard, behind the towering foundation cross. Living quarters, workshops, and storerooms form other sections of the quadrangle; in the distance can be seen the Indian *ranchería*. Within the mission compound the Franciscans exercised a well-intentioned spiritual and secular despotism, as they sought to mold native converts into a Hispanic community of Christian farmers and artisans. From George Vancouver, *A Voyage of Discovery*, 1798. Courtesy California Historical Society, FN-30519.

Priests organized their communities hierarchically, replicating part of Spanish society, so that Indians could learn their place in this complex order. In this hierarchy priests placed men in one of four groups according to occupation. First were the *skilled artisans* consisting of masons, carpenters, blacksmiths, cobblers, saddle-makers, cart-makers, weavers, plasterers, and tanners. Second came *fishermen, stockmen, and herdsmen,* who were also carters, tallow workers, hide cleaners, meat curers, butchers, and cowboys (*vaqueros*), as well as Indian auxiliaries used to return mission runaways. Third were the *horticulturists* who tended gardens along with mission vineyards and orchards, planting, pruning, and collecting materials weekly if not daily. They usually kept poultry and pigeons. And fourth were *the laborers and field hands* who made adobe tiles for building, cleared and plowed the fields, planted cereal crops, and harvested them. Children frequently weeded gardens and served the padres' table as pages. When needed, everyone helped with harvest. Within the mission compound priests created a new Indian elite group, the choir, the ability to join depending solely upon the ability to replicate European sound in song. These all-male groups in California eventually had their own uniforms to distinguish them from nonchoristers and they generally held better jobs, closer to the priests. They also learned Spanish well and formed an important bonding unit between priest and congregation.

To effect the division of labor and to instill correct behavior in Indians, priests employed several instruments of social control at their missions. The *escolta*, or mission guard, usually comprising six soldiers and their families, represented Spanish military power, while also reinforcing the proper mode of family life. A mayor domo, a retired military man and his family, helped to oversee daily life. To punish the disobedient, priests had the power to have Indians flogged,[12] shackled in irons, or placed in wooden stocks. Those who carried out such orders and who assisted the mayor domo were *alcaldes*, Indian officials. But the veiled threats of the soldiers or the routine use of punishments were only external corrective devices. In seeking to remake the Indian from within, the priests had other techniques. To persuade the Indian to accept personal responsibility for his behavior, the priest needed to replace the indigenous sense of shame with the Judeo-Christian concept of guilt. Thus external and internal corrections were supposed to accomplish the Indians' conversion and pacification that Franciscans and Spanish authorities sought.

Although the Sacred Expedition had been sent in 1769 to forestall a permanent Russian incursion into California, the Russians did arrive eventually. In 1811 about eighteen miles north of Bodega Bay, they established a colony called Rus, an ancient name for Russia, translated into English as Ross. The Russian-American Fur Company, which organized the colony, pursued two ventures in California: taking sea otter and other fur-bearing marine mammals for the international trade in their pelts, and planting and harvesting of foodstuffs (made possible in the warmer climate) to feed their Alaskan outposts. Although the Russian colony lasted only thirty years and was not a religious enterprise, the Russian errand in the California wilderness threatened Spanish ideas of social control, especially control of Indians.[13]

To begin with, the Russians scoffed at the notion of Spanish sovereignty over California, deriving as it did from late fifteenth-century treaties between the papacy and the crowns of Spain and Portugal. The supposed Spanish right meant that Indians were squatters on their own land. That principle the Russians rejected by negotiating a treaty with the Pomo to lease their land and to trade with the Pomo for their labor to build the stockade that would surround it and to clear and plant the fields that would produce foodstuffs. The Russian practice of treating the Indians as near equals did not suit Spanish sensibilities.

The Spanish and later Mexican missionaries and settlers, however, could not exist without the clandestine trade with Ross for the European goods demanded by them to continue their operations and which the mother country could not supply. Trade meant contact and knowledge of another European power's ways. To one foreign observer it seemed that the Indians at Ross fared better than did their missionized brethren to the south. According to Otto von Kotzebue, "The inhabitants of Ross live in the greatest concord with the Indians who repair, in considerable numbers, to the fortress, and work as day laborers, for wages. At night they generally remain outside the palisade." Kotzebue continued, "They willingly give their daughters in marriage to Russians and Aleutians; and from these unions ties of relationship have arisen which strengthen the good understanding between them."[14] Spanish and Mexican settlers worried that Russian treatment of Indians at Ross set a potentially dangerous example for mission Indians.

The primary purpose of the Franciscans in the missions was to mold good Christians. Their secondary aim was to mold as well a labor force to occupy the bottom social rung of the town each mission was to become. Secular interests valued the secondary goal above the Franciscans' primary objective, and nowhere was that conflict clearer than in the struggle over mission secularization or the cessation of priestly rule. Missions were supposed to be temporary, and beginning in the early seventeenth century newly baptized Indians were exempted from paying tribute to the Crown and tithes to the church for the first ten years following receipt of the sacrament.[15] To facilitate evangelization the Hapsburg Crown not only waived its tribute revenue but also paid missionaries for their efforts to offset their loss of tithe income. Bourbon Crown reformers in the eighteenth century, however, sought to increase royal revenues and viewed with concern the loss of revenue combined with financial outlay that missions entailed. While many missions had been secularized over the years, many more continued in mission status, and Indians still enjoyed the exemptions from tribute and tithe more than one hundred and twenty years after their missions had been founded. Bourbons sought to change that situation. Reformers pushed to accelerate mission secularization, and a 1749 law reflected a new, formalized royal policy that missions were to become *doctrinas,* the beginning of Indian parishes, ten years after their founding.[16]

In theory, but rarely in practice, missions were to become pueblos in about ten years. At that time, the vast amount of land originally given to the Franciscans in trust for their charges — generally more than 22 square leagues, or about 100,000 acres—was to be divided unequally.[17] Franciscan holdings, serving as the parish for the new town, would be reduced to the church building, living quarters of the friars, and some adjacent land.[18] The Indians were to receive all the lands the padres had held for them, and they could sell some of it to the Spanish settlers in the colony. The settlers envisioned a different scenario, one in which the Indians would be given small plots for subsistence around the former mission. The remaining mission land, about 97,000 acres, the civil government would give to the settlers and soldiers for whom the emancipated Indians would work. Despite the civil government's success in creating Indian offices, such as *alcaldes,* Franciscans denied that their charges were morally prepared for pueblo life and successfully prevented secularization during the Spanish period.

Franciscans themselves were subject to social control. As priests, they were expected to lead virtuous and celibate lives. As apostolic missionaries, they were dedicated to bringing their spiritual message to difficult areas and to work among potentially dangerous people. The apostolic college of San Fernando in Mexico City sent 125 missionaries to Alta California in the Spanish era. Even for men accustomed to hardship, the physical and psychological challenges of work in California proved daunting. Although legally obligated to stay for ten years, fifty-seven served less than that while a near equal number, fifty-eight, died at their missions. In the words of one Franciscan historian the preponderance of missionaries "might be classed as men of ordinary ability, zeal, learning and virtue." Compared to Franciscan behavior in New Mexico where sexual dalliance was common,[19] California missionaries, influenced by Serra's stern orders and example, lived conspicuously celibate lives. An examination of the fourteen missionaries who served at mission San Fernando is illustrative. Nine were classed as ordinary, two possessed superior virtue, one was a scholar, one an alcoholic, and one a womanizer. The alcoholic had been relieved at two previous missions before being sent from San Fernando to San Diego, where he eventually recovered his sobriety under the tutelage of the senior missionary.[20] No mention of Franciscan abuse of Indians by their biographer, however, does not mean that it did not occur. Civil records of Indian and military complaints abound with such charges. Priests and Indians negotiated social control at the twenty-one Franciscan missions—at times in apparent harmony, at other times in discord—as Indians converted, resisted, or practiced a form of protective ingratiation to get through another day; and priests tried to battle boredom, loneliness, and deprivation while trying to accomplish an enormous task.

The relatively peaceful negotiation of social control permitted the rise of seemingly successful mission establishments that produced surplus harvests to feed presidios and pueblos. Individual mission neophyte populations numbering from several hundred to nearly three thousand performed all work. Throughout the Spanish era, priests recognized that missionized Indians lived shorter lives than their gentile counterparts. Although the Franciscans could not accurately quantify the phenomenon, historical demography indicates that from 1771 to 1820 the mean annual birthrate stood at forty-one per thousand, the death rate at seventy-eight per thousand. Deaths exceeded births by thirty-seven per thousand. In the first decade under Mexican rule the figures worsened. From 1821 to 1830 the mean annual birthrate stood at thirty-three per thousand, the death rate at seventy-seven per thousand, meaning that deaths exceeded births by forty-four per thousand.[21] Such numbers indicate a crisis state for a population, and priests knew well that without active gentile recruitment deeper into the interior, the missions, no matter how prosperous in land, crops, and cattle, would fail. When New Spain achieved its independence as Mexico in 1821, the political leadership of the new country was divided over the fate of the California neophytes and the Franciscan missions. After fifteen years of internal debate an Enlightenment-influenced government ended in 1836 the work Serra had begun sixty-seven years earlier.

The Liberal Mexican government at the time complimented itself on its forward thinking and its decided break with the past. The remaining mission buildings generally and gradually fell prey to looters and the erosions of time. Mission ruins as artifacts and newly told histories became the subject of myths which Americans, following their conquest of California, wove about the past before their arrival. That general story portrayed valiant Franciscans laboring to upgrade a disordered if not depraved array of wild but generally peaceable Indians. By employing the methods of ethnohistory and theohistory, however, an attempt can be made to recognize both Indian and Franciscan worldviews, permitting this episode of human interaction to be more carefully assessed.

2

Indians at Contact

Although Spanish contact with California Indians began with the voyage of Juan Rodríguez Cabrillo in 1542, sustained interaction did not begin until two centuries later with the arrival of the Sacred Expedition in 1769. Given Spanish intentions to incorporate Indians into their society as laboring Christian subjects, as a new *peón* class that would help secure Spanish-claimed territory against foreign interlopers, contact inevitably meant conflict. Through the vehicle of religion these native peoples were to be brought into a new order and common culture not of their making. Missionaries cared not what Indians thought about religion because it seemed self-evident to Franciscans that without Christianity the Indians lacked "true" religion and lived in spiritual darkness misguided by superstition. Because the Indians except at San Diego proved peaceful compared to other native peoples Franciscans had encountered in New Spain, Sonora, Texas, and New Mexico, the missionaries seriously underestimated the challenge before them. An examination of the religious and cultural practices of the missionized tribes at contact, with a focus on conflict points with Franciscan Christianity, reveals the variety and sophistication of Indian worldviews as well as their ability to resist European pressure to change.

In 1769 an estimated 310,000 Indians inhabited the land now encompassed by the state of California with approximately 65,000, or 20 percent, of these living in or immediately adjacent to the coastal strip from San Diego to north of San Francisco, the area of mission influence.[1] Indians had been living in the region for 15,000 years and had been, in large part, migrants from elsewhere as their language families suggest. The Uto-Aztecan stock, for example, designates speakers from Mexico to Arizona. Those who moved into California spoke mutually unintelligible languages and belonged to Indian groups the Spaniards named for the missions to which they were attached: Luiseño (mission San Luis Rey), Juaneño (mission San Juan Capistrano), Gabrielino (mission San Gabriel), and Fernandeño (mission San Fernando). On either side of the Uto-Aztecan stock were those from the Hokan stock, with the Yuman family represented by the Diegueño (mission San Diego) language of the Kumeyaay and by the Chumashan family north of the Fernandeño. Mutually unintelligible dialects of Chumash were spoken at each of the missions in their territory and were designated as Ventureño (mission San Buenaventura), Barbareño (mission Santa Barbara), Ynezeño (mission Santa Ynés), Purismeño (mission La Purísima Concepción), and Obispeño (mission San Luis Obispo). Above the Obispeño and still from Hokan stock were the mutually intelligible dialects of Salinan called Migueleño (mission San Miguel) and Antoniaño (mission San Antonio). Other languages were spoken above Antoniaño but were designated differently such as Costanoan for many of the coastal inhabitants who belonged to the Utian family and the individual languages of the Indians of the central valley who spoke various languages of the Yokutsian family of Penutian stock.[2] In the greater San Francisco Bay Area, from Sonoma to San Antonio, for example, Indians at contact spoke dialects of five mutually unintelligible languages; in twenty years two more such languages were added as the missionaries extended their recruitment efforts affecting ninety-six tribes and villages.[3]

Altogether, six linguistic stocks encompassed sixty-four to eighty different, mutually unintelligible languages further subdivided into dialects, many of which were also mutually unintelligible. This prolific and baffling diversity reinforced the sense of Indian tribal identification through shared speech; outsiders spoke differently. California proved one of the most linguistically diverse regions in the world, and the missionaries soon found that the Indians they had brought from Baja to serve as interpreters were useless beyond San Diego. To Franciscans California must have seemed like Babel.

Franciscans as outsiders would have to learn the baffling array of native tongues of those they sought to evangelize. Yet the time of instruction—actually rote recitation of prayers—before baptizing an Indian into the new faith ran from eight to thirty days,[4] scarcely sufficient time to accomplish the task, especially in the years before the priests had learned the native languages.

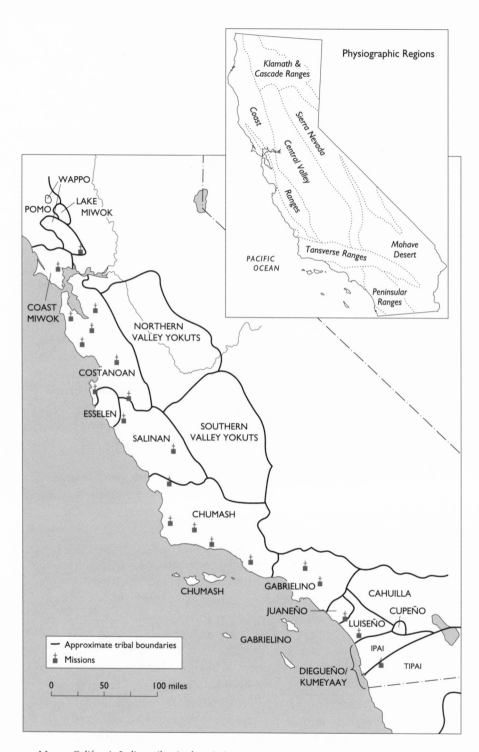

Map 2. California Indian tribes in the mission zone.

Despite the diversity of languages, however, Franciscans thought they recognized shared traits among the Indians—almost all of them unacceptable from a European perspective—such as laziness, sexual promiscuity, lying, and gambling. Despite this language separation most California Indian tribes shared similar attitudes toward the self and power. These shared values had profound impact on the process of conversion and also provided common ground for regional resistance, as in the Toypurina revolt.

In concentrating on imparting a prescribed doctrine to their potential converts Franciscans overlooked an important aspect of how Indians used their languages to describe themselves, a concept that underscored the difference between the native and the European worlds. For example, European notions of left and right, commonplace since the fourteenth century, both as directions and as locations for parts of the body, did not correspond to how Indians identified geography or parts of themselves. Orientation of the individual to the geography of place rather than an abstract sense of direction informed most Indian descriptions. Some California Indian languages did not mention left and right but noted instead directions such as east of the village or the west hand. When an Indian traveled up a river away from his village, for example, then the hills might be to the east and the river to the west. Upon returning to his village the hills would be to the west and the river to the east. If on the journey out an insect had bitten him on his east arm then on the return he would be scratching the itch on his west arm.[5] The geography invariably remained fixed while the Indian altered his orientation to it by his movement. The landform preexisted the Indian and doubtless would outlast him so it, not he, became the reckoning point. Humankind was part of the world, not superior to it. Thus Indians located geographic features relative to themselves in their descriptions of their journeys through the natural world instead of placing themselves in the center of activity and relegating landforms to an inanimate realm inferior and somehow subordinate to humankind.

Indians, moreover, described themselves as part of a group, a family, clan, or tribe and had few words with which to describe the individual apart from the larger relationship. This merging of the individual with the group, a fusion of part and whole, where a personal violation of cultural standards was repaired collectively ran counter to the missionary objective of instilling individual accountability for sinful behavior through guilt. To succeed in their goals missionaries had to detach Indians from their sense of community identification and reorient them to a cultural geography in which they were the center of determining proper conduct and ritual behavior. To convert the Indians would be to transform them, a process that one father president called "denaturalizing" them.[6] The meaning of that process of denaturalization has been described succinctly by one historian:

HOKAN STOCK
1. Pomoam Family
2. *Yuman Family*
   California group
      2a. Northern Diegueño
      Southern Diegueño subgroup (ipai)
      2b. Southern Diegueño (tipai) language
      2c. Kumeyaay language
3. Chumashan Family
   Island Chumash group
      3a. Roseño Chumash language
      3b. Cruzeño-Chumash language
      3c. Cuyama (Chumash language?)
   Northern Chumash group
      3d. Northern (Obispeño) Chumash language
   Central Chumash group
      3e. Purismeño Chumash language
      3f. Ynezeño Chumash language
      3g. Barbareño Chumash language
      3h. Ventureño Chumash language
      3i. Emigdiano Chumash language
4. Esselen language
5. Salinan language (or family?)
      5a. Antoniaño dialect or language
      5b. Migueleño dialect or language

YUKIAN STOCK
6. Wappo language

PENUTIAN
7. Utian Family
   Miwokan subfamily
   Western division
      7a. Lake Miwok language
      7b. Coast Miwok language
   Miwokan subfamily
   Eestern division
      7c. Saclan (Bay Miwok) language
   Costanoan (Ohlonean) subfamily
   Northern division
      7d. Ramaytush (San Francisco) Costanoan language
      7e. Tamyen (Santa Clara) Costanoan language
      7f. Chochenyo (East Bay) Costanoan language
      7g. Awaswas (Santa Cruz) Costanoan language
      7h. Southern Marin Costanoan (existence uncertain)
   Southern division
      7i. Chalon (Soledad) Costanoan language
      7j. Rumsen (San Carlos) Costanoan language
      7k. Mutsun (San Juan Bautista) Costanoan language
8. Yokutsan Family
   Foothill division
      8a. Buena Vista Yokuts language or group
      8b. Poso Creek Yokuts language or group
   Valley division
      8c. Northern Valley Yokuts language or group
      8d. Southern Valley Yokuts language or group

UTO-AZTECAN FAMILY
9,Takic Subfamily
   Cupan group
      9a. Luiseño-Juaneño language
      9b. Luiseño dialect
      9c. Juaneño dialect
   Gabrielino-Fernandeño group
      9d. Fernandeño language or dialect
      9e. Gabrielino language or dialect

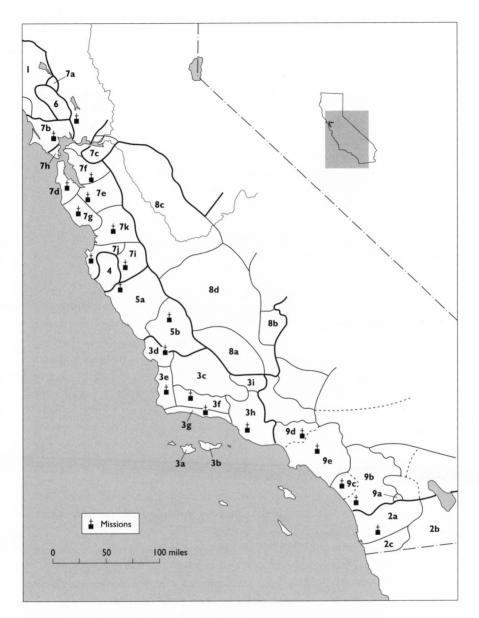

Map 3. California Indian languages in the mission zone.

Christian conversion required the native to accept both intellectual abstrac-
tions and psychological distancing alien to the Indian's sense of himself in
relation to others. For many spirits — friends, enemies, grandmothers, grand-
fathers, mothers, sisters, and brothers — substitute a single, exclusive, distant,
perpetually invisible, patriarchal God; for animal friends, enemies, and relatives, substitute animals as distinct and subordinate species; for a common
afterlife to which most relatives' spirits might make the final journey, substitute a final segregation between converted kin who go to heaven, and the
unconverted who go to hell. For visible violations of correct standards of
conduct, remediable by ceremonies that restore the individual's proper relations with his community and its guardian spirits — here and now — substitute
innate sinfulness and perhaps irremediable depravity.[7]

Franciscans undertook a challenging task in trying to transform the Indian
gentile into a Christian neophyte and Spanish subject, a task that demanded of
the Indian fundamental and thoroughgoing personal change.

Indian concepts of power, virtually undetected by their missionaries, provided
what in modern terminology would be called an alternate universe offering
spiritual and nonspiritual support in coping with the Christian God and in
reconciling European spiritual teachings and Spanish colonial imposition with
Indian lifeways. The Luiseño had the most elaborately articulated idea of
power that survived colonization and even an outline of its tenets suggests
how other groups viewed power in their lives. In Luiseño *ayelkwi* can be
roughly translated as "knowledge-power" meaning that the two were fused;
having knowledge meant having power and so knowledge became privileged.[8]
Ayelkwi had to be used in carefully prescribed ways and for a culturally determined appropriate end. Misuse of ayelkwi brought misfortune upon the user
such as accident, disease, or death. Because the world was an uncertain place
ayelkwi could not always be applied in a controlled manner, and its source
contributed to that uncertainty.

Ayelkwi came from several sources. Luiseño common knowledge, the lore
that belonged to them and not to other tribes, was available to all and thus was
the weakest form of ayelkwi. Inherited knowledge-power was passed down
from generation to generation, usually by males, and those who possessed it
were secretive. They sang their songs or danced at the important ritual ceremonies and in their acts released their knowledge-power for the good of the
tribe, but they closely guarded their displays of ayelkwi lest their songs or
dances be learned and stolen by another. Common and inherited ayelkwi
could be controlled. Two other types could not be. The knowledge-power that
each individual possessed could make that person exceptionally powerful.

Uncertain paternity, meaning that an individual might have been fathered by a shaman or a wizard, suggested that even a low-status person could possess amazing power. Thus no one knew with certainty the power potential of another. The final source of ayelkwi was residual, that knowledge-power that had been thrown away by the dying culture hero Wiyot as he wandered from village (*ranchería*) to village before he died, leaving it in virtually every part of the Luiseño environment. This unknown residual ayelkwi potentially could be obtained and used by anyone. Thus a prudent Luiseño watched all people carefully and maintained a respectful attitude toward others for fear that the other possessed more formidable ayelkwi and could use it to the observer's detriment.[9] The combinations of secrecy and fear that accompanied a careful appreciation of ayelkwi gave the Luiseño sophisticated tools for strategizing their relationship to the missions.

Franciscans established the first of two missions in Luiseño territory in 1776: San Juan Capistrano, which the Spanish called Juaneños when among the Indians. Fifty years later Franciscan missionary Gerónimo Boscana wrote a lengthy ethnographic essay on these people that, although unpublished in his lifetime, has come down to us as *Chinigchinich,* the name of one of their Gods. Although describing native customs and beliefs had been a well-respected practice in New Spain since the sixteenth century, Boscana was the only Franciscan to attempt such a project in California. California's native people lacked the monumental architecture, cities, and large armies of the Aztecs that had attracted earlier Franciscan writers. Perhaps the challenge inherent in such work proved daunting in California because unlike his predecessors in Mexico City, Boscana could find no happy ending, no assurance that the Indians he and his forebears had evangelized had truly accepted Christianity.

Boscana wrote after twenty years in the province, fifteen of them among the Luiseño, and he agreed with a colleague of forty years' experience who had said that he found these Indians "incomprehensible." Boscana compared them to a species of monkey who publicly imitated the behavior of superiors to secretly practice vice.[10] Boscana did not know it but he had described the "protective ingratiation" of Toypurina and other Indians when no alternative to living in the mission was available. For Luiseños as well as for other Indians, mission life provided another source of power—food, clothing, learning the knowledge-power of agriculture, stock-raising, and crafts—as well as the opportunity to study the priests closely to try to learn their power secrets. To the Diegueño and other native peoples Franciscans appeared as powerful shamans who needed some appeasement if an Indian wanted to continue to live, at least partially, his traditional life.[11]

Although Boscana ridiculed Juaneño religious belief and ceremonies he was shocked by the sexual content of some ritual dances and social behavior. He learned of three dances, all accompanied by music played on indigenous instruments, in which a young woman, either bare to the waist or completely naked, moved suggestively with her hands under her breasts, lifting them up toward the men in the crowd. In one dance she simply moved while the men sang. In another the men remained silent and she sang a song naming female and male genitalia — in Boscana's description it was "an infamous thing and a diabolical invention." The third dance was performed inside the compound, called the Vanquex, where religious ritual was performed. This was the first public dance of the son of a chief. It was also done for the son of a member of the village's councilors or of another high-status Indian. The two- or three-year-old boy's body was painted red and black and he was dressed in the ritual skirt of Chinigchinich with a crown of feathers set upon his head. He danced alone while musicians and singers performed for the assembly. The boy danced until he became too tired to continue, at which point the chief or a member of the council, dressed exactly like the boy, took him upon his shoulders and continued the dance while all the people watched. When the adult had completed his dance with the child, one of his female relatives — in Boscana's words, "A sister or aunt or some other one of his closest female relatives, single or married," it mattered not so long as she was young — "got up, stripped herself naked before all those who were assembled, who were always many . . . and naked thus with her hands underneath her breasts she began to dance." During this ceremony she offered herself to anyone who desired her, singing to the assembly that she was well, healthy, sexually experienced, and prepared for whatever might be wanted. Indian sexuality, especially female sexuality expressed publicly in rituals important to the societies that gave rise to them, shocked and baffled the Spanish Franciscan.

Boscana was aware that there were yet other rituals equally offensive to him that he did not describe and concluded his observation in the matter with an expression of hope undermined by a more sober sense of reality. "Through the mercy of God, since they have become Christians they are already abandoning them [these dances]," he wrote, "or at least they do not execute them in public."[12] In private and away from the Franciscan gaze, Boscana feared that the Indians did as they pleased especially when they consorted with their unbaptized brethren, the gentiles. Boscana's fears seem well founded. In the mid-twentieth century the Luiseño still had a word to describe such ceremonial dances that the Franciscans had called "obscene."[13] All other tribes had rituals equally repugnant to the missionaries. It seems that only in the San Francisco area, where the rapid collapse of Indian opposition to the missions, compared to the persistence of opposition in the southern region, were the missionaries able to succeed in controlling some Indian dances. When a foreign visitor arrived in 1806 at mission San José, the priest, Pedro de la Cueva, released the Indians from their duties to demonstrate a dance. All the sacred paraphernalia for the ritual including costumes, instruments, objects, and paints, material customarily guarded by shamans and chiefs, was kept by Cueva and given to the Indians only when he chose to have them perform.[14] In this area Franciscans, not the Indians, had control over some aspect of native culture and prohibited any public display of sexuality.

In the south, Juaneño sexual activity disturbed Boscana as Indian sexuality disturbed missionaries throughout California. Premarital and frequently extramarital sexual activity was commonplace. Marriage and divorce were casual. While most marriages were with one partner, chiefs frequently had more than one wife, and when women became chiefs they could have more than one husband. Some of this activity continued within the mission compound as one scholar has discovered in the records of mission Santa Cruz.[15] The Franciscan notion of female chastity before marriage and of monogamy by both partners afterward was affronted by such practices. Boscana noted that when Indian women traveled outside their ranchería, whether married or not and even if accompanied by their husbands or mothers, they were expected to yield sexually if they encountered a shaman who so desired them.[16] Convinced that the Indians were sexually promiscuous, the missionaries invested no small amount of their energies trying to reform native peoples according to their own standards of proper sexual conduct.

The greatest concern to the missionaries about Indian sexuality lay in their discovery of men who dressed as women, did women's work, and were found among women when explorers visited rancherías and later when groups of Indian women visited Spanish camps. The first observer was perhaps the most balanced. Fray Juan Crespi, a member of the Sacred Expedition, accompanied an exploration party north toward Monterey. After visiting the villages along the channel of the Chumash area, Crespi noted, "We have seen heathen men wearing the dress of women. . . . We have not been able to understand what it means, nor what its purpose is; time and an understanding of the language, when it is learned, will make it clear."[17] Such an inquisitive, nonjudgmental view disappeared quickly. In 1775 military commander Pedro Fages observed in each village of the channel area two or three male Indians dressed and behaving as women. Fages reported that they "pass as sodomites by profession (it being confirmed that all Indians are much addicted to this abominable vice) and permit the heathen to practice the execrable, unnatural abuse of their

Figure 2. Indian neophytes at Mission San José perform a dance in a drawing by the physician and naturalist Georg Heinrich von Langsdorff. Langsdorff, who visited California in 1806 with a Russian expedition commanded by Count Nikolai Rezanov, was much interested in the ceremony, noting that in preparation the men smeared their bodies with charcoal dust, chalk, and red clay and that the music consisted "of singing and the clapping of sticks split at one end." As part of his effort to control Indian behavior, the mission priest Pedro de la Cueva kept the ornaments and other articles associated with ritual dances under lock, distributing them to the natives only when he authorized a performance. Courtesy Bancroft Library.

bodies." Having expressed his Spanish male revulsion for sexual practices European Christians considered aberrant, Fages continued with a description of the phenomenon that seemed to amaze him. "They are called *joyas* [an attempt at Chumash that translates as "jewels" in Spanish]," he wrote "and are held in great esteem."[18] The facts of male cross-dressing and male-on-male sex, combined with community acceptance and even high regard for such persons caused Fages to think that Christianizing them would be very difficult.

A year after Fages made his account, mission Santa Clara was established. During the initial period of pagan and new Christian interaction, the mission-aries observed an individual working with the women and dressed as one of them who lacked breasts although old enough to have them. They told the corporal of the guard to watch this person and use any pretext to take that individual to the guardhouse, have him or her disrobe, and determine the person's sex. The strip revealed the individual to be a man, and so the priests ordered that he be left naked and fed well but imprisoned. He was ordered to sweep the small plaza, and the guard harangued him to act like a man and dress like one too, and to quit the company of women "with whom it was presumed he was sinning." After three days the dispirited fellow, who had grown very depressed, was released. In subsequent conversations with the neophytes the missionaries learned that this man had resumed his old role in his ranchería. At mission San Antonio two pagans, one a man and the other dressed as a woman but suspected of being a joya went to visit a neophyte. Immediately one of the priests accompanied by the corporal and a soldier entered the neophyte's house and found the two pagans engaging in "an unspeakably sinful act." When the priest admonished them, the pagan dressed as a male indignantly replied that the joya was his wife.[19]

By the time of Boscana's observations, recorded fifty years after these initial reports, Franciscans had a more sophisticated perception of the joya's sexual orientation. Among the Juaneño/Luiseño they were called *cuút* and had been selected as youths to fulfill this role, spending much of their time among the women. A chief would take a "hombre muger (man woman)," in Boscana's words, as one of his wives because in household work he was stronger than any woman. Instead of being corpulent, weak, and impotent, as a celebrated Franciscan had written of such people in Mexico, the joyas Boscana had seen were the opposite. One of them Boscana knew had married a neophyte woman and fathered two children. Boscana learned that a joya's power within the village was such that if he decided to have consensual sex with a woman even her husband could not object.[20] Joyas expressed Indian male and female sexuality and stood apart from the group constituting their own elite.

Traditionally, anthropologists have called cross-dressing men and women *berdache,* a word derived from Arabic designating young male prostitute. The term, however, omits women transvestites and assigns the role of prostitution not found in the historical records, at least for California. Reversing Boscana's phrase of "man woman," which placed the sex at birth as the defining characteristic of such people, some anthropologists now favor "woman-man" or "man-woman" to give priority to the chosen gender role of the individual over sex at birth. Use of the proper pronoun then becomes confusing, perhaps intentionally so.[21] Clearly, however, in most Indian societies gender identity was fluid and Indians bestowed high status upon those who filled special roles. Creation of mixed gender roles gave those who expressed them great power within their communities and made them important people to consult in times of strife. In many societies berdache became shamans in addition to fulfilling their cross-gender assignments.

Shamanism encompassed a broad array of activities, all of them specialized, practiced by men and some women. These individuals distinguished themselves from others by their degree of power. Such specialized activities required specialized knowledge, and all shamans underwent lengthy training to achieve their status. Franciscans sometimes thought of shamans who participated in Indian religious rituals as their Devil-inspired inverted twin, Indian priests for a pagan cult. At other times Franciscans regarded them as medical quacks, counterfeit doctors who cured ill patients by blowing smoke over them or by sucking some foreign object from the patient's body such as a rock, twig, or feather by trickery.[22] Franciscans generally classed all suspected shamans into the category of wizard, or *hechizero,* and dismissed them as unimportant, sometimes irritating nuisances and at other times as outright threats. At mission San Gabriel, for example, Padre José Zalvidea, who arrived twenty years after the Toypurina revolt and served there twenty years more, treated Indians with special powers severely. According to one observer Zalvidea chained suspected shamans "together in couples and kept them well flogged." Others he kept "like hounds in couples," putting them to work as sawyers with one positioned above the other in the pits where large beams were sawed.[23] Forcing them to work in an enclosed space belowground and with a metal saw that could do mechanically the magical work of tree splitting seemed to be one Franciscan's way of trying to discredit native power wielders. Most Franciscans did not appreciate either the shaman's importance to the village or the diversity of services he or she provided.

Individuals usually became shamans because either elders selected them or they experienced a dream that called them to the task and sought out an existing shaman to apprentice with. Typically, young people between the ages of nine and fourteen, customarily but not exclusively male, studied for a year or more learning the lore appropriate to the type of shaman they would become such as a healing doctor, a midwife, an herb curing doctor, a seer, a war councilor, or a dream interpreter. The culmination of this training was access to the world of spiritual power through the drug called *toloache* by the Spanish, a concoction derived from the roots of the green shrub with the white trumpet-shaped flowers known as *Datura meteloides.* Through ingesting that liquid beverage, supervised by a sponsor, the initiate had a hallucinogenic experience that connected him or her to a parallel world of power not visible to the unaided eye. Experienced shamans administered the drug to learners, since the amount of narcotic poisoning sufficient to enter the dreamworld was only slightly less than a fatal dosage, and in all cultures it was appropriate, albeit dangerous, for surviving family members to kill a shaman who made a mistake. Failure by a shaman to cure the ill or to fulfill a prophecy also merited death.[24]

The experience of a Diegueño dream doctor is illustrative. His maternal grandfather, a dream doctor, selected him at the age of nine to follow the older man in his spiritual work. The grandfather did so because of the boy's precocious dreams about success in hunting, his interest in magic and his grandfather's life, and because the boy was healthy and intelligent and possessed common sense along with an abnormal amount of physical and libidinal energy. After a year of training his grandfather determined that he was ready. His two-day toloache ritual began with an oral test of all that he learned. Approximately thirty minutes into the questioning, the boy was feeling happy and sleepy. Crowds of people began to gather around him; some he knew but most he did not. Grandfather, explaining that those he did not know had not yet appeared in his life, questioned the boy about how to engage each one appropriately. Initiates were given water during the experience and were prevented from wandering free lest they inadvertently hurt themselves. During the hallucination the boy learned that his animal guardian and future dream helper was the mountain lion. He also dreamed of the five pieces of magical quartz that would help him to read the dreams of others, he learned his secret sexual name, and he dreamed the dream of "world knowledge" that would enable him to connect and interpret the dreams of individuals with the wider Diegueño world.[25]

During the toloache initiation ritual, individuals also learned whether or not they had the power to strike others dead from afar or if, in addition to what they had trained for, they had other powers, especially prophecy. Both of these were among the characteristics attributed to the female shaman Toypurina by the Gabrielinos. Specialized healing doctors such as bear doctor or rattlesnake doctor often learned to use their animal helpers against others or to shift their shape into that of their animal familiar. The deer doctor, important to hunting, for example, could assume the shape of the deer to lure animals closer to men in hunting parties. When shamans worked their magic for the common good they were shamans; however, when they used their power for personal ends they were wizards or sorcerers. Their power within Indians communities was vast for they played important roles in communitywide public ritual and privately gave comfort to individuals needing help.

Among the Diegueño, Luiseño, Juaneño, Gabrielino, Chumash, and Southern Yokuts, *Datura* use was widespread and nearly all males and in some cultures females underwent a modified toloache initiation at puberty to learn their future roles in society.

All who used *Datura* learned the identity of their dream helper, usually an animal spirit, who would guide them in their first and any subsequent visits to the supernatural world. Each *Datura* user also learned the materials from which he or she could make a talisman that would be their source of power and aid that person in time of danger. Sometimes shamans had talismans that could not be worn—like the crystals of the Diegueño dream doctor. Most talismans, however, were made from materials that could be carried on the body. In mission times Chumash routinely wore their talismans under their shirts with the Christian rosary clearly visible on top of the shirt. One dying man's wife inverted that order by placing his talisman around his neck outside his shirt and placing the rosary so that it hung down his back.[26] She sought thereby for her husband to reach the Chumash supernatural world by the aid of the *Datura* symbol, reinforced by the talisman to the Christian spiritual world.

While in many societies *Datura* was taken only once by the average person, among the Yokuts annual toloache ceremonies were held where men and women drank it together. Gabrielino, Salinan, and Chumash, however, took the drug year round, and for the Chumash, at least, it was an individual and not a communal activity. Individuals used the drug within the Chumash village rather than at separate ceremonial houses. The primary purpose was to connect with one's supernatural guardian to obtain power or to avert danger such as reversing the prophecy of hearing an owl that foretold a person's death. Chumash took *Datura* for limitless reasons: to seek advice in love, to have luck in hunting, to secure advantage in some endeavor, to communicate with the dead, to learn the future, to become more manly if a man and to make a woman more courageous in childbirth and free from danger during the delivery. For the Chumash *Datura* was practically a recreationl drug, inducing a dreamlike trance that lasted from eighteen to twenty-four hours and differed sharply from the longer hallucinations experienced by shamans.[27] As in all societies in which *Datura* was used, shamans administered it. Some became specialized in that art and were known as toloache doctors to the Spanish. Such practitioners emerged because knowing the correct amount of *Datura* to administer meant preparing the dosage according to the user's age, weight, and sex, and watching over the user through the experience. Among the Diegueño, one male in ten became a shaman.[28] For the tribes geographically above them more active in the toloache rituals and especially among the Chumash, the percentage must have been much greater. In many of those societies women, too, became shamans.

While each *Datura* vision was personal and doubtlessly private, the act was a shared ritual by which a guide enabled the user to leave the visible world and enter a realm of power. Access to such a world meant that Indians of southern California had a significant, power-generating alternative to the Christian world being imposed upon them as long as *Datura* grew wild, something it still does today in lower-altitude habitats from the tip of South America to the Canadian Shield. Indeed, *Datura* shaped and fueled religious movements that anthropologists have labeled Toloache Cults.

The Toloache Cults consisted of the Chinigchinich and Datura Cult (*ʔantap*) religions, both of which were undergirded by *Datura* usage. The primary centers of the Chinigchinich religion were located among the Gabrielino, where it allegedly began, the Luiseño-Juaneño, and the Diegueño of San Diego.[29] Each culture had its own version of the basic story, which began with a creator God who made brother sky and sister earth. Following an incestuous act Mother Earth brought forth the prototypes of all beings and things. In that early time, all things lived including flora and fauna and rocks and water. When people appeared, the distinction between them and the animals was fluid and unclear. In time a culture hero named Wiyot appeared. He possessed great power, more than any other being, and called himself the son of the creator, born of a virgin impregnated by lightning. Wiyot loved all creatures and regarded himself as their father or caretaker. One-day Frog, who could read his mind, learned that Wiyot thought the legs of human women more beautiful than hers and Frog became jealous. She decided to kill him by injecting poison from her body into the water he drank. Wiyot could read all minds and knew of Frog's scheme but accepted her desire, permitted the act, drank the water, and slowly died. While dying Wiyot journeyed to all the villages that accepted him, casting away bits of his tremendous power as he went. He announced that upon his death he should be cremated and promised that he would return to watch over the people. All the people gathered at Wiyot's death to confer about power and what should be done next. A guard was posted to watch the body until the funeral pyre could be built. When the fire finally had been lit Coyote leaped over the guard and snatched the heart of Wiyot from the flames, ran away, and consumed it. Coyote became the symbol of inconstancy and trickery and Wiyot was transformed into the Moon. In memory of Wiyot his Indian successors cremated their dead until the Franciscans forbade the practice at the missions. With Wiyot's death life was thrown into chaos, since now power could not be controlled and its sources were uncertain.

Sometime after Wiyot's death another powerful being appeared who called himself God and whom the Indians called Chinigchinich. He taught the people to celebrate rituals in an enclosure, the Vanquex, rather than in an open space and abjured them to live by the moral code he gave them. After spending some time among them he then departed. Chinigchinich monitored and punished human behavior after he had gone by means of animal spies and avengers. Raven reported to Chinigchinich human mistakes in ceremony, disobedience to the moral code, and indiscreet revelations of secrets so that the God might punish wrongdoers through his avengers (rattlesnake, tarantula, bear, sting-ray, and raven). All Indian groups worshiping Chinigchinich held large annual mourning ceremonies and conducted other rituals combining veneration for Wiyot and propitiation of Chinigchinich. Indians regardless of tribe intoned the key words in these rites in Luiseño, attesting to the origin of the religion. In some open rituals, as opposed to private tribal ceremonies, they invited their neighbors to participate.

The Chinigchinich religion had some parallels with Christianity that could facilitate Indian acceptance or at least comprehension of the new story once the language obstacle had been overcome. The Diegueño manifested the great-est resistance to Spanish religious and physical colonization. While allowing their Christian members to be buried, in the backcountry of San Diego county the Diegueño continued until at least the 1870s to cremate those who followed the old ways.[30]

The Luiseño, however, gave the Spanish the least trouble. Mission San Luis Rey became the most populous of all the mission communities, with over 2,800 neophytes at its peak.[31] The Indian population was not viable, just like the populations of the other missions, because deaths outnumbered births. But the size of the mission compound, the numbers of its herds, and the yields from its fields counted this as the "most successful" of all the Franciscan enterprises in California. Two reasons probably account for that. One missionary, An-tonio Peyri, served as senior priest from its founding in April 1798 until his departure on the eve of secularization in December 1831. While Peyri estab-lished a village at the mission site, he varied from the Franciscan preference to concentrate neophytes around the church and generally permitted the Luiseño to remain in their own rancherías after baptism. Peyri's decentralized ap-proach to missionization permitted the Luiseño to continue their religious practices beyond the sight of priests. Like his colleague Boscana at mission San Juan Capistrano, Peyri strove to change his neophytes but always felt frustrated by their inscrutability. Sixteen years into his ministry Peyri observed that the Luiseño "never reveal more than that which they cannot deny. We are uprooting some of these ideas in the neophytes," he wrote, then concluded glumly "yet they always remain Indians."[32] And so they remained even after his departure, preserving significant elements of their old culture well into the twentieth century.[33]

North of the Chinigchinich sphere of influence lay the Chumash of the islands, the coast, and the interior who participated in the Datura Cult (*ʔantap*) religion, so named from the Chumash word for the secret society that administered it.[34] All tribal leaders belonged to the Datura Cult as well as all singers, dancers, shamans and other performers at the large public rituals the Chumash held several times a year. The largest of these rituals occurred at the solstices (the winter solstice was believed to have been the time of the beginning for the Chumash) and at harvest. Their function was to renew the world and to begin again a new series of seasons.

The Chumash viewed the world as an eternal struggle between a threatening male sun deity and the female earth deity in her aspects of wind, rain, and fire. The forces of life and death in the heavens that affected humans were arrayed in opposing teams playing a gambling game called *peón*. Their counterparts on earth were represented by Datura Cult members and the principal ceremonies were designed to aid the earth in her struggle against the sky Gods. One of the Indian female deities was Momoy, the Ventureño and Yneseño word for toloache or *Datura*. This celestial game of chance involving the forces of good and evil could be affected by correct ceremonial behavior by the Chumash as a group guided by their leaders, and ceremonial participation was important for all. Datura Cult officers spoke their own language unintelligible to commoners, and Datura Cult members were chosen at birth or selected later when an uninitiated individual did something to win distinction. The talented individual then became a lucky element for humankind who could be inducted into Datura Cult secrets and aid in the peón game.

Chumash believed that there were three worlds floating in an abyss, the middle world being inhabited by humankind and supported by two giant snakes whose occasional movement caused earthquakes. Unlike the Chinigchinich account, the Chumash lacked the story of a single creator and the Chumash do not mention an incestuous relationship between two significant supernatural beings. Like the secret societies of the Chinigchinich religion that performed at public rituals and guarded their power, the Datura Cult organized and integrated people across space and kinship lines since people had to leave their villages to gather for the large collective ceremonies. Village headmen and their advisors, the political leadership of the village, along with the other specialists mentioned all belonged to the Datura Cult. So powerful was this religion that a non–Datura Cult member could still describe its form and the part of its function known to commoners to an anthropologist early in the twentieth century.[35] Thus the Toloache Cults with their hallucinogenic access to another world of power, their secret societies, and even secret language provided a strong, flexible, integrating force in the Indian societies of southern California that were not found elsewhere. They also offered their followers a respite from the storm of missionization.

The Toloache Cults, like the use of *Datura*, attenuated sharply the farther north from the Salinan one moved. The Salinan influence, the Indian group above the Chumash, extended to lower Monterey County. In the remainder of northern central California variants of another religion prevailed, the Kuksu, so named for the Eastern Pomo word for the major God impersonated in its ceremonies. Kuksu rituals performed the same tasks as those of the Toloache Cults and included numerous secret societies of men, and some women, who exercised all the diverse powers of shamans to the south. Among Kuksu adherents, status was achieved through membership in several of these secret societies. Those commoners lacking access to any or to only one were regarded as low-status. The more democratic access to power through a hallucinogenic drug was not available to people here, and individual merit and birth determined a person's success. The strongest of the Kuksu centers lay in the Sacramento area and in the foothills.[36] Thus many of the Indians of the San Francisco Bay area were more easily intimidated by Spanish power and incorporated themselves piecemeal into the missions in ways that their southern counterparts did not.[37]

Finding the California Indians not violently combative like the Apaches and not as sophisticated and intricately organized as the Aztecs, Franciscan missionaries seriously underestimated the task of evangelization before them. Converting California did not prove to be what they expected.

3

Junípero Serra and Franciscan Evangelization

California's missions cannot be understood apart from their evangelical purpose of bringing Native Americans to Christianity. In that effort Junípero Serra, first father president of the missions from 1769 until 1784, made an imprint that lasted with but little modification through the Spanish era that ended in 1822. During his tenure, nine of what would be twenty-one missions were begun, with Serra personally founding six. At his death more than 4,600 natives had been baptized, and all of the older missions except San Diego had met the problems of survival and were producing surplus foodstuffs. Spanish officials at the time judged that the Franciscan enterprise had been successfully initiated.[1]

Serra's religious motivation, background, and worldview provide an appropriate theological and historical context within which to consider his accomplishments. Born in 1713 to humble parents on the Balearic Island of Mallorca, off Spain's east coast, Serra turned to a religious life early and took his vows in 1731. A delay in admitting him to the Franciscan order stemmed from his having an ancestor named Abraham. The name suggested that he came from a Jewish family, called *chueta* in Mallorquin, which caused the reviewers to consider his application more closely in order to ensure that he was not a backslider, a closet Judaiser.[2] Serra was eventually admitted to the order. His exceptional zeal first in his personal piety and studies and later as a missionary

Retrato del Rev. Padre Fray Junípero Serra Apostol de la Alta California, tomado del original que se conserva en su Convento de la Santa Cruz de Querétaro.

Figure 3. Fray Junípero Serra, the courageous and indomitable Franciscan who helped lead the Sacred Expedition to Alta California and who established the first nine missions in a chain of twenty-one that ultimately stretched from San Diego to Sonoma. An able administrator and a powerful preacher, Serra served as the father president of the missions from 1769 until his death in 1784. His mystical, medieval vision of a sinful world, in which God and Satan contested for the souls of men, informed his entire adult life, and he drove himself relentlessly to gather souls to salvation on the California frontier. Courtesy Santa Barbara Mission Archive-Library.

may have reflected an ongoing desire to prove his worthiness for Christian religious life and to transcend any doubters. He pursued religious studies avidly, securing a doctorate in theology. He taught philosophy and theology at San Francisco de Palma, Mallorca, where from 1740 to 1743 he instructed, among others, Juan Crespí and Francisco Palóu, two young Mallorcans who would later follow Serra to the New World.

Serra's advanced training, combined with his growing reputation for oratorical excellence, won him a professorial appointment teaching sacred theology at the Lullian University in Palma, Mallorca, in 1744. Five years later, at the age of thirty-five, with a frame lean from years of physical deprivation, a swarthy complexion, and standing five feet two inches tall, he left his native island for the first and last time to work as a missionary in the New World.[3] His former student and friend, Palóu, accompanied him.

Both men initially had been deferred from missionary service owing to an alleged "instability" of Mallorcans that prevented their fulfilling such duty. However, when five of the priests recruited for the New World by the Apostolic College of San Fernando in Mexico City abandoned their vocations upon encountering the sea and becoming fearful of sailing upon it, Serra and Palóu were permitted to fill their vacancies.[4] Need for missionaries overbore any considerations of unsuitability. In New Spain, Serra served in the Sierra Gorda region northeast of Querétaro as a missionary and as an administrator for the College of San Fernando in Mexico City. After twenty years of these labors, at age fifty-five, he led the Franciscans into Alta California in 1769 both as missionary and as first father president, staying there the fifteen years remaining to him.[5]

In Serra's experiences before 1769 lie the keys to understanding his conduct in California. The example of Francis of Assisi, the teachings of John Duns Scotus, the writings of María de Agreda, and the missionary experience in Querétaro all shaped the worldview Serra brought to the religious enterprise he commanded in Alta California, "this last corner of the earth."[6] The intellectual movement known as the Enlightenment came of age during Serra's lifetime, and that secularizing impulse promoting the liberation of humankind from priestly domination forced Serra to shape himself in opposition to the Enlightenment, the dominant thought of his time. The Enlightenment appealed to European elites while generating suspicion among the poor and humble who resented its attack upon religion. The new thinking had some impact on Spain although the Balearic Islands and especially Mallorca with its Franciscan conservatism experienced a cultural lag from the mainland.

Francis of Assisi (1181–1226) although born into a wealthy family renounced his social and economic position as a young man and chose to embrace poverty and simplicity in imitation of Christ and the Apostles.[7] As a mendicant he wore the cheapest of tunics, begged for his daily bread, and wandered the countryside preaching penance as the means for personal salvation. Francis was widely ridiculed and reviled. Only later did people acknowledge him as "God's holy fool." To further renounce the temptations of the body he wore a hair shirt under his tunic that constantly irritated his flesh.

In a remote, small stone church dedicated to Our Lady of the Angels that had fallen into decay and lay abandoned by Benedictines, Francis found a refuge. It was situated on a tiny parcel of land known as the *porziuncola* (*porciúncula* in Spanish), and here Francis cultivated a special devotion to the Virgin and experienced his vision of what to do. In this chapel that Francis repaired with his own hands he founded the Franciscans. Given to visions and self-flagellation in imitation of the suffering of Christ, Francis drew men and women to him who sought to share his hard and simple life of sacrifice for Christ. He called them the Third Order of Friars Minor, to indicate the humility and unworthiness of these men who married only Lady Poverty. He also acknowledged the Poor Claires, making them the female equivalent of the Franciscans. Because he was not a priest, an ordained monk, he struggled to secure papal approval to preach. But once he had secured that approval he submitted completely to papal authority. Two years before he died he received the stigmata, lacerations in the hands, feet, and side that bled regularly, marks of the five wounds Christ had received on the Cross. Such an experience of Christian mystery, never before observed, convinced those who knew him that because of his piety Francis had been marked by God the Father as His "second son." Within two years of Francis's death Pope Gregory IX proclaimed him a saint, someone who had died and gone to heaven and was now able to intercede with Christ for the faithful.

The pope tried to smooth out some contradictions in Francis's approach by permitting Franciscans the *use* of money and property, *not* ownership, to carry out their missionary work. Subsequent leaders of the order decided that training for ordination to the priesthood and rigorous schooling were desirable and necessary for future Franciscans. Serra's own education, which he could never have obtained without joining the Order, reflected those newer ideas. When Serra completed his novitiate he dropped his given name, Miquel, for Junípero, the name of an early follower of Francis noted for his simplicity and humor. Juniper, an evergreen symbolizing constancy, was also thought to be the *retem* of the Old Testament, a shrub/tree that bore white flowers, symbolic of chastity and integrity.

Imitating Francis, Serra adopted a particular devotion to the Virgin Mary and the practice of self-flagellation. This was a ritual that involved removing the tunic from his shoulders and striking his bare back repeatedly with a small braided whip, called a discipline (*la disciplina*), all the while deep in prayer and meditation upon Christ's sufferings for humankind. Although the act was private, other Franciscans witnessed it while at common prayer and it distinguished Serra as one of a small group of ascetics within the Order known as "fervents." To increase the pain and further mortify the flesh, Serra embedded pieces of metal into the cords of the discipline as well as into the hair shirt he wore to curb what he regarded as a tendency to commit the sin of pride.[8]

John Duns Scotus (1265–1308), a Scottish Franciscan philosopher and theologian, argued that God's love for humanity was the primary reason for the Incarnation, for making God visible in the human form of his only son, Jesus. In return, man's duty was to respond to Christ's redemptive suffering through love of Him. Duns Scotus proposed the doctrine of Mary's Immaculate Conception, meaning that she, as the mother of Jesus, had been conceived without the taint of Original Sin just like her son. This Marian doctrine, however, did not win church approval until 1870 so that the Scotists held a unique, perhaps more aptly a parochial, view for seven centuries. In its Marian emphasis Scotism concerned itself with the Nativity from two perspectives. One perspective considered the synoptic gospels' of Matthew, Mark, and Luke telling of Christ's birth as a historical event to be remembered and celebrated. The other perspective addressed the view of the Apocalypse of Saint John as an event witnessed outside this temporal world to remind men and women of their duty to love God through Jesus.

These two views had practical implications for evangelization. Francis of Assisi first secured the right to display a replica of the nativity scene, or synoptic gospel view, in churches during the liturgical season of Advent. Francis believed that depictions of the Holy Family surrounded by live animals in a simulated stable would inspire peasants and princes to translate to their daily lives the message of devotion depicted by the worship of shepherds and kings. Francis also wanted to show the sufferings of Christ for humankind as expressed in His humble birth. According to Franciscan legend the first such depiction was made on Christmas Eve 1223 for the Midnight Mass at the village of Greccio. Francis preached a sermon on the birth of the poor King and, while Francis spoke the Infant Jesus, signifying His approval, miraculously took the place of the doll Francis had placed in the crèche.[9] Franciscans, in addition to the creation of crèche displays, later developed a pastoral play commonly known in the Americas as *Los Pastores,* to represent the apocalyptic vision, and had it performed during Advent by congregation members.

Duns Scotus profoundly affected the Franciscans. In 1633 in Toledo, Spain, the general chapter of the Franciscan Order directed four learned priests to write a manual of Scotism. All those who taught philosophy "were obliged to teach from this course under pain of irremissible removal from office."[10] Serra immersed himself in Scotist thought and later taught such a course during his tenure at the Lullian University. Theologically speaking, Serra did not question the training he both received and inculcated in others. His carefully cultivated medievalism, the very source of his intellectual and moral strengths, was at odds with the Enlightenment.

Serra also drew inspiration and comfort from the writings of a Spanish Franciscan nun and mystic, María de Jesús de Agreda, known as María de Agreda (1602–1665). She was descended from *conversos*, converted Jews. Her most celebrated work, *The Mystical City of God*, first published in 1670, became an important source of devotional reading. It was published in more than sixty editions in all the Romance languages. Her four volumes purportedly contain the true story of Mary, mother of Jesus, as revealed to María de Agreda. It took the nun ten years to record it all. In it Mary confirms her own Immaculate Conception. Moreover, Mary affirms that she is, along with her son, the co-redemptress of humankind.[11] *The Mystical City of God* was immensely popular with Franciscans. Serra had a copy with him in the Sierra Gorda and his companion in the New World, Francisco Palóu, brought one to California with him.[12] Serra's personal devotion to the Immaculate Conception then derived from Duns Scotus reinforced by *The Mystical City of God*.

María de Agreda had further influence on Serra. From 1620 to 1631 she had experienced the Christian mystery called the miracle of bilocation, being in two places at once. While she never left her convent in Agreda, she nevertheless was borne away to the New World on the wings of Angels and St. Francis where she helped in the missionization of Indians in New Mexico and Texas. Indians reported seeing a beautiful young woman, a Lady in Blue, who spoke to them in their own language and urged them to find the Franciscans for baptism. She attributed her language facility to divine grace. As a nun she could not baptize and, perhaps to remove any earthly temptation, God made her invisible to the friars.

During this period she made no fewer than five hundred visits, sometimes four a day, preaching to diverse Indians. She claimed that God was so enthusiastic for this missionary work that He told her that Indians would convert spontaneously simply at the sight of a Franciscan. Until the end of the seventeenth century Franciscans from Texas to Arizona encountered Indians who spoke of visits from a beautiful Lady in Blue. Even though she later repudiated her stories, her widely publicized experiences increased vocations among priests to become missionaries.[13] According to his biographer Palóu, Serra drew inspiration and comfort from the writings of María de Agreda before committing himself to the New World.[14]

Serra arrived in Mexico as a man of iron resolve whose personal motto, derived from St. Paul, was: "Always go forward, never turn back (*Siempre adelante, nunca atrás*)."[15] Upon landing in Veracruz in December 1749, Serra declined the bishop's offer to travel to Mexico City expeditiously by horse and instead decided to walk the two hundred and seventy miles, relying on Divine Providence to get him through. Along the way a series of insect bites caused an itching rash on Serra's leg. In his sleep he scratched the rash so severely that by morning it had become lacerated. The laceration soon became infected, and this affliction remained with him until his death, often causing him severe discomfort, sometimes crippling him to the point that he could not walk.[16] Serra continued forward, however, undaunted by any physical discomfort.

The apostolic college of San Fernando in Mexico City, to which he had been assigned, sent him to work in the missions among the Pamé Indians of the Sierra Gorda, near Querétaro. During his ensuing twenty years of service both in the countryside and in the capital, he earned a reputation as an excellent administrator and a powerful preacher, one able to move those who heard him to fervent displays of emotion. In condemning his own sinfulness, Serra employed a variety of techniques to communicate to his listeners their obligations to repent and to love God.

His former student, missionary companion, and confessor Palóu recounted how Serra would confess to him publicly before the congregation seeking to encourage others to make their private confessions frequently. Additionally, with a stone kept in the pulpit Serra would strike his sternum with his right hand while holding a crucifix in his left, making an Act of Contrition, the blows echoing from the walls and floors of the stone churches in which he denounced his sins. On other occasions he opened his tunic to bare his chest, lit four candles from one taper to illustrate souls suffering in Hell because they had not repented, and then held the candles to his own chest, burning the flesh to imitate that pain. Parishioners sobbed in response. At other times, Serra would pull down his tunic to expose his shoulders and lash himself with a metal whip, drawing blood, to demonstrate to his Indian audience his own unworthiness before his God, all the while repenting his sins.[17]

On one occasion in Mexico City his demonstrations had an unforeseen effect. While imitating the Peruvian missionary St. Francis Solano by scourging himself with a chain, and thereby moving the congregation to tears, a man suddenly approached the pulpit. The congregant seized the chain from Serra, retired to the back of the church, stripped to the waist, and began beating himself shouting: "I am the sinner ungrateful to God who ought to do penance for my many sins and not the Padre who is a saint." He continued flagellating himself until he dropped to the floor. The congregation thought him dead but Serra administered the Last Sacraments to him before he expired. "Of this soul," Palóu wrote, "we can believe with pious Faith that he will enjoy God."[18]

For children and adolescents Serra had a different approach. Serra enjoyed singing and involved children early in participating in the *Alabado,* the daily hymn of praise to Jesus, Mary, and Joseph. During the Lenten season the Stations of the Cross, a devotion to the suffering, crucifixion, death, and resurrection of Jesus, would be performed on Fridays. This Franciscan-initiated devotion, like the nativity at Christmas, became a vehicle for drawing people closer to the mysteries of Christ and a proper Christian life by participation with the priest in the veneration of the Christian God. To complement the nativity scene in the church during Advent, Serra also had young people perform *Los Pastores,* a pageant about the visit of the shepherds to the Christ child, outside the church. Serra taught the young people their parts in both Spanish and Pamé and used the play as a way to communicate the humility of the shepherds as a model for adult parishioner behavior.[19]

Serra's arrival in the Sierra Gorda coincided with the decline in a belief that had given the Holy Office of the Inquisition much work over the previous century: humans making compacts with the Devil. Despite the decline in reported, or at least adjudicated, cases from the area preceding Serra's assignment, in September 1752 Serra reported evidence of witchcraft among the *gente de razón* in the region around Jalpan. He named a mulatto woman and a Mexican woman, both of whom implicated others, including some Indians, in devil worship and sacrifice to demons. They claimed to fly through the air to nearby caves to perform their rites. The Inquisition promptly appointed Serra as an official, authorizing him to exercise his powers anywhere he was preaching in New Spain where he found the absence of a regularly appointed Inquisition officer.[20] Significant here was Serra's direct encounter of evidence of the Devil in the New World and of the potential temptations the Evil One might offer to new Christians as well as to those more established in their faith.

As a missionary Serra had left the comforts of home and country in order to bring religion to pagans, to live among them simply, and to earnestly work toward their conversion. Serra was shorter than the Pamé Indians, and he had to place a bundled rag on his shoulder to match the height of the Indian with whom he carried beams to equalize the burden.[21] Although Serra suffered the afflictions of age and asceticism he frequently served his fellow priests when living at the College of San Fernando, a service from which age and experience as an apostolic missionary would have exempted him. He did so to demonstrate his humility as a servant of God.

When the time came for new labors, Serra seized the opportunity to expand the Apostolic College's missionary territory first into Baja California in 1767 and two years later into Alta California. He was zealous, optimistic about God's blessing upon the new Franciscan endeavor, and impatient to get on with it. Obstacles were irritants to be overcome, not messages to turn back.

Missionaries, at least of that era, were not tolerant people. They believed that their religion had exclusive claims to Truth that mandated they spread that Truth among nonbelievers. Those to be missionized might resist; the missionary, however, believed that if he worked hard enough, conversion would result. An ascetic who struggled to subordinate his body to his spiritual will, an educator, a doctor of philosophy who knew his spiritual purpose without question, and a man determined to show his love for Indians by changing forever their way of life for what he knew to be their own improvement, Serra came to Alta California as an irresistible force from and for his God.

Serra wrote his initial report to the College of San Fernando from "this port and new mission that will be San Diego." His letter brimmed with optimism despite his discovery upon arrival that several seamen had died from scurvy and many others lay ill from it. He had joined them by coming overland with the last of four groups sent by land and sea to initiate what the viceroy had called the Sacred Expedition. En route, Serra had seen gentile Indians naked, "just as their mothers brought them into the world," people who knew not the shame of Adam and Eve, living in lands "that had never before been trodden by a Christian foot." Serra believed that with "very little difficulty" a rich "harvest of souls" could be gathered into "our holy Mother the Church." In a clear reference to María de Agreda, Serra enthused, "It seems to me that we may work to our hearts' content, and our Lord God will fulfill the promise made to our Seraphic Father Saint Francis that merely at the sight of his sons, in these last centuries, the gentiles will be converted." Tempering his enthusiasm slightly, he concluded that the missionaries he needed for this spiritual conquest "should not imagine that they have come here for any other purpose than to endure hardships for the love of God and the salvation of souls."[22] Within two weeks Serra, with the help of the few able-bodied soldiers, had built and erected the large, wooden foundation cross on the dual feast day of the Holy Cross and Our Lady of Mount Carmel. Serra dedicated the new site with a High Mass and singing as he had done before in founding a mission in Baja California and as he would at subsequent foundings. A rough hut had been built to serve as a temporary church.

Serra had noted that the Indians visited the Spanish camp frequently but put aside their bows and arrows before doing so. That situation, however, would not last. Although wanting to believe that the Indians were warming to their presence, Spaniards began to find the pagans taking things from them. Palóu claimed they stole clothing and even cut pieces from the ship's sails.[23] These Diegueño, doubtlessly annoyed that they had not been given the presents they expected in the reciprocity customs of their culture, compensated for the Spanish rudeness or oversight by taking the gifts that they expected.[24] They overcame any initial fear of Spanish firearms and skirmished with the soldiers at least twice in ensuing weeks.

On August 15, 1769, the Feast of the Assumption of the Virgin Mary into Heaven, the Indians attacked the weakened Spanish camp while some soldiers and a priest were on board the ship. Serra and a fellow missionary took refuge in their rough quarters as the Indians fired arrows into the camp, charged it, and began to plunder what they could, even taking the sheets from the sick. During the fighting Serra's Spanish servant darted into the priest's hut, shot through the throat by an arrow. Serra administered the Last Rites to the boy before he died, holding the youth's head in his lap. Serra, not daring to move either to disturb the corpse or to draw attention to himself, sat in a pool of the young man's blood while the skirmish lasted. Once attacked, the soldiers responded by quickly arming themselves and returning fire. Although the Indians had the advantage of surprise and outnumbered the soldiers twenty to four, they lacked the discipline of European warfare and the Spanish fought them off, sustaining one dead and three wounded. The Indians suffered five dead and many wounded.[25] Because of this attack the Spanish built a stockade around their camp.[26]

Such an assault, launched on a feast day important to the cult of Mary, stiffened Serra's resolve. Despite the language obstacle, Serra believed that he had made contact with a fifteen-year-old boy by a combination of signs and some Indian words. Serra tried to persuade the lad to bring him a baby to baptize, to initiate into the Christian faith, and explained that the ceremony included the need for a godfather and the pouring of water on the infant's head. The new convert would wear Spanish clothes, something that seemed desirable to the Indians, and would become as a son to the priest and a relative, through baptism, of the soldiers. If the young man could secure a child, Serra would do the rest. The boy left. A few days later some pagans came to the camp with a baby, indicating that they wanted it baptized. On short notice, Serra arranged for a soldier to serve as godfather. With great excitement Serra approached the baptism of his first "convert" in Alta California. But as he prepared to pour the water from a silver shell over the infant's head, the parents snatched the baby from the arms of its would-be godfather and fled to their village. Serra stood holding the shell, his hopes for a new beginning crushed, at least temporarily.

Rather than condemn the Indians for rudeness or profanation, Serra blamed himself for the incident, seeing in it a rebuke to his sin of pride for thinking he could bring them to his God so quickly. Palóu noted that in later years, when retelling the story, tears always came to Serra's eyes.[27] At that moment, however, he resolved to work harder. But the struggle for survival curtailed proselytizing. The lack of irrigation meant little planting and food enough for those then in port, but no surplus.

An exploring party that had gone north to find Monterey Bay had failed to do so, although it had located San Francisco Bay. Discouraged Spaniards returned to San Diego and its dwindling commissary in late January 1770. The supply ship had not arrived, and by mid-February Gaspar de Potolá, the expedition's military commander, decided to wait for it only until March 19, the feast day of the expedition's patron, San José. If no ship had appeared by then, the Spanish would withdraw and attempt the colonization of Alta California at another time. Serra reluctantly agreed, but privately he made his own plans to remain even if the others left. Meanwhile Serra proposed a *novena* to San José, a nine-day devotion, which would culminate on his feast day. The morning of March 19 dawned clear, and after Mass and throughout the morning nothing was seen of a ship. Discouraged and preparing to depart, soldiers noticed a sail on the horizon at about three o'clock in the afternoon. Serra and the others took this as a sign from their God to continue: the Sacred Expedition had been saved! Thereafter, for as long as he lived, Serra celebrated a High Mass in thanksgiving to San José on the nineteenth of each month.[28]

Emboldened by what he believed was the miraculous appearance of the relief ship, Serra pressed forward with mission building. Easter followed quickly after the feast of San José in 1770 and when he had fulfilled his obligations in San Diego, Serra sailed north to Monterey where he established the second mission. On June 3, the feast of Pentecost, he had the foundation cross raised and celebrated a High Mass in the hut built as a church. This mission, named San Carlos Borromeo, would become his headquarters; the governor would assume his office in the presidio of Monterey when it was constructed. Writing to Palóu for candles, needed for the Mass and other services, Serra remarked that he intended a procession for June 14, the feast of Corpus Christi, the Body of Christ. Serra thought that that procession together with the Mass he would celebrate "ought to drive out any little devils (*Diablillos*) that might lurk in the land."[29]

As that letter and the one he sent to his superior attest, Serra dreaded the prospect of being alone, of enduring "this cruel solitude" occasioned by the need for priests to separate to build new missions. It had been a year since Serra had received a letter from "Christian lands" and those missionaries who would be sent to California had better be prepared to suffer. "Hardships they will have to face. . . ," he wrote, "and although I am not going to cry over it, it is childish to pretend that what I have had to put up with, and what I now endure, is any mere trifle. Where distances are so great, hardships must be faced."[30]

Serra's sense of the mystical fueled his actions. In July 1771 he led an expedition to establish mission San Antonio. After finding a suitable spot Serra ordered the mules unpacked and had the bells hung in the trees. He immediately started to ring them, crying out, "Come you gentiles, come to the Holy Church, come receive the Faith of Jesus Christ." His priestly companion asked why he did this since there were no pagans around. Serra replied that his heart overflowed and he needed to express it. Serra then exclaimed that he wished "that this bell were heard throughout the world, as the Venerable Mother, Sister María de Agreda, desired it, or at least that it were heard by every pagan who lives in this sierra."[31]

Within two years of the mission's founding, Franciscan missionaries at San Antonio had baptized 158 Indians and had learned the local languages in the process. María de Agreda, at least so Palóu and others believed, played a significant part in preparing the Indians of that region to accept Christianity. An elderly woman called Agueda came to be baptized saying that she believed what the Franciscans taught because when she was a young girl her parents told her that they had been visited by a man dressed as the Franciscans. This man had not traveled on foot; he flew through the air. The skeptical missionaries asked other Indians about this story and they confirmed it as part of their ancestors' lore. Palóu concluded that this flying monk was one of two whom María de Agreda said that St. Francis had sent to missionize this broad region but who had suffered martyrdom after many successes.[32] In this instance Franciscans accepted an Indian legend because it supported a Christian mystical belief. Belief in the supernormal helped encourage missionaries to continue in the daily struggle to evangelize a new and diverse people.

Serra had specific thoughts about how he would evangelize this new province in which he believed he had a free hand. His first altars yield clues to his vision. Critical was the Foundation Cross, a fifteen-foot icon erected outside the hut and later adobe building that housed the church. Upon the altar, in central position, stood an image of Mary. Typically she was represented as the woman from the Apocalypse, the vision of St. John in which a woman appears standing on a crescent moon. She either has or is about to have a child. A beast frequently depicted as a dragon or serpent threatens her. Archangel Michael brandishing a sword, however, protects her. Medieval interpretation of these images, an interpretation adhered to by Duns Scotus and Serra, held this woman to be Mary, the child to be her son Jesus, and the beast to be the Devil. St. John's vision was taken as another version of the nativity, not the chronological version but a view from outside the world, looking back upon that event. This apocalyptic view of the nativity addressed what humans must do to help the woman and her son to prevail over the beast. Archangel Michael alone would be insufficient. Humankind must do its part, the aggregated effort of each individual soul, to atone for the sufferings that child will endure on the Cross, sufferings He will make in reparation for humankind's Original Sin. Franciscans sought to instill in those who did not have it or to arouse in those who had become complacent about it this sense of personal responsibility and the obligation of each person to make reparation for Christ's suffering. This message had to be taught to new Christians. The Foundation Cross at each mission represented this apocalyptic view outside the world with an image of Mary on or above the altar inside the church representing the sublunar world of humankind; together these images constituted the primary coordinates of this iconographic system.

Mary could be represented in many ways, but those with particular signifi-cance to the Apocalypse were La Purísima (the Immaculate Conception) and Guadalupe. As La Purísima, Mary stood on a crescent moon, usually without the Christ child, a halo with stars above her head and clothed in finery, usually white. As Guadalupe, the dark Virgin who allegedly appeared to the Indian Juan Diego outside Mexico City in 1531, Mary, a blue cloak embroidered with stars around her shoulders, stood on a crescent moon crushing the ser-pent beneath her feet. Any image of Mary, however, could be converted into a Purísima by adding a halo with stars, as Serra did when he brought such a device along with two statues of Mary with him to California, only one of which was a Purísima.[33] Mary's flexibility of representation enabled the Fran-ciscans to communicate a variety of her role models to churchgoers.

Serra's iconographic system, in the tradition begun by St. Francis, sought to teach churchgoers important Christian messages every time they went to Mass. As had been done since medieval times, Franciscans segregated their neophytes by sex and by age, with the youngest placed closest to the altar. Men stood on the left or Gospel side of the altar where Truth was proclaimed, and women stood on the right or Epistle side of it to receive the Word. Generally, men were placed in line to view cross *santos* (images of saints) while women could see birth santos. Men also usually were given to contemplate a birth santo in the form of a male saint, like St. Anthony, holding the Christ child. In the medieval approach to church art that Serra brought to California, the content of the art far surpassed any concerns about its quality. Cross santos emphasized Christ's suffering and crucifixion, and those images were intended to teach male Indians their new role as head of a Christian family, the role of suffering for that family. Birth santos were to teach female Indians to model their behavior after the Virgin and to help maintain the integrity of the family. The most commonly used birth santo for women was the Guadalupe. The message of remolded behavior, especially for women, was rooted in the medieval saying that "sin came [to the world] through a woman, but salvation through a Virgin."[34]

These images, placed on side altars to the left and right of the central celebratory space, were visual reinforcements of the verbal instructions of the priests—not so subtle reminders that pagan behavior would have to be changed for the neophytes to become good Christians. Indians saw these images frequently. In preparing for baptism, they learned to recite the *doctrina,* or list of standard prayers, by rote twice a day, once in their native language and once in Spanish. This was usually done in the church. Moreover, everyone in the mission compound was obligated to attend Mass daily and all neophytes recited the doctrina at least once a day.[35] Franciscans believed that exposing Indians to these images at least twice, if not three times, daily for as long as the Indians lived in the missions would help teach them their proper roles as men and women, husbands and wives, and guide their behavior as Christians. One historian describing the altar and sanctuary arrangements at mission San Antonio suggested that similar designs applied to the altar arrangements for all the missions. "San Antonio's sanctuary design in mission times was unquestionably built to bring to mind the *Apocalypse* of John, the nativity of Christ, and the scholastic worldview [of Duns Scotus and Serra], to such a degree that it must be considered a most precious vestige of medievalism in America."[36]

Serra introduced medievalism and his apocalyptic view in the nativity play *Los Pastores,* a simple liturgical drama that recounted the visit of the shepherds to the Holy Family the night of Jesus's birth. During their journey the shepherds, male and female, encounter the Devil, St. Michael, and a Franciscan carrying a cross. The characters were invested with the quirks and idiosyncrasies of the Indians in the audience. Among the shepherds were Bartolo and Golita. Bartolo is a lazy man, frequently joking, who fails to take seriously what is happening. He becomes the Devil's primary target. Golita, a loquacious woman who sometimes misses what is happening because she is talking, is the female equivalent of Bartolo. The storyline has the shepherds traveling to Bethlehem (*Belén*) distracted by the Devil who tries to prevent their arrival. Along the way, the Franciscan assists them. Finally St. Michael defeats the Devil and brings the party to a stage covered by a curtain. St. Michael pulls the curtain back to reveal the Holy Family and the basis of humankind's salvation. Bartolo, however, is asleep and must be awakened and brought inside to have the mystery made clear to him. *Los Pastores* was performed in the mission churches following midnight Mass on Christmas Eve and at other times during Advent.

Figure 4. In *The Last Judgment,* a huge allegorical painting that formerly hung in the church of Mission Santa Barbara, Christ and a heavenly court float above an Earth in tumult, while souls writhe in torment before the mouth of Hell. The Franciscans used paintings and prints as didactic devices in their apostolic labors among the California Indians, seeking to convey the teachings and precepts of the Church and to guide the neophytes in their temporal lives as Christian men and women. The French explorer the Comte de la Pérouse, who expressed deep reservations about the mission system after a visit to Monterey, nonetheless appreciated the importance of such art, writing, "It is absolutely necessary to strike the senses of these new converts with the most lively impressions." Courtesy Santa Barbara Mission Archive-Library.

Franciscans intended that Indians see themselves in the play and to correct the bad behavior of the Bartolo or Golita in each of them. Moreover, they were supposed to see in this depiction that they were part of a larger story, a larger struggle between God and the Devil in which the Franciscans were helping them and so too would St. Michael and Mary. The Franciscan carrying the Cross was not an anachronism because this play, even when performed on Christ's birthday, was not merely about the historical fact of Christ's birth but, more important here, about the interpretation of the apocalyptic message that everyone needed to make reparations for Christ's sufferings. The Franciscans would help Indians in making their reparations. Indians, in turn, must do their part and *Los Pastores* was a way to learn how to do that.[37]

Serra, Palóu, and many of their colleagues shared a vision of apocalyptic hope. Even though historically they were situated in what Serra called "these last centuries"[38] there was no gloom or foreboding about Christ's return. Serra and his companions were helping bring together a new congregation of faithful for Christ, a congregation located in newly founded missions that would be filled, as María de Agreda had foretold, merely by hearing the voices of the sons of St. Francis. Apocalyptic hope, rooted in medieval Franciscan and Spanish mysticism, placed Serra firmly in the tradition of St. Francis and María de Agreda, as his first biographer, Palóu, carefully framed it.

To reinforce his point about Serra's humility, Palóu recalled that whenever Serra preached in the Sierra Gorda he removed his leather sandals and replaced them with humbler foot coverings made of hemp (*alpargatas*) in imitation of Christ's preaching. Serra wore the alpargatas until they fell apart. Palóu reminded his readers that our knowledge of Christ's footwear came from His mother, the Virgin Mary, through María de Agreda.[39] In Franciscan lore, then, Serra literally walked in Christ's shoes. On another occasion, while returning from preaching missions in the Huasteca (rugged terrain in eastern San Luis Potosí and northern Veracruz) Serra and his companions found themselves at dusk far short of their destination. Having determined to sleep in the open, they saw a light not far from the road and, walking toward it, found a small house. The Franciscans were greeted by an older man, his much younger wife, and son. The missionaries were well fed, attentively treated, and permitted to sleep in the house. The next morning they continued on their journey and after a few miles encountered a muleteer, a man whose knowledge of the roads he traveled was extensive and detailed, for his trade depended upon such information. He asked the missionaries where they had camped, and when he was told of the little house and family he remarked that there was no house in the entire area that the priests had traveled the previous day. The missionaries concluded that the Holy Family had given them sustenance.[40] Miraculously, Jesus, Mary, and Joseph had given Serra and his companions refuge and encouragement, thereby further sanctifying their work. Serra both imitated Christ down to the Savior's footwear and had received a miraculous favor from Him.

With the expulsion of the Jesuits from the Spanish Empire in 1767, the Franciscans had been elevated to the highest level of Spanish religious hierarchy. Serra had been chosen to lead the religious component of the Sacred Expedition. He was impatient to pursue the task because history soon would end. Serra and the Indians he baptized, whether they realized it or not, were to be part of the fulfillment of a Divine plan. Perseverance, hard work, and self-sacrifice would result in a restoration in California of something like the primitive Christian church: all souls living, working, and praying together under Franciscan guidance, ready for the reappearance of Jesus.

Serra's insistence on primacy in ordering the newly created mission communities put him at odds with civil authorities. He intended that Franciscans have complete control over the Indians and their punishments except in cases involving criminal matters such as assault, theft, robbery, killing horses and cattle, insurrection, and murder. In those instances he allowed civil authorities to deal appropriately with Indians. Room for disagreement, however, existed. Supplies sent from Mexico for the missions and the military, for example, became subjects for disputes over ownership. While the military role was to support the missionary endeavor, concerns over safety and logistics prompted commanders to question the timing and pace of mission founding.[41]

To accomplish their spiritual objective the priests needed to satisfy the material wants of those they missionized. Thus as populations at the missions grew, Franciscans divided labor in a manner that guaranteed food and clothing for everyone. Serra envisioned a mission chain, spaced roughly twenty-five leagues (65 miles) apart that permitted a traveling priest to spend every third night in a mission settlement.[42] Serra implemented in California the system he had used in the Sierra Gorda and that Franciscans before him had established in Texas. The goal was a self-contained economic unit that permitted the instruction, baptism, development, and maintenance of the religious life of the Indian turned neophyte, undisturbed by outside influences.[43]

The Mass, said daily as well as on Sundays, became central to spiritual and physical life. Attendance for all was mandatory, and priests or their assistants rounded up stragglers, pinching their ears or striking their ears and heads with a long stick that was also used to awaken those who fell asleep during the service. After Mass roll was called, and each Indian, upon hearing his or her name, approached the Franciscan to kiss his hand. Attendance accounted for, priests or their representatives assigned Indians to their tasks. Indians absent without an excuse were pursued and returned to their mission. Franciscans meted out punishment for desertion and for other matters such as insolence, tardiness or absence from Mass, carelessness in learning the doctrina, gambling, and bickering between spouses that led to violence, laziness, fornication, adultery, and concubinage. In medieval thought sexual transgressions violated the basic covenant between a monotheistic God and his people; Indian monogamy therefore meant fidelity, whereas Indian promiscuity signaled idolatry.[44]

Punishments included flogging, shackling, or incarcerating in stocks any mis-creant. Priests usually had assistants, frequently Indian, administer their punishments.[45]

The Franciscan approach to punishment was rooted in medieval thought and practice. New Christians were prone to backsliding — to reverting to ear-lier pagan practices that the priests tried to teach their new coreligionists was sinning. Sinning needed to be corrected in two ways: by the sacrament of Confession and by physical chastisement. The Mass was the daily participa-tory act of the entire community, and through it churchgoers made known their sinfulness publicly by the Act of Confession (*confiteor*). Punishment, except in the case of flogging for women, was also public and frequently administered following Mass. The public humiliation of sinners,[46] a wide-spread medieval discipline, was recapitulated in California — softened, how-ever, in Franciscan eyes by its association with the Mass. The ceremony of the Mass permitted reconciliation between God and sinner in a general way through the confiteor, but the temporal punishment accrued to each sinful act had to be atoned for either by additional time in Purgatory in the afterlife or by suffering corporal punishment in this world. Franciscans saw public punish-ment before the assembled community as a means to inculcate individual personal responsibility for sin that in turn would be confessed privately in the confessional. To maintain that sense of a closed community, outsiders were not to be present when neophytes were punished.

Some civil authorities appointed by the French kings of Spain tended to re-flect the newer ideas of the Age of Enlightenment, viewing the peculiar ar-rangement of priestly control in California simultaneously as backward and irritating. Although highly diverse intellectually and ultimately politically, Enlightenment thinkers shared a passion for the application of reason to hu-man problems and sought individual emancipation from older paternal con-trols such as those exercised by the functionaries of organized religion. The Swiss-born Jean-Jacques Rousseau had enormous influence on European elites through his thoughts on "natural man" and the rise of inequality. The "noble savage" if left to his own devices lives morally, argued Rousseau, but subject him to society and its "civilization" and he will lose his natural morality and become corrupt.[47] Thinking such as Rousseau's could not have been more different from Serra's medieval belief that only civilization could teach the Indian morality.

One of those Spaniards influenced by Enlightenment thinking was Pedro Fages, the first military commander of the presidios of San Diego and Mon-terey, whose interactions with Serra proved difficult, not least of all because they were equally strong-willed men. Fages disliked the upper hand the king had given the Franciscans in California, a situation unique for the time. Fages commanded two types of soldiers, his volunteers from Catalonia and the line soldiers, *soldados de cuero*, known as leatherjackets. The former, like Fages, were Spanish and professional; the latter, born in the New World, were more experienced in dealing with the frontiers of New Spain and were more casual about military regulations. Fages's reputation as a stern disciplinarian caused resentment and desertions among the leatherjackets, something the new venture could ill afford.[48] Soldiers were needed to protect the priests, and diminution in their number caused Fages to try to slow the founding of new missions. Any hesitation or delay angered Serra. At one point Serra took advantage of Fages's four-month trip to San Diego presidio to bring supplies back to Monterey to refound Carmel mission and to establish two new missions, San Antonio and San Gabriel, in the commander's absence.[49]

Serra found the soldiers' sexual immorality with Indians appalling and wanted the power to remove any guard whose behavior he deemed offensive. He had reports of soldiers molesting Indian boys when they came to visit mission San Gabriel and also learned that a soldier had sexually assaulted an Indian man there. Same-sex fornication Franciscans believed an abomination, something peculiar to Indians,[50] and so Serra concentrated on leatherjacket immorality with women. Serra was upset by and disapproved of two types of behavior: concubinage (*amancebamientos*) and rape. At San Antonio and San Luis the respective corporals of the guard lived with Indian women even after having been exhorted not to. The previous corporal at San Antonio had been removed for concubinage yet reassigned to San Luis. Later he was removed from San Luis for the same reason, and then reassigned to San Antonio! The persistent sinfulness of these men set a bad example for the neophytes and reinforced pagan customs. Since Indian women cooperated in these relationships they too scandalized female neophytes.

Rape, however, was worse. Serra had not known that such men could exist. Shortly after founding the mission of San Gabriel a soldier and companions set out ostensibly to round up cattle. Serra thought the real reason was to catch women. In the course of their activities they shot and killed the primary Gabrielino chief in the area, decapitated him, and brought the head back to the mission for display. Fearing reprisal, Fages reinforced the San Gabriel mission guard to nearly twenty men. Morale plummeted from inactivity and the corporal could not control the leatherjackets who went out in the mornings in groups of six or more to plunder the countryside. When Indians saw them they fled, but these riders used their skills with rope to lasso women like cattle and then rape them. The situation to the south was no better. In San Diego, a soldier named Camacho had killed an Indian girl in the course of raping her, and so terrible was his reputation among the Indians that when the priests passed through their territory their first question was whether Camacho accompanied them. Although he and another man judged equally bad by the priests had been punished by banishment to Baja California, the troop scarcity in Alta California meant that they were going to return.[51]

Serra's distress and anguish over troop behavior and what he regarded as Fages's lack of respect for the priests and lack of support for the religious enterprise prompted the father president to seek redress at the highest civil level, from the viceroy in Mexico City. Serra decided to travel in person to plead his case in late 1772. On his way to meet the viceroy, Serra suffered two bouts of an undiagnosed fever, each attack of which threatened his life. Serra was given Last Rites on the first occasion in Guadalajara, and following a relapse after he continued to travel he was about to be given them again in Querétaro when he recovered. His will to continue permitted him to prevail in such matters. While in the Sierra Gorda someone poisoned his altar wine, and on another occasion he narrowly averted a plot against him on the steps of his church in Jalpan.[52] Serra let nothing stand in his way, and in this matter of California he deeply wanted to prevail.

Serra had a plan for California, and he needed Viceroy Antonio María de Bucareli Ursua's approval. They met and talked in March 1773, and Serra later, at Bucareli's request, sent the viceroy a written request, or *representación,* of what he wanted. Of the thirty-two points Serra made, near the top of his list was the removal of Fages, primarily because of the desertion of the leatherjackets and because of Fages's haughty attitude and his overwork of the line troops. Serra thought that regular soldiers were inappropriate for command on frontiers and recommended that José Francisco Ortega — a leatherjacket sergeant whom he had known since the beginning of the Sacred Expedition and worked well with at Carmel — replace Fages. Serra also specifically asked that missionaries be given the power to request removal of any soldier from the mission guard who was a bad example to the Indians, especially in sexual matters. The missionary need not disclose the reason he asked for the removal, but the new commandant would order the soldier back to the presidio and send in his stead another, or others, who would not create scandal. Many other issues were addressed, involving logistics, supplies, weights and measures, and pay.[53]

On May 6, 1773, the viceroy and his counselors met, acted on Serra's request, and issued a new regulation (*reglamento*) concerning California. Fages and his Catalonian volunteers would be removed and those troops replaced by leatherjackets. Any soldier of the mission guard who was a bad example to the Indians could be removed to the nearest presidio at a missionary's request without the need for the priest to explain himself. Upon submitting that request to the commandant or governor that official would act upon it immediately. Sergeant Ortega was promoted to lieutenant and given charge of San Diego presidio. The new commandant, however, would be a regular army officer who had served with the Sacred Expedition and was then sent to Baja California, Fernando de Rivera y Moncada. And when the new regulation was reviewed in Spain, concern arose over the power of the missionary to have a soldier removed. Secrecy proved the sticking point. Such removal, it was feared, would weaken military discipline since not all priests would have Serra's integrity and in ten, fifteen, or fifty years the practice could degenerate into priestly dominion over the military. For this reason subsequent governors would quarrel over this point with missionaries. Yet at the time and in the historical literature it seemed as though Serra had obtained nearly all that he had requested.[54]

Palóu thought that Bucareli had endorsed Serra's proposal, even to the point of desiring that missionaries accompany future naval explorations along the northern California coast, because he had been moved by Serra's story that pagans would come to their Holy Faith merely at the sight of the sons of St. Francis. Bucareli had not known previously of this prophecy by María de Agreda.[55] He may have had other than religious reasons for his action. The viceroy could see what a powerful motivator for accomplishing difficult objectives in a very remote frontier this belief in the nun's prophecy had upon the father president. Serra returned to California relieved and renewed.

Serra had accomplished a conservative restoration. Officially, missionaries had complete control over their Indians except in crimes already mentioned. Legally the priests stood as parents to children or as guardians to wards; Indians were their adult children or charges, not independent adults. As such, Indians were subject to the authority of their religious superiors. "The management, control, punishment, and education of baptized Indians pertain exclusively to the missionary Fathers," as the reglamento clearly stated.[56] Priests had charge over every aspect of a neophyte's religious and social life. Serra's bailiwick, however, remained an anomaly in an empire undergoing reformation by Enlightenment ideas. While King Carlos III had written Bucareli that the primary purpose of the colonization of California was Indian evangelization, the king nevertheless pursued a policy of regalism in Spanish America, of tightening state control over the church.[57] Although that policy had taken a detour in California because of the political need to move quickly to fill a void that foreigners might exploit, it was still the central direction in which the state moved. In colonizing the province of Nuevo Santander along the gulf coast between Tampico and Texas in the late eighteenth century, for example, Jose

Escandón wanted Indians to become Christianized and Hispanicized by living with families of established Christians, the gente de razón.[58] He enjoyed some success using colonists instead of missionaries, but it was an example Serra abominated. Escandón had tried this experiment before, in the Sierra Gorda as a rival model to the program of the College of San Fernando. Serra and his fellow Franciscans had opposed it then as well.[59] Fraternizing with settlers, Serra believed, would harm new Christians. Franciscans like Serra believed that keeping Indians in the missions protected them from exploitation by colonists; colonial authorities, however, came to see Indian isolation as missionary exploitation that prevented Indian assimilation into the empire. Such conflicting views colored the entire missionary experience in Alta California.

4

The Indians of San Diego Say "No!"

The tension among Indians, missionaries, and soldiers is best revealed in the events surrounding the Indian revolt against mission San Diego in 1785.[1] The Spanish occupation of San Diego adversely affected Indians in several ways. Soldiers and missionaries established their presidio and original mission in an Indian village. Spanish soldiers turned cattle, horses, and mules out to graze on what they took to be open land; the land Indians used to cultivate grasses for food. Spanish animals competed directly with Indian people for scarce food supplies. Consequently, Indians began to shoot Spanish animals and soldiers responded with punishments and reprisals, a cycle that continued for years. At San Diego the issue of food for neophytes critically and directly affected the ability of the missionaries to proselytize because of a long-standing policy of accepting no more candidates for baptism than could be fed and clothed. Padre Luis Jayme counted only fifty-five total baptisms from mission founding in July 1769 until early summer 1772, when he stopped seeking or accepting more for want of food. Soldiers contributed to the food shortage by taking the mission mules for work on the presidio. When returned to the mission, the exhausted animals were too weak to plow. Without plowed fields there could be no crops. Jayme therefore had to send or allow his Indians to leave the mission to hunt and range the countryside for sustenance.

Beyond taking their land and disrupting their struggle for survival, Spanish soldiers also took Indian women as sexual partners. When it was done forc-ibly — rape — the action outraged the entire Indian village. Jayme reported discovering that an Indian woman, after being raped by three soldiers, had become pregnant. When she told the priest that she intended to abort the child, a distraught Jayme implored her not to do it. Later, however, he learned that she killed the infant following its birth; other Indians told him that the child had a light complexion, confirming her story. On another occasion three soldiers serially raped two Indian women in a corral, then put in stocks a neo-phyte male who happened to be in the Indian village when they did it. Punish-ing the neophyte, they thought, would keep him silent. They were wrong. Jayme defied the corporal of the guard, released the Indian, and learned of the incident from him, from both women, and from other villagers. Incensed Indians demanded of Jayme how these men who called themselves Christians, *gente de razón,* could transgress their own moral code when the Indians, before hearing the word of the Christian God, had believed such behavior reprehensible and had refrained from it. Jayme had no answer.

Indians could identify by name some of the soldiers, and one man had participated in both events. Punishment by the commander, however, was erratic. Soldiers were not to be publicly punished for fear of emboldening Indians to resist them. Fages incarcerated them instead. Yet when they prom-ised to work on the construction of the presidio, Fages released them. Over time, Fages ceased punishing or reprimanding them at all in San Diego, de-spite the long-standing orders against mistreatment of Indian women. By the early 1770s Diegueño Indians had many reasons for resenting the Spanish sol-diers and priests. Soldiers took their land, Spanish cattle and horses took their foodstuffs, and some soldiers sexually violated Indian women. Spanish-introduced disease began to kill native people. The new religion of Christ offered no improvement upon their own, and its vaunted moral superiority was undermined by the hypocrisy of its followers, all of whom considered themselves superior to any Indian.

As head missionary at San Diego, Jayme wanted to move the mission away from the presidio and soldiers to a site more conducive to agriculture and more removed from potential moral scandal. He felt that soldier abuses of Indian women and the reprisals these abuses provoked, created a condition in which, "what the Devil does not succeed in accomplishing among the pagans, is accomplished by Christians." Serra and the College of San Fernando agreed and by August 1774 the mission had been effectively relocated two leagues (five miles) east, in a valley, at a spot visible from the presidio should soldiers be needed for any reason. Once again, however, the Spanish occupied a site inhabited by Indians, and their intrusion along with the foraging of their large

Figure 5. Tribesmen defend their village against a leatherjacket Spanish dragoon in a drawing titled *How California Indians Fight* by the artist José Cardero, who visited Monterey in 1791 with the Malaspina expedition. Native Californians usually fled in the face of superior Hispanic arms and tactics, but they were able warriors, who on occasion were capable of large-scale military actions that required cooperation among smaller tribes as well as between neophytes and pagans. Not long after midnight on November 5, 1775, a force of 600 Diegueños, seeking to drive the Spaniards from their lands, attacked Mission San Diego, killing two artisans and Padre Luís Jayme and burning the compound to the ground. Courtesy Museo Naval, Madrid. Photograph Courtesy Iris Engstrand.

animals provoked resentment. With a better but still precarious food base, priests increased the number of total baptisms gradually during the remainder of 1774, rising to 116 Indians, double the figure of 55 two years earlier.

Diegueño leaders decided to rid themselves of the Spanish presence and devised a comprehensive plan to achieve it. Indians needed to learn more about the working of the mission before acting against it, and that could happen only if Kumeyaay villagers agreed to join it. They began in 1775 by coming to the mission seeking baptism in ever greater numbers, overwhelming Jayme and his fellow missionaries with their sheer body count. Jayme and his fellow missionary Vicente Fuster found themselves forced to adopt, at least temporarily, the Jesuit practice from Baja California of allowing baptized Indians to live in their own *rancherías,* or villages, because the priests could not feed them. The missionaries believed that permitting neophytes to live among the gentiles was an odious but necessary concession since the Indians' professed love for Christianity seemed so strong. The more advanced among them would lead the rest in prayer within their rancherías, and the entire group would come to the rough mission church of thatch, brush, and wood for Mass on Sundays and feast days. The catechumens visited the mission daily to recite the *doctrina*. As a result Indians came and went with scant control over their movements by the Spanish, a condition Fages had tried strenuously to avoid and which the new commandant, Rivera, now could scarcely prevent. It was an unstable situation for evangelization since neophytes continued to attend pagan dances in their rancherías and the priests could only threaten and admonish them for their backsliding. Military expeditions to return runaways and punish thieves encouraged Indian plotting.

By early November missionaries had baptized a total of 480, more than 100 of whom were baptized during the previous month. Since the beginning of the year the mission population had increased threefold. Despite the difficulties in managing such numbers, the missionaries believed that finally success was upon them. Franciscans saw in this harvest of souls the hand of their God, not the calculated plan of a disgruntled people seeking intelligence about their oppressors. Yet the missionaries received warnings. Interpreters alerted them to a large conspiracy by neophytes and pagans to attack and destroy the mission, kill the priests and soldiers, and drive out the Spanish. Jayme dismissed such reports as gossip and, following several warnings, told the Indians plainly that the next person to report such lies would be whipped. Jayme loved his Indians and could not believe that they did not love him in return, that they might want him dead.

Meanwhile, plans to found a new mission, San Juan Capistrano, went forward albeit unevenly. Ortega, the commander of the presidio at San Diego thanks to Serra's intervention, was to take Padre Fermín Francisco de Lasuén and several soldiers with him north where he would join a party of priests and a guard sent from Monterey to initiate this project. Most soldiers did not want to leave San Diego, fearing that there would be even less to eat at the new site and complaining that they did not want to work building a mission. Several flatly refused to go, declaring themselves to be soldiers of the king not his manual laborers. Ortega used his sword point to roust these men to do his bidding. Thus on October 19, 1775, Ortega, Lasuén, and twelve soldiers, half the presidial guard, left San Diego. Of the eleven soldiers remaining in San Diego, six stayed at the presidio and five formed the *escolta,* or mission guard, stationed at the new site. One of those mission soldiers, complaining of illness, returned to the presidio in late October and was not replaced.

The Indians observed everything. Sending messengers as far away as the Colorado River, Southern Diegueño village headmen and shamans plotted a two-pronged attack on the presidio and the mission. Out of twenty-five rancherías located within twelves leagues (thirty-one miles) of the presidio, fifteen contributed warriors, and throughout the second half of October Indians stockpiled weapons at selected sites and gathered information on the foreigners' movements. Ultimately three of the four primary conspirators came from so-called Christian rancherías, the most prominent of whom had been given the name Carlos at baptism. Carlos had enlisted men and support from many pagan villages as well so that the combined effort reflected the resentments of many but not all of the Southern Diegueño [Ipai], whereas most of the Northern Diegueño [Tipai], both neophytes and gentiles, declined the invitation to join the conspiracy.

On the afternoon of November 4, 1775, neophytes from two nearby rancherías came to spend the night before attending Mass the next morning. Following dinner, Padre Jayme adjourned to the priest's room adjacent the church and Padre Fuster retired to the warehouse/granary at the rear of the compound. Also staying at the mission were two boys, the son and nephew of the recently departed Lieutenant Ortega, two blacksmiths, one master carpenter, and the four-man escolta. The number of Spaniards able to fight stood at seven. The night proved cold and the soldiers built an open fire in front of their roughly made guardhouse. Since they suspected nothing, however, the entire group went to sleep without posting a guard and the sentry stayed by the fire.

While the Spanish slept, Diegueño warriors in various-sized groups totaling 600 crept silently toward the mission. They surrounded first the nearby rancherías and secured their silence by threatening to kill anyone who gave an alarm. The attackers then divided their forces so that half continued on toward the presidio. At the mission the Indians encircled the entire compound, then entered and quietly looted the church before setting the structure afire and raising a war cry.

At about one o'clock in the morning Fuster awakened to the noise of yelling and gunfire. Half asleep, he stumbled outside to see the church aflame and rushed to the guardhouse to learn what was happening. Fuster had scarcely blurted out his question when "I saw on all sides around me so many arrows that you could not possibly count them. There we were," he continued, "surrounded on all sides by flames." Soldiers, priest, and the two boys made their way to the warehouse, where one room had been finished on three sides just the day before. One soldier who did not have his leatherjacket, an effective piece of body armor against arrows, suffered so many wounds in the initial assault that he was unable to fight. Another became similarly disabled. As the two remaining soldiers fired their muskets at the Indians, Fuster took the two boys into an adjacent room where they fell to their knees and Fuster led them in prayer to God, Mary Most Holy, San Diego, and other saints to deliver them from the Indians and the flames.

At that point Fuster wondered about his fellow missionary and rushed out of the granary and back toward the priests' quarters. Although the room was aflame and smoke-filled, Fuster entered and searched above and below the bed for Jayme but found no one, then fled before the roof beams collapsed. Fuster returned to the granary to secure the boys when a soldier asked for the store of mission gunpowder. Astonished and frightened, Fuster realized that it lay in the now burning granary and, recognizing that if he did not secure it the resultant explosion would surely kill them all, he boldly ran in and retrieved it. For the remainder of the fight the soldiers had Fuster hold the powder bags for them to reload and to prevent flaming arrows from striking them. No place provided refuge, for the Indians torched every retreat. As Fuster wrote, "It was necessary to move elsewhere; but in the whole of the mission there was nowhere to go, because everything was on fire, and not even the smallest building escaped." Finally they made a stand in a loosely packed adobe building finished on three sides that served as a cookhouse. By piling up boxes they could close the opening to about chest height. When the Indians discovered them, as Fuster witnessed, "with united forces they hurled such a storm of arrows, rocks, adobes and firebrands that it seemed they were determined to bury us under them. The two soldiers who alone were fit to fight kept up a constant fire." At that point Fuster sustained "a terrible blow from a piece of rock" that hit his shoulder, giving him "plenty of pain."

Fuster knew the desperateness of the situation. One of the blacksmiths had already died, the master carpenter lay mortally wounded, only two soldiers and a blacksmith could fight, and the enemy gave no sign of retreat. "We were all longing for daylight—there was plenty of the other kind," he wrote, "and that night seemed as long to us as the pains of Purgatory. The arrows stopped coming for a while, but not the rocks and firebrands." Fuster sensed that the Indians held their arrows back for a dawn attack. "And sure enough my suspicions were well grounded," he noted. "Scarcely had dawn appeared than they let loose such a storm of arrows as to overwhelm us. I could hear numbers of the enemy, who until recently had been my trusted children, giving orders that now they should once and for all make an end of us." But, in Fuster's view, Divine Providence saved them in the form of a well-timed volley of musket fire from the Spanish defenders that disheartened and scattered the attackers. Actually, the Indians feared attack from the presidial soldiers. When the hostile Diegueño withdrew, local neophytes returned and assured the priest and his companions that the danger had now passed.

Jayme's whereabouts became Fuster's principal concern. When the violence against the church began, Jayme, awakened by the noise, went forth greeting the Indians with the customary Franciscan salutation, "Amar a Dios, hijos" (Love God, my children), and disappeared among them. Loyal neophytes searched for him at Fuster's request and reported that they had found him, a short distance from the mission, dead. The news filled Fuster with grief and sorrow; then the Indians brought him the corpse. "If the news that he was already dead was a blow to me," he wrote, "how much harder it was to bear when I saw he was quite unrecognizable. He was disfigured from head to foot, and I could see that his death had been cruel beyond description and to the complete satisfaction of the barbarians." Luis Jayme had been stripped naked, shot through with countless arrows, and his face, to Fuster, appeared "one great bruise from the clubbing and stoning it had suffered. The only way my eyes could recognize him to be Father Luis was from the whiteness of his skin and the tonsure on his head." Upon seeing his fallen comrade Fuster fainted, slumping over the body of Jayme, where he remained unconscious for a long time until some Indian women revived him with water.

The original Indian plan had called for the group assaulting the presidio to burn the buildings there. Those flames would signal the warriors at the mission to burn it at the same time. But someone had lit the fire at the mission before the attacking party at the presidio had taken up their positions. Upon seeing the flames they feared that the presidial soldiers would ride to the relief of their comrades in the valley, so the second band of warriors returned to the mission to help their brothers. The soldiers at the presidio, however, claimed to have seen nothing and continued in their unguarded sleep, learning only in the morning of the events at the mission. Priests and soldiers attributed the failure of the two-pronged assault to their God's will. More than two centuries later and despite the advances made in weaponry and communication, a simultaneous attack on two sites was regarded as extraordinarily challenging.[2] The eighteenth-century Diegueño, therefore, had accomplished a difficult military action, with human initiative seemingly more responsible for the outcome than Divine Providence.

Angry Diegueño warriors had burned the mission compound to the ground, leaving only the bells unscorched. They killed one-third of the potential fighting men at the post and a priest. They had killed a Spanish carpenter and blacksmith, although the soldiers they wounded later recovered. The Indians had ritually executed missionary Jayme by shooting more than twenty arrows into him and desecrated his body with blows from wooden sabers and stones in a multi-authored, ritualized destruction of the man and his religion. Moreover, they had taken religious objects from the church, destroyed or taken most of the grain supplies, and killed mission cattle. They sent a clear message of rejection of all things Spanish. That was a message, however, that most Franciscans could not hear. Palóu was with Serra when the news of San Diego arrived. Upon reading the reports the father president exclaimed, "Thanks be to God! Now indeed that land has been watered [with a martyr's blood]; certainly the San Diego Indians now will be converted."[3] Jayme, who died for his religion at the hands of the enemies of Christ, was a martyr and a saint to Franciscans. When Serra said the Mass in his honor he told the congregants not to pray *for* Jayme but rather *to* him so that he might intercede on their behalf with God. More than any other act, this martyrdom made San Diego irrevocably Franciscan territory.[4]

Repercussions from the revolt rippled outward in ever enlarging circles. Ortega, the first to learn of it on November 7, had his men bury the bells and supplies, thus effectively abandoning work at San Juan Capistrano, and returned to San Diego. The arrival of Fathers Lasuén and Gregorio Amurrió, who had been with Ortega and who were to become missionaries at the new site, afforded some comfort to the distraught Father Fuster. Ortega began immediately to lead soldiers into the countryside to query natives and to round up suspects. He used the lash and the torch to secure his information; military reprisals had begun.[5] Ortega also had to prepare a report to Rivera, his superior, in Monterey, and Fuster had to do the same for Serra. This process consumed the remainder of the month.

As Fuster wrote: "What upsets me most is that I cannot place full confidence in the Christians [neophytes] who remain with us." Rumors abounded for several months that the Indians would strike again, that the mission was but the first of their targets, and that more sites would be attacked to expel the foreigners. In that climate the mission was relocated back to the presidio, in temporary quarters. Since the priests felt distrustful of all natives, they temporarily suspended proselytizing.

The reports from San Diego did not reach Monterey for more than a month. Rivera immediately rode to Carmel to give Serra the grim news. Rivera allegedly told Serra that the only good thing about the incident was that the Indians had not killed any of his soldiers. By implication civilians were expendable. Rivera blamed Ortega for the incident because he was off doing Franciscan business and not minding the military affairs of the presidio. Serra wanted to accompany Rivera on his trip south to San Diego, but the commandant demurred, claiming that he would be traveling too fast for the priest.

A frustrated Serra reconciled himself to traveling to San Diego later and resorted to the pen to flank his military adversary. Serra wrote to Viceroy Bucareli, who had confirmed his position in the *reglamento* of May 6, 1763. Serra began by correctly concluding that the Indians had destroyed not one but two missions in their assault and then stated that the lack of Rivera's support prompted him to seek the viceroy's commitment to reestablish these two missions immediately. Serra described what he knew of the attack, and although he did not know the identities of the murderers he nonetheless recommended mercy and not punishment for the guilty Indians. At the beginning of the Sacred Expedition, Serra wrote Bucareli, "One of the most important requests I made . . . was that if the Indians, pagan or Christian, killed me then they should be forgiven." Serra observed further, "While the missionary is alive, let the soldiers guard him . . . but after the missionary has been murdered what can we gain by military campaigns?" Serra answered his own rhetorical question with the military argument that such campaigns frightened the Indians and deterred their further aggression. Serra argued that preventing future death could be accomplished by soldiers' guarding the priests better than they had. As to the murderer's fate, Serra replied, "Let him live so that he should be saved for that is the reason that we came here and the justification of our claim [to evangelize and colonize]."[6]

It would be months before Bucareli received Serra's letter and months more before Serra got a reply. In that interval Serra discovered the reason behind the San Diego uprising. By luck, an expedition of colonists and soldiers from Mexico City, led by Juan de Anza and accompanied by a Franciscan chaplain, Pedro Font, encountered Rivera at mission San Gabriel. Anza, who was headed north to help found San Francisco, immediately reversed direction and went with Rivera to San Diego. As part of their company, Font kept a diary of what he had seen and heard. Font noted that among the icons taken from the altar had been a statue of La Purísima, the woman of the Apocalypse. It was never recovered.[7] Serra now recognized his true enemy: the beast who threatened the woman, the Evil One, the Devil. Earlier, Jayme had blamed soldier abuse of Indian women for contributing to the Devil's interference in the missionary endeavor, for aiding Satan in making Indian conversions difficult.

Padre Palóu expressed the problem succintly. "The enemy [Satan]," Palóu wrote, "envious and resentful, no doubt because the pagans in that territory were being taken away from him, and because the missionaries, with their fervent zeal and apostolic labors, were steadily lessening his following, and little by little banishing heathenism from the neighborhood of the port of San Diego, found a means to stop these spiritual conquests."[8] Ignoring the role Indians themselves played in joining the mission in unprecedented numbers during the first ten months of 1775 to gain intelligence on Spanish activities, Palóu instead saw the Franciscan evangelical effort thwarted not by Indian resistance but by the Devil's manipulation.

Although Diegueño insurrectionists communicated clearly their rejection of

Spanish imperial and religious colonization, Serra and his companions could not hear them. Franciscan love for their Indians, consistent with the paternalism from which it sprang, could not allow the beloved freedom of choice. Priestly fathers knew best. Indians may not have been aware of it but they possessed an innate and deep-seated longing for the Christian God, a spiritual hunger that the Franciscans could help satisfy. Indians could remain gentiles only until such time as the missionary system, staffed with sufficient priests and producing enough food to feed them, could remove them from their pagan environment and remake them as Christians. Time, in Serra's view, favored the Franciscans; he could not imagine the circumstance under which Indians would say no to Christianity's "good news." Indian violence against missionaries, therefore, was misguided behavior and not a deliberate rejection of Christ. To Serra Indians were Satan's pawns. That Indians also could be seen as Franciscan pawns was a point Serra could not admit and perhaps not imagine.

Serra and his fellow missionaries understood in this instance that the Indians were absolved from full blame for what they had done because of the theological precept of "inculpable ignorance." This precept meant that Indian actions that transgressed Christian or natural law but which the Indians did not recognize as wrong were to be forgiven and such Indian misbehavior corrected by the priests.[9] Serra's plea to the viceroy for leniency was reconfirmed by this principle once he learned that Satan had been the author of the attack. Serra also redoubled his efforts to succeed in San Diego now that the real evildoer had been revealed.

The priestly view of their true adversary, however, found little sympathy among the military. Secular men saw the Indians as murderers, thieves, cattle killers, and rebels, not misguided followers of Satan. Indians were real or potential insurrectionists, as the military sorties of Ortega and Anza repeatedly revealed.[10] Font noted that Rivera ordered Indian suspects brought back to the presidio be "greeted" with fifty lashes. One Indian died from the flogging. When Font saw smoke from fires in the distance he mistakenly thought they were Indian signal fires instead of villages set aflame by Anza's and Rivera's troops.[11] Soldiers could visit their justice or their vengeance upon men but not upon a cloven-hoofed beast. To the military San Diego was an area that needed pacification by arms before any proselytizing could continue, and Rivera would not spare men to rebuild San Diego mission for eight months.

Bucareli received Rivera's report before Serra's letter had arrived, and initially Bucareli approved of Rivera's plan of punishment for the Indians. The viceroy ordered that more troops be recruited from Baja California to reinforce the northern presidios "since this outbreak convinces me how little trust one can have in the Indians under instruction, and much less in the pagans, when both groups unite to inflict hardship." Upon receiving Serra's letter, however, Bucareli was impressed by Serra's vision of returning anger with mildness, of treating the San Diego prisoners with leniency rather than harshness. Thus Bucareli ordered Commandant Rivera "to carry this out in consideration of the fact that it is the most feasible means for the pacification and tranquility of those souls, and perhaps the best method to convert the pagans, since thereby they will receive kindness and good treatment rather than the punishment and destruction of their villages which they had to expect because of their revolt."[12]

By the time the viceroy's letter favoring leniency reached California, however, the pattern of punishment had already been instituted and Commandant Rivera and the Franciscans had clashed over a neophyte Indian leader of the uprising accused of participating in the murder of Jayme — Carlos. Spanish authorities had been searching for Carlos since November without success. On the night of March 27, 1776, nearly five months after the attack and with guard duty unimproved by the recent experience, Carlos entered the presidio compound and hid in the back of a warehouse that served temporarily as the church. A startled Fuster found him there the next morning when the missionary went to say Mass. Carlos, a cagey neophyte, clearly knew that he would be better treated by the priests than by the soldiers. It is unclear whether he knew of the principle of sanctuary — the right of an accused criminal to seek asylum from civil authority in a church — or Fuster advised him of it, but when Fuster reported his presence to Rivera at the presidio, Fuster claimed that right for Carlos. Rivera demanded that Fuster turn Carlos over to him and Fuster, for the reason given, refused. If Rivera were to remove him from the church he would incur excommunication. Among other points, Rivera argued that the building was not a church but a storehouse made up as a church only when the Mass was said. An upset commander then took Carlos from the makeshift church forcibly; Fuster, after conferring with his fellow missionaries, countered by declaring Rivera excommunicated — unable to receive the sacraments and to participate fully in the spiritual life of the community. Military-religious relations had plummeted to a new low.

Rivera returned to Monterey to talk to Serra about his excommunication while Carlos remained imprisoned at San Diego. During the course of lengthy discussion Rivera argued that Carlos was too valuable and important a leader to allow to go free — he might incite further trouble. Ultimately, however, Rivera accepted Serra's judgment that he had behaved improperly. So Rivera returned to San Diego, and on May 18 in a single ceremony he returned Carlos to Fuster and received absolution from the censure of excommunication from

Lasuén. Then he requested that Fuster return Carlos to him, and this time the priest did. Thus ended an episode that contributed to Rivera's desire for retirement and transfer, to Fuster's further disillusionment with San Diego, and to a legacy of continuing contention between Cross and Crown in California.[13]

Serra arrived in San Diego in July 1776 anxious to rebuild its mission and to refound San Juan Capistrano. Everywhere he turned, however, he encountered frustration. He visited the Indian prisoners to comfort the neophytes and to convert the gentiles. The sergeant of the guard told Serra that one of the gentile prisoners had been an organizer of the attack upon Serra in 1769 and was held now as a suspect in the murder of Padre Jayme. Serra summoned all his energy to try to engage the man in conversation. He sought this unnamed Indian's conversion above all others and came repeatedly to the jail to exhort him to repent and guaranteed that he would be forgiven by the Christian God and the Spanish king. Other Indians responded to Serra and sought baptism; this man, however, said nothing at all. On the morning of August 15, the Feast of the Assumption, this Indian was found dead, strangled by a rope; Spanish authorities judged the deed a suicide although no one — soldier or Indian — had seen the prisoner do it.[14] Since it was exactly the seventh anniversary of the attack of 1769, the death of an unrepentant Indian participant in that event by his own hand might have aroused Serra's suspicion that soldiers had retaliated by murdering the Indian. Serra chose to ignore it and turned to other matters, this time involving his missionaries.

The College of San Fernando had sent Serra a lengthy document of regulations, a *patente,* seeking to limit his power, among other things, to move missionaries. Complaints from priests in California had clearly informed the new directive. Serra's response to the patente provides an unusual insight into missionary behavior in the early years of the spiritual conquest. Serra raised three instances of difficulties with missionaries that he was then experiencing and asked how the new requirement that the father president could move a missionary only upon that missionary's request could handle the situation. At one mission the two priests did not get along, and each asked Serra to remove the *other.* Without giving details, Serra described the behavior of both as scandalous. After Serra admonished them to improve, one of them corrected his behavior and the other did not. Scandalous behavior was coded language for immorality with women. The college in the same patente sought to remove temptations against chastity by forbidding the serving of food to soldiers' wives or to any other women at the houses of the missionaries.[15] At another mission one priest tormented the other in the hopes that his victim would request a transfer. It seemed just to Serra that the tormentor be removed, not the one tormented.

Serra's final case involved Fuster. He had sought to retire after Jayme's death, and when Serra denied the request because he needed Fuster in San Diego, Fuster then asked to have his fellow Catalonian, Padre Juan Figuer, transferred from mission San Luis Obispo to San Diego to be his companion. Figuer, however, was happy at San Luis Obispo and did not wish to leave. Figuer said he understood Fuster's loneliness and would do whatever Serra commanded in the spirit of Franciscan humility. Serra asked Figuer to write a formal request to be transferred to San Diego; Figuer would not do that because he genuinely did not want to go, but he would do so if Serra ordered. What, Serra asked his superiors, should he do in these cases? The issue was dropped, and Serra retained his right to assign missionaries where he needed them.[16] He then sent Figuer to San Diego.[17]

Fuster's emotional problems following the attack — his moodiness, irritability, and mistrust of those he came to save — proved emblematic of the disaffection that had crept into some other missionaries also. Fathers Amurrió and Lasuén joined Fuster in requesting to return to Mexico and the college. Serra, needing them in California, ignored their requests. Fuster's case, however, proved more severe. Fuster had expressed in his reports and in his conversations with Font a feeling of remorse that he had lived and Jayme had died. In describing Jayme's virtues he exalted those of the martyr and diminished his own: "I could see to my shame how shining were his virtues and what a weak imitation were my own poor efforts."[18] It would be two centuries, however, before any medical authority would classify Fuster as suffering from posttraumatic stress disorder, complete with survivor guilt, feelings of unworthiness, irritability, and mistrust of those he served.[19] Serra may have been impatient with Fuster because the first father president, too, had been attacked by these Indians and had held a dying servant in his arms while the assault surrounded him. At some point, however, Fuster's condition moved him. In the summer of 1777 Serra reassigned Fuster to mission San Gabriel.[20]

Serra's frustrations, however, continued with Carlos, one of the major leaders of the 1775 uprising. In a letter to Bucareli thanking him for granting leniency and for authorizing the rebuilding of missions San Diego and San Juan Capistrano, Serra reported that he had been forced to remind commander Rivera of the viceroy's amnesty so that Rivera would rescind his order sending Carlos into exile in Baja California.[21] When Felipe de Neve became governor and replaced Rivera, the viceroy repeated his decree of leniency for the San Diego Indian rebels.[22] Two years after his letter to the viceroy Serra again wrote Bucareli with the good tidings that clemency had worked. Serra had just been to San Diego, where he baptized several Indians including leaders of the 1775 attack. Moreover, he wrote movingly, "The two brothers who were the ringleaders of the whole uprising [Carlos and Francisco] are now such models of loyalty that they are the main support of the padres and have now been confirmed."[23]

Carlos's model behavior did not persist. Thirteen months later Serra expressed his exasperation at Carlos's continued poor conduct and that of another former Indian rebel. They had been involved in plotting against the Spanish, stockpiling bows and arrows, attacking neophyte rancherías, and even killing one Christian Indian. Perhaps what they needed, he mused, was to be sentenced to life imprisonment so that they could be told daily of the virtues of conversion and the benefits of Christ's love. Professing deep affection for them both, Serra averred that his only goal was to see them "die well"—that is, in a state of Christian grace so that they could go to Heaven.[24] Carlos, however, continued to be a troublemaker. He disappeared from the documents in 1782 following Serra's protest to Neve against the governor's plan to assign Carlos to seaman duty on ships exploring the coast. This would pervent him from scheming with others against the Spanish. Serra feared that Carlos might die at sea with no one to hear his final confession. Neve finally did banish Carlos to Baja California, and six years later Lasuén obtained his release.[25]

If any priest did hear Carlos's last confession there is no record of it. Carlos had participated in the attack upon the Spanish and Serra in 1769, then joined the mission. Yet he continued to plot trouble, becoming a ringleader of the 1775 uprising. Despite having received Confirmation—recognition of his maturation as a Christian—he continued to resist. Carlos apparently remained an insurgent to his end. Yet Serra could not hear him, could not believe that Carlos would reject the faith that Serra knew would save him. In Serra's paternal view as this Indian's spiritual father, Carlos really did not know his own mind.

5

Serra Refuses to Turn Back

Governor Felipe de Neve proved to be Serra's last major challenge. In Neve Serra encountered a most forceful expression of Enlightenment thinking and its criticism of his mission system.[1] Neve saw Indians as victims of Franciscan paternalism — adult children who should be allowed, even encouraged, to become adults. He disapproved of punishments for Indians, preferring instead to offer gifts, which he gave to every Indian he encountered — paid for from his own resources. Only if Indians proved rebellious did he think they needed punishment, and that would be administered by the military. Mindful of his king's insistence that Indians learn Spanish to become assimilated into the empire, Neve thought that Indians should have more contact with Spanish settlers, *gente de razón*, to learn the empire's language. Missions isolated Indians from contact with nonmissionaries, and Neve regarded that as retrograde. Neve valued Indian emancipation and assimilation over their salvation as defined in quarantine for religious instruction. This new approach, the Bourbons believed, would integrate Indians into society and dissolve the antipathy, if not horror, with which Indians viewed the name "Spaniard" in South and North America.[2]

Serra's missionary approach, rooted in scholastic thought and medieval practice, contrasted sharply with Neve's Enlightenment thinking and the Bourbon reforms such thinking produced. Neve did not make policy; rather, he tried to implement the policies of his superiors — policies with which he agreed. Since Serra had made his life these missions, they could be changed only if he changed. The man who never turned back would not alter a plan that he believed conformed to the Divine Will.

Given their differences and the strength of their respective convictions, these men could barely maintain civility in their interactions. Serra dreaded being in the governor's presence and once complained that the experience made him ill.[3] During one period of particularly intense pain from his infected leg, pain that prevented him from standing long enough to celebrate the Mass, Serra wrote that his sleeplessness and discomfort were caused "more by the head (*"del real,"* or Neve) than the legs."[4] Neve wrote of Serra's "unspeakable artifice and cleverness" and noted "there is no mischief these religious [under Serra] will not attempt if exasperated, such is their boundless unbelievable pride." Serra, Neve continued, "knows how to feign compliance in matters put before him, as well as how to avoid it."[5]

The conflict began because the priests, at Serra's direction, did not give the governor the inventories of their missions as he had requested. Without that information, Neve claimed, he could not plan for the colony, especially in its secular affairs. Priestly silence Neve correctly interpreted as secretiveness and a lack of cooperation with the civil authorities. Neve served as governor of both Californias, and although he eventually got the inventories from Baja California, Serra never gave him the reports from Alta California. When pressed, Serra told Neve he had sent them to his college in Mexico City as his duties demanded. Neve, however, interpreted this act as a refusal by Serra to recognize Neve's authority. Neve had to pursue his policies with only impressionistic data on mission populations, food production, animals, especially mules, and building materials.[6] Serra's silence concealed a base of rations for potential settlers, the newcomers Neve wanted for town-building, an important goal of Bourbon reforms. To Serra, towns would be a source of sin and scandal for neophytes and he opposed their creation. Eventually Neve succeeded in founding two pueblos, San José in the north near mission Santa Clara on November 29, 1777, and in the south El Pueblo de Nuestra Señora, la Reina de Los Angeles del Río de Porciuncula. This southern California town established on September 4, 1781, on the banks of the river that Padre Juan Crespi had named for the site in which St. Francis had founded the Franciscans, has become more commonly known as Los Angeles.[7]

Of all the controversies between the two men, the most important revolved around treatment of the Indians. Neve wanted a more measured pace in mission founding than Serra desired and began by increasing the number of soldiers at the presidios of San Diego, Monterey, and San Francisco. With more men he could dispatch punitive expeditions to reprimand Indian trouble-makers. To achieve his goal of concentrated military force, he resisted using soldiers to pursue runaway neophytes and limited the size of the mission *escolta*. Believing that mission "Indians' fates [were] worse than that of slaves" because the Franciscans were "independent and sovereign" in their control "without recognizing any other authority than their own religious superiors," Neve resolved to undermine that Franciscan authority through modernization.[8]

From 1749 the general Spanish plan for missionization envisioned that after about ten years of that experience Indian people would be ready to live on their own.[9] The mission would be secularized and become a *doctrina,* or proto-parish, because it would become a place where Indians would recite the doctrina on their own, without the mission's total immersion. Becoming a doctrina meant that the mission lands the priests had held in trust for their wards would be given over to the Indians to form a pueblo or town. Missionaries would move on to create new missions in other parts of the frontier and secular clergy would replace them. Religious property then would be reduced to the church buildings and priestly living quarters. Spanish settlers, however, had a different goal. They wanted the civil authorities who would dispose of the land to grant them large tracts and give Indians small plots for personal use, thereby forcing the former neophytes to labor for the newly land-rich settlers. The basis for Neve's approach to changing the status of California's missions came from the multivolume compendium of legal statutes entitled *Recopilación de leyes de los reynos de las Indias* (1681), more commonly known as the *Recopilación,* that theoretically regulated every aspect of Indian life under Spanish rule. While his interpretations may have been incorrect, Neve's frequent references to the *Recopilación* prompted Serra to beseech his College of San Fernando to send him a copy of the five-volume set for missionary use in the province.[10]

Without announcing his intentions to Serra but with the approval of his superior Teodoro de Croix, Neve announced in December 1778 that early in the new year missionaries should begin to give Indians experience in Spanish government. At the oldest missions of San Diego (1769) and San Carlos (1770) Indians were to elect two *alcaldes* (magistrates) and two *regidores* (councilmen); at the more recently founded missions of San Antonio, San Gabriel (both 1771), and San Luis Obispo (1772) Indians were to elect one alcalde and one regidor. After being chosen by their peers the new Indian officials were to report to the nearest presidio for their installation in office in the name of the king, to receive their instructions from the governor, and to accept for each alcalde a wooden staff of authority. These Indian officials would have jurisdiction in punishing their fellow neophytes; they, however, could be punished only by military authority. The most recently founded missions — San Francisco, San Juan Capistrano (both 1776), and Santa Clara (1777) — temporarily remained exempt from the experiment.[11]

As one historian has noted, "Despite the acceptance of Indian officials in missions elsewhere in New Spain, the Franciscans in Alta California bitterly opposed the elections."[12] Serra's reasons were obvious; priests would lose power and Indians would lose respect for them. Serra asked Neve to cancel the elections and he refused. The issue came to a head on Palm Sunday 1779 when, after a sharp exchange with Neve, Serra had to calm his emotions before saying the Mass. Later that night, as he tossed and turned, it came to him to behave as admonished in Matthew X: "Be prudent as serpents and simple as doves." Thus inspired, Serra wrote to his fellow missionaries, "Whatever the gentleman [Neve] wishes to be done should be done, but in such a manner that it does not cause the least change among the Indians or disturb the regimen you Fathers have established." Thus in San Diego Serra directed that Francisco, the brother of the conspirator Carlos, be made the first alcalde and "another might be from one of the *rancherías* that visit the mission every fifteen days." Regidores likewise were to be chosen from neophyte villages, preferably but not necessarily the chief. Serra concluded feelingly: "I hope in God that in this way the disadvantages will not follow that under the other arrangement would, almost of moral certainty, have resulted." The governor would have his elections but the Franciscans would choose the office holders.[13]

Serra's plan to thwart Neve with sham elections of friars' puppets as Indian officials quickly backfired. The puppets would not obey the puppeteers. In the first five mission priests found themselves powerless to punish the new officials without first consulting Neve. At San Carlos, Serra's headquarters, forty-five-year-old Baltazar, who had been a Christian for only four years, was selected the first alcalde and then complained of priestly mistreatment directly to the governor, who believed him. Apparently encouraged to independent action, Baltazar did as he pleased. He impregnated one of his relatives although he was already married, and he flogged a Baja California Indian for carrying out a priest's order that Baltazar disapproved. After finally being punished by the priests, Baltazar fled the mission for the mountains. To Franciscans Baltazar was a deserter, an adulterer, and an abuser of his office and of Indians. Nonetheless he exhorted those neophytes while on pass visiting relatives in the mountains to abandon the mission and join him in plotting against it. Indians who resented mission punishments or those with other complaints joined him, increasing the ranks of mission enemies in Serra's view. Within eighteen months of having been elected alcalde Baltazar died in a gentile ranchería an apostate.[14]

Serra did not elaborate on the numerous instances of alcalde abuses at San Diego, except to note the alcalde's role in getting older Indians to work at the presidio in violation of his idea of priestly control of Indian labor. Yet, Serra thought the proximity of the presidio and the possibility of quick military punishment of their wrongdoing limited alcaldes' misuse of their authority there. A mission forty or fifty leagues (104 or 130 miles) from their presidios, such as San Gabriel and San Luis Obispo, lacked such proximate corrective force. At San Gabriel the priests claimed to have positive proof that alcalde Nicolás worked as a pimp, supplying "women to as many soldiers as wanted them." At San Luis Obispo the alcalde kidnapped another man's wife and fled. Serra asked the governor whether such behavior could be permitted to continue unchecked since Franciscans had found evidence of disturbance at four of the five missions in which Neve had ordered elections.[15] Obviously it could not, and by April 1780 Neve relented. He allowed the missionaries to punish alcaldes and any other Indian officials when the circumstances warranted it while also giving the friars more latitude in the selection of Indian officers than his previous order had permitted.[16]

Serra's apparent victory gave him a measure of comfort but failed to restore the status quo. Annual elections became the norm and were introduced in all missions over five years old. Moreover, elections continued after Neve left and alcaldes gradually became a powerful internal force, sometimes cooperating and sometimes opposing the system in which they functioned. Under Mexican rule alcaldes would lead major revolts against the mission system and apply pressure from within that, complemented by the pressure of Enlightenment thinking from without, would lead to mission secularization in the 1830s. Serra did not know it, but Neve's wound ultimately would prove fatal to his enterprise.

Neve's concept of the missions deeply offended Serra because Neve viewed them as parishes, as established Indian churches requiring little more than the land of the church buildings and the priests' quarters to function. In that misunderstanding he cited the *Recopilación* to justify his call for Indian self-government and elections in the late 1780s. To Neve these establishments were what the *Recopilación* called doctrinas and certainly not missions, as Serra adamantly insisted his operations were. Serra took his objection to Neve's nomenclature and with it the corresponding diminution of his spiritual and temporal authority to Neve's superior. Once again Serra's position was sustained; to the commandant general of the Internal Provinces charged with oversight of New Spain's far northern frontier, Serra's enterprises indeed were missions and not doctrinas and Neve would have to help those already built and support the creation of more.[17]

While awaiting that judgment, however, Serra had to respond to Neve's charge, generated largely by Indian complaint, of priestly abuse of Indians through punishment, particularly by the whip. Serra wrote to Neve that "spiritual fathers [priests] punish their sons the Indians with lashes seems to be as old as the conquest of these kingdoms [the Americas] and so widespread that even the saints were no exception." Serra went on to invoke his personal role model St. Francis Solano. In Solano's biography Serra noted, "We read that while he had a special gift from God to soften the ferocity of the barbarous by the sweetness of his words, nevertheless in operating his mission in the province of Tucumán in Peru . . . when they failed to carry out his order he had his Indians whipped by his *fiscales* [Indian officials]." Neve found the practice of whipping an alcalde in California appalling, which Serra found surprising since the old Franciscan custom was all the more necessary in a land so recently Christianized. As to the severity of the whippings Serra remarked: "I am willing to admit that in the infliction of the punishment we are now discussing, there may have been inequalities and excesses [committed] on the part of some of the priests and that we are all exposed to err in that regard." Serra said that punishments with the whip, and occasional abuse, applied to all Indians, not just alcaldes, yet all Indians knew that the Franciscans were in California only for their salvation and they in turn knew that the missionaries loved them.[18]

Neve was unmoved by Franciscan protestations of love for their Indian children yet ultimately he could not interfere with Franciscan punishment of their legal wards. Invoking St. Francis Solano to a secular audience may have been bold for Serra given his own record of preaching missions in Solano's style in Mexico City. In one instance, it will be remembered, a male parishioner had grabbed from Serra the metal whip Serra had been using to scourge himself and then went to the back of the church, bared his chest, and began beating himself so severely with it that he died. In chastising Indians Serra unflinchingly employed the punishments used by his order, believing that he followed the practice of saints; Serra found having to explain such long-standing and repeated behavior to a governor a time-consuming irritant.

Serra was offended at Neve's permissive attitude toward fornication between soldiers and Indian women. Serra complained to Lasuén that he had heard from Neve's own lips that such fornication was "permitted in Rome and tolerated in Madrid" and for that reason, despite its being an offense against God, Serra could not use this as an argument against Neve.[19] Serra was as powerless to interfere in soldier–Indian sexual relations as Neve was to meddle in priestly punishment of neophytes. Neve had been, however, a strict disciplinarian regarding his soldiers' treatment of Indians. In building the presidio at Santa Barbara, for example, when a soldier mistreated an Indian Neve subjected him to the punishment of the cueras before the chief and other Chumash Indians. This punishment consisted of the guilty soldier parading in the hot sun wearing several layers of leather cuirasses, body armor made from skins, from which the name *soldados de cuero,* or leatherjacket soldiers, derived.[20] Neve thus humiliated publicly a Spanish soldier, a violation of the *Recopilación,* to show Indians his fairness. Indian rights would be respected and no soldier would be above Indian or Spanish law.[21]

Another Spanish experiment in settling the frontier during the Serra–Neve conflict, however, seemed to underscore Serra's successes. An inadequately provisioned and staffed mixed force of soldiers, settlers, laborers, and four Franciscans set out for the Colorado River in late 1780 to establish two hybrid presidio-pueblo-mission settlements among the Quechan Indians, whom the Spaniards called Yumas. These two settlements — Purísima Concepción across from present-day Yuma and San Pedro y San Pablo de Bicuner ten miles upriver — imposed the same deprivation on the Quechans as the Spanish settlement in San Diego had had upon the Diegueños. Quechans, linguistically related to the Diegueños, attacked Concepción on the morning of July 17, 1781, as Padre Francisco Garcés said the Mass. The Quechans killed over one hundred Spanish men, women, and children, enslaved the survivors, and completely destroyed the six-month-old settlements. They clubbed to death Garcés and the three other missionaries, then surprised and killed a military force led by Captain Rivera y Moncada, the same captain who had earlier caused Serra much grief and endured excommunication for violating the right of sanctuary of the Diegueño rebel, Carlos. With this military act, the Quechan effectively closed the land route from Sonora to California for the remainder of the Spanish and Mexican eras, making California solely dependent upon the sea for external supply.[22]

When news of the Quechan expulsion of the Spanish, events that the Spaniards regarded as a massacre, reached San Diego, Serra worried about its impact on the Diegueño. The martyred Franciscans had had nothing to do with his enterprise and had been drawn from the Apostolic College of Santa Cruz in Querétaro. Serra took pains to express his regret for the loss of life of priests, soldiers, and civilians — he said nothing of the loss of Indian life — but expressed his disapproval of the venture indirectly. "About what happened on the Colorado River," he wrote, "both in regards to the new experiment as well as to the deeply saddening disaster that followed, what can we say?"[23] Although covered with the blood of martyrs, Spanish authorities decided to regroup their frontier forces to deal with more pressing enemies like the Apache and so abandoned the Colorado River experiment. Nevertheless, the commandant general of the Internal Provinces thought that a substantial expedition should be sent to the Colorado River to punish the Quechan before the Spanish retired entirely.

The commandant general chose Neve to take his reassembled troops from California, march to the river, and there join with other forces sent to meet him so that a war of fire and blood could be waged on Spain's enemies under Neve's direction. All this took time and planning, so it was not until late August 1782 that Neve, at the river, met with those other forces, one of them under the command of Pedro Fages, who had been first commander of the presidios in California. While there in the field Neve received notice that he had been promoted to captain general of the Internal Provinces, requiring his removal to Sonora, and that Fages had been appointed to replace him as governor of both Californias. Neve's attempt at punishing the Quechan proved futile as the Indians evaded contact, took what food they had with them, and left him little to destroy. Chafed by the disappointment but anxious to assume his new duties, Neve nonetheless took the time to draw up detailed instructions for Fages to follow as governor.

Neve's instructions reflected his experiences and his goals. To him, the primary objective of government was "the preservation of the peninsula in perfect peace and tranquility, maintaining friendship and good treatment for all heathen peoples, and not allowing them to be molested in any way." To woo the Indians he had given gifts of beads and trinkets, stores of which he left behind for Fages. Neve described the use of the punishment of the cueras on soldiers guilty of Indian mistreatment so that all gentiles might understand "our [policy of] punishing with severity any transgression against them." Indians did, however, have a propensity to shoot horses and livestock, which was considered a crime against the common good. Neve had the culprits seized, brought to the presidio, and punished by shaming them publicly in the stocks for eight to ten days and giving them twenty to twenty-five lashes. Afterward "I admonished them with great kindness," Neve wrote. He then released them with a ration of shelled and fresh corn taken from his own stock. Neve believed that this practice was bringing success. He thought, however, that Serra did not sufficiently admonish the neophytes against such practices and that Fages should exhort him again to do so.

Neve told Fages that military relations with the missions were tense. Neve had curtailed the use of soldiers to pursue runaways, and he had insisted that the missionaries themselves assume that responsibility. Missionary requests for military escorts to hear confessions should be treated warily, since Neve wanted the soldiers back before dark and Serra and another missionary, on separate occasions, had used the protection afforded by the guard to extend their stays overnight in violation of Neve's policy. Moreover, Serra had still not supplied those mission inventories that Neve had requested repeatedly and he urged Fages to continue to press the point.

To Neve, "The continued growth of the towns is very important to the colony. Very soon their harvests and those of the missions will be able to supply the presidios with corn, wheat and beans relieving us from the need of transporting these foodstuffs from San Blas [on the coast of New Spain in the present Mexican state of Nayarit]." Although Neve did not then know that the Quechan attack had closed the overland supply road, he understood well the role the mission harvests, more than the harvests of the fledgling towns, could contribute to stabilize presidio life. Neve wanted Fages to develop sufficiently good relations with the missionaries that cooperation rather than conflict might ensue so that the presidios would be fed from local sources. Serra's age argued that he could not remain the father president much longer, and for the interim Neve urged Fages to remain "aloof," as he claimed that he had tried to do.[24] While Neve meant his *instrucción* to be a blueprint for his successor, Fages chose to use it as a guide. After all, he knew Serra from his earlier tour of duty.

For Serra the return of Fages, whose removal the father president had engineered ten years earlier, must have seemed like a nightmare revisited. Although Fages's governorship would be remembered more for the plotting of Gabrielino neophytes and gentiles against mission San Gabriel led by Toypurina than for his dealings with Serra, Fages's new relationship with Serra revealed a change in the governor's approach to the missionaries. Instead of going through the father president, Fages took his concerns directly to the priest involved.

From Teodoro Croix, the outgoing commandant general, Serra learned of the promotions of Neve and Fages and of Croix's concern that Serra do his part in implementing Croix's orders regarding punishment of neophytes and gentiles for robbing or killing livestock. "Though," wrote Serra, "I do not know what that might be." Serra wanted to answer Croix with his own set of questions. "I would certainly ask him to tell me, " Serra wrote, "if his program directs them [the soldiers] to castrate the gentiles, hang the gentiles, disembowel the gentiles, and butcher the gentiles indiscriminately, for having eaten some mares that had strayed into their home many leagues away. All these sad occurrences have been done under Señor Fages' administration."[25] Serra's complaints, however, went to the College of San Fernando, and he seemingly had little direct dealing with Fages.

In compiling his fifteen-year summary report and inventory for his head-quarters at Carmel mission, Serra had to rely on an assistant, Padre Mathías Antonio Noriega, because his health was failing. This report illustrated what Bourbon accountants wanted to hear: stories of quantitative success at mini-mal cost to the king. Beginning with a year-by-year summary of activity and culminating in a description of the total number of baptisms at Carmel of 1,006 — nearly 20 percent of total baptisms at all missions of 5,308 — Serra could point to spiritual success along with material accomplishment. In mis-sion building, construction had progressed from early reed structures to adobe churches, harvests had increased from small-plot farming to large-acreage cultivation, and herds had grown from a handful of animals to several hun-dred.[26] Under Serra's leadership and administration Franciscans had created nine missions in fifteen years, most of them judged successful by the standards of their day.

Although wracked by sickness Serra continued to fulfill his religious obliga-tions. On August 19, 1784, he celebrated the Mass in honor of San José, commemorating as he had each month for fifteen years the anniversary of the original Feast Day of March 19, 1770, when a disheartened group of Spanish soldiers, sailors, and priests saw the sail of the supply ship on the horizon off San Diego Bay that signaled the salvation of the Sacred Expedition. Nine days later, and one week after Neve, Serra died on August 28. The two men who had shaped early California more than anyone else found common ground only in death.

Serra's imprint on California mission history was significant both in his re-ligious intent and in his definition of success. He can be seen as a man margin-alized from the larger society of which he was a part. Although a Spaniard, he came from an island where relative isolation permitted a cultural lag with peninsular social thought. Throughout his life and despite his personal accom-plishments, Serra was ever the outsider. An islander for whom Spanish was a second language, a short, sickly intellectual of partly Jewish ancestry, Serra seemed possessed of a deep desire to succeed and could clothe or moderate his ambition only through the humility of the Franciscan life. Through study and learning he became a doctor of theology and later teacher of prescribed Fran-ciscan philosophy and theology at the Lullian University in Mallorca. That experience made him religiously medieval and antisecular at the very time that modernity, in the form of Enlightenment thought, sought an end to religious control over people and a thoroughgoing secular control over religion. Al-though Serra opposed the Enlightenment, his asceticism and seriousness of purpose combined with his vast religious knowledge and powerful speaking abilities made him charismatic rather than erratic within the conservative confines of the Franciscan world.

Teaching, contemplation, and personal cultivation alone, however, proved insufficient for Serra. At an advanced age for missionary work Serra moved to a marginal part of the Spanish Empire, the Indian frontier of the Sierra Gorda above Mexico City. From that outpost he learned the practice of missionization over twenty years, restlessly seeking a newer place to implement what he had learned. Finally, with the expulsion of the Jesuits for what the Bourbons' believed to be their refusal to submit to secular authority, Serra secured his best chance: beyond the established realm of Christendom lay a territory never before evangelized. A charismatic outsider had the opportunity to bring his marginalized ideas into a wilderness where his determination and administrative skills would permit them to grow.

Upon the theological clean slate of California Serra sought to inscribe his well-ordered understanding of the medieval world. In "these last centuries" before the Apocalypse, Serra would build a model of the primitive Christian church, a community of Indians and Franciscans clustered in their mission settlements learning and teaching Christian doctrine, preparing themselves for the return of Christ. Franciscans, free of external meddling by secular authorities and yielding fully to no authority but God's, would teach Indians their responsibility to pay for the sufferings of Christ. Together Franciscans and Indians, with the help of the Virgin Mary, Mother of God, would struggle against Satan in anticipation of the final victory because María de Agreda had prophesied that these pagans would come to God at the sight of the sons of St. Francis.

Serra, however, believed that this vision needed to be tempered by practical considerations. To create such a general community with its constituent communities, Indians would need to be fed. Only by feeding them regularly would their minds be freed from earthly distractions to contemplate life's larger truths as revealed in the accepted word of the Christian God. Temporalities — fields of grain and pasture, adobe churches, work buildings and houses, herds of livestock, flocks of sheep, looms to weave wool into blankets and garments to clothe the naked child of the forest — were all but instruments to free Indian minds to contemplate Jesus. Franciscans believed that the only way to accomplish their goal was to break the cycle of Indian life in which hunter-gatherers pursued alternating patterns of ceaseless labor for food followed by profligate indulgence afterward. The characteristics of gentile life in the forest must be expunged by neophyte life in the missions in which Indians would learn a

European division of labor and new skills. Serra's practicality and the material accomplishments of his system have tended to obscure the religious premise undergirding the whole enterprise.

Serra's religious convictions informed all his actions, and the threat of the Enlightenment lay not only in its emphasis upon secular control over religious authority but also in its struggle to abolish all aspects of the Medieval world. The challenge Enlightenment thinking posed to the medieval worldview in one minor illustration reveals the vast extent of this conflict. In medieval thought science could be explained theologically. In the Scholastic worldview, Serra taught, the universe was geocentric: spheres orbited an immovable earth as presented in the Ptolemaic system. The Copernican school that emerged in the fifteenth century, however, argued against this, saying that the earth and other planets revolved around the sun. In his lectures in Mallorca Serra taught the Scholastic view against upstart ideas. "Contrary to Copernicus," Serra wrote, "I suppose it absolutely manifest that the earth remains immovable and that all the heavens . . . are moved in a circle. I say, moreover, that the Spheres are not moved by themselves but by certain Intelligences or Angels."

Serra's thinking followed the teachings of Duns Scotus and others. One of those was the "Seraphic Doctor," St. Bonaventure, for whom Serra named his last mission in California, San Buenaventura. St. Bonaventure had written, "These [Angels] according to the philosophers move the celestial bodies, and according to the theologians, rule the universe in accordance with the powers of the supreme God *with respect to the work of reparation.*"[27] A copy of Serra's geocentric universe diagram and notes on his lectures were taken to mission San Antonio in California by Buenaventura Sitjar, one of Serra's former students, where he in turn attempted teaching it to the Indians.

Serra and his students could not accept a challenge to the Scholastic geocentric universe because it would destroy their theological explanation of how the universe behaved. God had Angels motivate the seven spheres described in the Apocalypse of John and represented on earth by the seven star-topped angels of the Christmas play *Los Pastores.*[28] Tampering with Scholastic science meant tampering with Scholastic theology — it meant violating the Apocalyptic message and the need for Indian reparation assisted by the Franciscans, which Serra would not and could not do. Enlightenment thinking, however, advocated the Copernican system that Serra abominated. Copernicus's system and later Newton's law of inertia, if accepted, would wreck havoc upon the Scholastic worldview and the critical role of and need for human reparation for Christ's suffering in preparation for His return. Let the new thinking advance and something as basic to communicating that message as *Los Pastores* would be doomed. On the frontier of a new province Serra could deal with

Figure 6. Father President Fermín Francisco de Lasuén and several other Franciscans receive the great French explorer Jean-François de Galaup, Comte de la Pérouse, and his staff at Mission San Carlos in September 1786. La Pérouse characterized Lasuén as "one of the most worthy and respectable men" he had ever met, declaring that "his mildness, charity, and affection for the Indians are beyond expression." Nonetheless, as a son of the Enlightenment, La Pérouse was troubled by the temporal and secular bondage of the neophytes and wondered if it would not be possible for the missionaries to select a few of the brightest and teach them "the advantages of society founded on the rights of the people." The drawing, a copy made of the original in 1791, is the earliest known image of a California mission. Courtesy Museo Naval, Madrid. Photograph courtesy Robin Inglis.

Enlightenment secular officials through his passive-aggressive behavior, never risking the open opposition that would earn him the dreaded label of "Jesuitical," and he could protect his fledgling community from dangerous and undermining thought. Serra adamantly defended Franciscan independence in controlling the Indians in their missions for deeply held religious reasons.

In punishing Indians Serra followed the example of his much admired forebears including St. Francis Solano rather than trying anything new. If whipping worked in Peru, in New Spain, and elsewhere, then it would work equally well in California. Flogging was merely an instrument, a means of correcting behavior the priests deemed sinful, especially behavior manifesting Indian cultural practices such as fornication, gambling, and native deity worship. Flogging also seemed the appropriate way to punish inattention at or avoidance of the Mass, lying, theft, laziness, insolence, unauthorized absences, fighting, and any other imaginable offense not punished by civil or military authority. Priestly life was filled with challenges, obligations, and sufferings, and if a priest occasionally abused his Indians that was an incidental but unintentional cost of missionization. Routine Franciscan practices after Serra confirmed this point.

No priest guilty of abusing his Indians was removed for it, as the case of Serra's assistant at mission Carmel reveals. While governor, Pedro Fages heard accusations that Padre Noriega punished his Indians excessively for the least infraction of missionary rule. Not wanting to believe it, Fages nonetheless conducted his own investigation. Determining that the charges were true, Fages wrote Noriega asking the priest to stop this mistreatment of neophytes in the name of the king, of Spanish law, and of humanity.[29] By avoiding the father president Fages hoped to secure cooperation through a direct personal relationship. Noriega doubtless showed this letter to the father president as Franciscan regulation dictated, but no reprimand has been recorded and Noriega continued in his post for another two years before returning to Mexico. His Franciscan biographer made no reference to this matter,[30] although another Franciscan historian cited it as an example of the "uncontrovertible testimony that delinquent Indians were whipped, sometimes excessively, by the padres."[31] Periodic charges of excessive punishment of neophytes by missionaries first arose under Neve and continued throughout the life of the missions. Serra's attitude in the matter clearly reflected his lack of concern: Indian eternal salvation outweighed their temporary earthly discomfort.

Serra began the practice in California of counting each baptism as another body won in the battle for Christianity against Satan. Baptism meant ipso facto conversion despite the evidence that neophytes had not yet truly forsaken their old ways and belief systems for the new ones. By counting baptisms as victories Franciscans regarded any return to gentile behavior as sin, or backsliding, that needed physical along with moral correction. In Serra's missions, as in those of his successors, death stalked and hobbled the missionary effort. More Indians died in the missions than were reproduced there, and that population shortfall caused the missionaries to expand their areas of gentile recruitment. Each new infusion of Indians meant restarting the conversion process and continuing the Franciscan belief that Indians were no more than adult children.

Following Serra's death a new father president was chosen, Padre Lasuén. He would take a more conciliatory attitude toward secular authority but continued Serra's religious vision. A new chapter in converting California had begun.

6

Fermín Francisco Lasuén and Evangelization

Fermín Francisco Lasuén, twenty-three years Serra's junior, had been tested and proven himself over a decade in California. Serra groomed the younger man as his replacement, and the College of San Fernando elected Lasuén the second father president of the missions. That early period in California, however, had been hard on him as he observed to a friend before he assumed his new post. Although only forty-six, Lasuén wrote, "I am already an old man and completely gray; although it is the toll of years, the price has been accelerated by the heavy burden of [my] office . . . and especially by the five years I am completing as superior at San Diego."[1] He had sought to escape Alta California shortly after he arrived by requesting a return to the College of San Fernando in Mexico but Serra had denied the petition. Serra thought Lasuén a better missionary than he did himself. From his entry to Alta California in 1773, Lasuén waited for a mission of his own until 1777, when Serra finally assigned him to San Diego, the worst of the missions situated in the midst of the hostile Diegueño, which had launched the 1775 Indian uprising. Confronting all the challenges of San Diego, Lasuén experienced a period of depression. In the spirit of Franciscan humility, however, he reconciled himself to his plight and endeavored to become a good missionary. By 1780 he had been able to get the Indians to erect a stone church there, finally leaving behind the temporary structures of wood and reed, and harvests had begun to increase. While Indians still lived in their own *rancherías* because there was yet insufficient food to feed them all, Serra nonetheless approvingly acknowledged Lasuén's accomplishments.[2]

Still it had been a rocky road for Lasuén because his temperament was different from Serra's. While stationed in Baja, Lasuén developed a friendship with Fernando Rivera y Moncada, commandant of the military forces in both Californias but then residing at Loreto. When Rivera moved his headquarters to Monterey in 1775 he discovered that Lasuén had no assignment (his posting to San Diego was two years away) and so asked Lasuén to ask Serra if he could be assigned to the presidio as Rivera's chaplain. Lasuén genuinely wanted that assignment, both to enjoy his friend's company and to have some constructive work. Serra, however, emphatically disapproved; he did not want to create a precedent of apostolic missionaries serving as presidial chaplains, and he disapproved both of Lasuén's request and of Lasuén's friendship with Rivera. When Rivera threatened to leave California if Lasuén were not assigned as his chaplain, the College of San Fernando acquiesced and Lasuén incurred Serra's coldness for two years before the irritant in the mind of the father president subsided.[3] Serra, unlike his subordinates Francisco Palóu and Lasuén, never developed a friendship with any senior army officer commanding in California, yet this ability would prove an indispensable asset for Lasuén and for protecting and furthering the Franciscan enterprise in the years following Serra's death.

The Franciscans needed a diplomat in their dealings with secular authority. They also needed one in dealing with one another. Lasuén, drawing on his personal experience, changed the policy of the father president assigning missionaries only at his discretion and allowed priests to request assignment at a mission of their choice. Lasuén actively tried to promote harmony among his fellow missionaries, although their individual pettiness and squabbles made the task more challenging than it had been for Serra if only because there were more of them. Lasuén wanted to avoid scandal of any kind among the missionaries and would accede to their requests if he could, not because he found their arguments persuasive but because he sought to avoid quasi-public griping and the gossip of scandal. Those who knew him described Lasuén as cultivated, generously outgoing, and possessed of a sweetness of character that made his company a delight — attributes that further distinguished him from Serra.[4]

As suggested by the building at San Diego, Lasuén proved to be a church builder, leaving behind many of the distinctive structures associated with the missions today such as the stone church with bell tower at Serra's mission Carmel and the distinctive brick and stone edifice at mission San Gabriel.

Lasuén founded a number of missions equal to Serra, nine, and together they founded eighteen of the twenty-one total in the first three decades following initial settlement. Comparative figures illustrate both men's accomplishments. At Serra's death in 1784, eighteen missionaries labored at nine missions; at Lasuén's death in 1803 forty priests served at eighteen of them.[5] Mission growth under Lasuén proved phenomenal. Mission harvests of cereal crops increased from 1784's 9,052 *fanegas* (1.3 bushels to a fanega[6]) to 44,926 fanegas in 1803, distributed among crops of wheat, barley, and corn. Mission cattle in the same period went from 6,813 to 77,578, with horses, mules, sheep, goats, and pigs showing similar gains. These animal and field products served a growing mission population. The number of neophytes living in the missions witnessed a corresponding increase, from 5,125 in 1784 to 15,562 in 1803.[7] Lasuén also introduced arts and crafts instruction that developed over time to a level sufficient to make the neophytes useful in supplying needed food and skills to presidios and towns.

Although Lasuén presided over a period of consolidation and growth for the missions, it would be a mistake to suppose that those were untroubled times. Under his cultivation three important future fathers president — Mariano Payeras, Vicente Sarría, and José Señán — learned to cope with the challenges of California. These very successful missionaries, however, were among a succession of troublesome missionaries reflecting hard times in New Spain and in Franciscan recruitment in Spain. Criticism of the order in Spain for its attachment to papal authority and for its success in adding recruits had made it vulnerable to questions of regal loyalty by the Bourbon kings. In Enlightenment thought, population growth meant economic development, and young men who joined mendicant orders and kept their vows of celibacy did not contribute to newly defined national goals. Franciscans had begun voluntarily to restrict the numbers of novices they would accept as testimony to their royal allegiance during and after the time the Alta California missions were being founded. Thus new missionaries would be needed at the very time when there were fewer to be recruited. Enlightenment thought heavily influenced many members of the smaller, younger groups of priests who came to the College of San Fernando in the 1780s. Internal dissension within the College of San Fernando ensued. A group of seven disgruntled friars, known as the *padres descontentos,* emerged who agreed with themselves and disagreed with all others. The crux of their complaints revolved around priestly administrations of temporalities, that contradiction at the heart of Franciscan operations that dated from the time of St. Francis. These *temporalistas* believed that the college should renounce its holdings, support secularization, and return to the abject poverty in which the order had been founded. Rebuffed by the majority

Figure 7. Mission San Gabriel in 1828, as portrayed in an oil painting made several years later, from a field sketch, by the German supercargo and naturalist Ferdinand Deppe. Founded in 1771, San Gabriel, like the other missions, flowered under the presidency of Fermín Francisco de Lasuén. During his years in office the magnificent stone church that still stands was constructed. When Deppe made his drawing, San Gabriel was at the height of its material prosperity. More than 26,000 cattle ranged the surrounding hills and plains, and the vineyard was the largest in California. But symptomatic of the unhealthy living conditions prevailing throughout the mission chain, the number of neophytes had been in decline since 1817. Courtesy Santa Barbara Mission Archive-Library.

of their colleagues, all the padres *descontentos* sought to disaffiliate themselves from the college and most eventually succeeded. Some of those friars, however, came to California, resulting in dissension in the mission field. A priest influenced by them made the most serious complaint against the Franciscan effort in the history of their California operations, an indictment made seemingly credible to secular authorities because it came from one of their own.[8] Lasuén had to deal with it.

Thirty-year-old Padre Antonio de la Concepción Horra arrived in San Francisco in April 1797. Lasuén sent him as companion to the experienced Buenaventura Sitjar to found mission San Miguel, and they did so on July 25. Sitjar, a remarkable linguist, baptized some adult Indians on the founding day, something his companion found distressing. Within a month and in a move unprecedented at the founding of a mission, Sitjar left his post and traveled to see Lasuén personally. Sitjar revealed that he thought the younger man was insane. Among other problems, Concepción Horra considered himself a great military leader. To show his might he ordered the mission *escolta* to fire their arms in salute and for the Indians to likewise fire their bows. He also possessed a large lance that he kept by his cot and used it one day to threaten an Indian who the priest believed had slighted him. Concepción Horra experienced fits of screaming alternated with passivity, causing the mission community to fear him and prompting the new neophytes to leave the mission.[9] The longer Concepción Horra remained at San Miguel the more likely it was that this missionary effort would fail. Lasuén succeeded in having Concepción Horra removed from San Miguel and brought before the governor in Monterey. It took the governor nearly a month to find him demented and then agreed that the missionary should be returned to the college immediately. Concepción Horra had been in California seven months.

Back at the college, Concepción Horra wrote a lengthy letter directly to the viceroy. "Your Excellency," he began, and proceeded with an attack upon Franciscan practices that would resonate with any Enlightenment-influenced official. Describing his role in the founding of mission San Miguel, he accused Padre Sitjar of being "completely opposed to everything that is mandated by the Royal Decrees of Our Sovereign King with respect to the care and education of Indians." Sitjar, avowed Concepción Horra, "not only speaks with the Indians in their own language but also is in the habit of teaching them the *doctrina* in their own language and he wanted me to adopt those practices. This is contrary to the mandates of our King." Moreover, charged Concepción Horra, Sitjar "baptizes them (Indians) without teaching them the very explicit and essential information one needs to comprehend to receive this holy sacrament." As proof Concepción Horra observed that Sitjar had "engaged in this practice with a number of adults the very day that the mission was founded." After claiming that he was of sound mind and that charges of insanity against him were mere devices by his superiors to silence him, Concepción Horra continued to the core of his allegations. "I would like to inform you of the many abuses that are commonplace in that country [California]. The manner in which the Indians are treated is by far more cruel than anything I have ever read about. For any reason, however insignificant it may be, they are severely and cruelly whipped, placed in shackles, or put in the stocks for days on end without receiving even a drop of water."[10]

He expressed four broad areas of complaint. While he had been in California Concepción Horra claimed that he had been poorly treated, that the missionaries were derelict in their instruction of neophytes (frequently baptizing the same Indian more than once), that the missionaries abused their Indians, and that they administered their enterprises without respect for the needs of settlers and soldiers.[11]

The viceroy ordered an investigation made by the governor, Diego de Borica, who in turn secured responses to his questions from the four presidio commanders. Borica used the opportunity to revisit the conflict between Cross and Crown over access to Indians. At issue for the secular authorities was what Indians did with their time away from the missions. Were they in the forest, visiting relatives indefinitely? If so, why could they not also come to the presidios or towns to work? The commanders' reports agreed that the Franciscans tried to keep Indians away from other Spaniards and punished those Indians found to have associated with soldiers and settlers. The superior at the College of San Fernando sent the results of Borica's investigation to Lasuén, who combined it with reports from missionaries and his own vast knowledge to compose a lengthy reply he entitled "Refutation of Charges."[12] Composed over a seven-month period and completed on June 19, 1801, this reply and defense ran to forty printed pages and refuted Concepción Horra's and Borica's charges in detail. Time passed slowly as the viceroy's office in Mexico City considered the report and, failing to resolve the contradictions between the claims of the military and the Franciscans, called for further study. The new governor, José Joaquín Arrillaga, called for a report — this time, from only one military man who was favorable to the Franciscans. He accepted that account, and on November 3, 1803, he forwarded it to the viceroy, who by now was José de Iturrigaray. Nearly six months later Iturrigaray adopted Arrillaga's position and closed the Concepción Horra complaint by exonerating the California Franciscans and encouraging them to continue the course they had been pursuing.[13] Soldiers and settlers resented the official rebuff of their desire for more access to Indian labor.

Lasuén's richly detailed "Refutation of Charges" provides insight into everyday mission life together with a more focused and reflective view of how the Franciscans saw their task. Since it was a defense, Lasuén began with a minor confession followed by the beginnings of a vigorous offense. "At the outset I admit that defects exist, and inevitably so," he wrote, "but not one is in the category of a crime, not one is beyond the normal, not one remains uncorrected once it is recognized, and if any are permitted it is but to avoid greater evils."[14] Specific charges by Concepción Horra were readily dismissed. Both civil and religious authorities had agreed that the priest was demented so there was nothing arbitrary in his removal to the college. Combing all 27,000 baptismal records and talking to friars, Lasuén found only three instances of rebaptism — all infants, two female and one male — and Indians had been carefully admonished not to present their tiny children to a priest a second time after the baby had received the sacrament.

To the charges of excessive punishment Lasuén declared that twenty-five stripes or lashes was the upper limit of Franciscan-directed punishment,[15] and he insisted that the lash come only after every other means of correction had been tried repeatedly. A missionary from San Francisco wrote Lasuén, "In an average school [in Spain or New Spain] a person would receive more punishment for not knowing his lesson than he would receive here for living in concubinage."[16] Lasuén outlined the problem for his superiors. "Here are aborigines whom we are teaching to be men, people of vicious and ferocious habits who know no law but force, no superior but their own free will, and no reason but their own caprice." To Lasuén they were "a people without education, without government, religion, or respect for authority, and they shamelessly pursue without restraint whatever their brutal appetites suggest to them. Their inclination to lewdness and theft is on a par with their love for the mountains." Having dismissed California Indian culture as without value by this generalization, Lasuén continued, "Such is the character of the men we are to correct and whose crimes we must punish." He then described their offenses as "of all kinds; crimes against religion, against approved customs, against the peace of the community, against private and public security. These they commit with the greatest alacrity, and with an incredible tendency to keep on doing them." A "barbarous, fierce, and ignorant country" to Lasuén needed punishments different from one that would be "cultured and enlightened, and where the way of doing things is restrained and mild." Nonetheless, Lasuén asserted that the missionary "treatment of the Indians is normally very mild." "Sometimes," Lasuén acknowledged, "a missionary violates it [the mild treatment of Indians]," but such violations he claimed were not the norm.[17]

Having depicted the California Indian as savage and deserving of strong punishment, Lasuén then portrayed the Franciscans as punishing the Indians less than they truly deserved. Then, in the language of blaming the victim, Lasuén defended the missionaries even in their excesses. "Is it to be wondered at if a missionary should sometimes fall a victim to uncontrolled passion and for a moment upset the even balance of his mind and disposition?" he wrote. "We must keep in sight that he is weighted down with more cares than would keep all the departments of a government busy, for he is in charge of aborigines such as we have been speaking of, amid the most baffling surroundings." Having provided a context for priestly aberration Lasuén pushed his argument farther. "So, I do not deny that there ever was or ever will be an instance of harshness or even the threat of cruelty," he observed. "I do say in regard to such impulses as are sudden and almost entirely indeliberate, that the missionary, so far from defending himself detests what he has done. They are matters of great sorrow to him." Lasuén had conflated the physical and psychological suffering of the flogged Indian with the psychological suffering of the priest who had ordered it done. In the language of abusers across culture, time, and space the victim deserved it, brought it upon himself, and inflicting the pain hurt the abuser more than the abused.[18]

Lasuén then illustrated his point with an example. An unnamed missionary of great experience, well informed and known for his mildness, engaged Lasuén in conversation. "We spoke for some time on the question," according to Lasuén. "Was it not unbecoming for us to pull the ears and rap the heads of any neophyte, even though parents usually do these things to their children, and teachers to their pupils? We discussed the matter and were still in complete agreement that this was the right attitude." The missionary returned to his work, met a young Indian boy whom he liked, a very good linguist and very helpful around the mission, and discovered that he had to reprove the neophyte for "some negligence." The boy, in the words of the friar, replied in "a haughty and impudent manner. . . . You are a liar!" With that, the priest struck the lad on the shoulder with a stick he had been carrying, breaking it. The priest returned to Lasuén in tears and confusion to confess what he had done. Lasuén offered as extenuating circumstances that the stick was "a slender willow rod, very dry and perhaps worm-eaten" and that the blow had not injured the Indian and possibly caused him no pain.[19] Lasuén gave the missionary the benefit of every doubt and presented the Indian as the offender who had been only slightly chastised. No possibility of missionary error could be admitted despite the possibility that this "good Indian boy" may not have been guilty of the negligence charged and replied sharply only in his own defense. To Lasuén, sympathy for the neophyte in this case — and by extension for all those to which he had just referred — had been misplaced. Priests, not Indians, needed sympathy.

For Lasuén, as it had been for Serra before him and as it would be for the Franciscans who followed him, punishment was but one of many means to an end, the salvation of Indian souls. Being forced to defend punishment of Indians against charges of abuse, whether from inside or outside the order, was irksome. Criticism of mission punishment was misguided or the product of self-interest by soldiers and settlers who wanted more Indian labor and brought their charges of missionary excess to secure Indian release from the missions. Lasuén took umbrage at the charges of excessive punishments lodged by soldiers who, in his view, acted hypocritically as though they were innocent of any abuses themselves. When Indians worked at the presidio Lasuén charged that they were forced to labor from dawn to dusk with only a short break, all the while being chided with the epithets "*Lazy, ill-bred, spoiled brat;* and then, in an undertone 'It's the Fathers who are to blame for your laziness.' "[20]

Lasuén contrasted the heavy work required of Indians at the presidios with the regimen in the missions. Mission Indians worked five to six hours a day during summer and four or five during winter, not the ten or twelve hours they put in at the presidios. Usually no more than half of the Indians worked at the same time. As Lasuén explained it, "Apart from those who have run away, or been given leave to go [on pass], and the sick and those who take care of them, the healthy are clever at feigning sickness, and they know that they are generally believed, and that even when there is doubt" the missionary generally would dispense them from work. Piecework proved the most common form of labor, and those few Indians who were enterprising had release time when they finished. If Indians worked at the presidios, however, when they finished the task assigned they could not leave but were compelled to remain for a fixed amount of time and were assigned to other work.[21]

As to contact with soldiers and settlers, Lasuén pointed out that in the presidios, "from the very beginning could be found [Indian] cooks, laundry-men, millers, water-carriers, and wood-cutters. And in case of need they have [been] given Indian women to serve as wet nurses. In the nurseries little Indian girls are used as babysitters, and employed to sweep, and to do work usually done by maids and servants and for no other remuneration than what they feel like giving them."[22] Lasuén acknowledged punishment for Indian artisans, "a shoe-maker perhaps, or a tanner, a deer-skin worker, or a worker in some other craft" who was found shirking his duties at the mission in favor of doing the same thing at the presidio.[23] No Indian, however, had ever been punished simply for going to a presidio, Lasuén avowed, unless that Indian was suspected of going for sinful purposes or if the *gente de razón* he or she would associate with might cause the Indian to fall into sin. Franciscans discouraged Indian contact with the gente de razón because old Christians taught the new Christians Spanish vices. Drawing on his personal experiences Lasuén claimed that "neither in the missions of [the] Sierra Gorda . . . nor in those of Lower California . . . have I ever seen Indians who were card players, or drunk with Spanish liquors, as I see here."[24]

Franciscans had a different attitude, however, where good, older Christians could be found. "When there is a chance of associating and communicating with a better class of people who live in these establishments [presidios and towns]," Lasuén noted, then "we not only permit it [contact], we use every effort, yes every effort to induce our neophytes to engage in it."[25] Such opportunities merely proved less frequent than the military and civilian community desired.

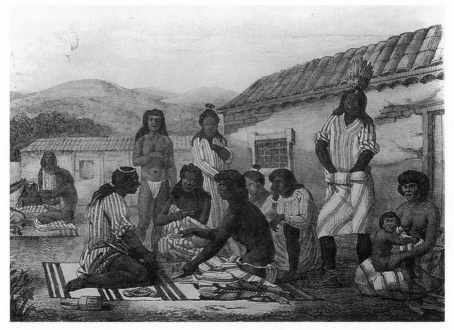

Figure 8. Jeu des habitants de Californie, one of a series of lithographs based on watercolors made in 1816 by the expeditionary artist Louis Choris, shows several neophytes at Mission Dolores entertaining themselves at a game played with half-round sticks. Although Franciscans feared that mission Indians would pick up such European vices as card playing if they associated with presidial soldiers or other *gente de razón,* gambling was in fact deeply entrenched in native culture, a favorite amusement of men. Despite prohibitions imposed by the missionaries, neophytes continued to game when opportunity arose, not only for pleasure but as a subtle resistance to Hispanic authority. From Louis Choris, *Voyage pittoresque autour du monde,* 1822. Courtesy California Historical Society, Templeton Crocker Collection, FN-30509.

In the single clearest expression of their task ever formulated, Lasuén explained "the greatest problem of the missionary" as: "how to transform a savage race such as these [sic] into a society that is human, Christian, civil and industrious." His answer went directly to the heart of the matter. "This can be accomplished," he argued, "only by 'denaturalizing' them. It is easy to see what an arduous task this is, for it requires them to act against nature. But it is being done successfully by means of patience, and by an unrelenting effort to make them realize that they are men."[26] Such a lucid explanation directly challenged Enlightenment thinking, which held that Indians were corrupted by "Civilization" and they, along with others in society, should be free to make their own associations independent of the control of another.

Lasuén understood the enormity of the challenge. In a letter to his superior he acknowledged that "the majority of our neophytes have not acquired much love for our way of life; and they see and meet their pagan relatives in the forest, fat and robust and enjoying complete liberty." Only the force of the mission guard and the promise that runaways would be pursued and returned kept the neophytes from reverting to the pagan life to which they were "still much addicted."[27] To Lasuén that pagan way of life "was free and it was lazy. Who can keep them from murmuring after it."[28]

Indian love of liberty lay at the core of the missionary problem. "If we cannot gently withdraw their hearts from their own way of living," Lasuén observed, then "how are we to get them to appreciate ours? How shall we teach them Christian obedience, and the ways of a civil society?" The answer began with food followed by instruction. "The effort entailed in procuring a sustenance from the open spaces" was, in Lasuén words, "incomparably greater than what is now enjoined on them so that they can sustain themselves; but the former is free and according to their liking, and the latter prescribed, and not according to their liking." In Lasuén's view reflecting long-standing Franciscan thought, Indians in their pagan state "disregard[ed] the law of self-preservation which nature implants in us. . . . Hence, as a rule, they live without providing for what is indispensably necessary for existence. . . . They satiate themselves today, and give little thought to tomorrow."[29] Missionaries saved Indians from themselves by missionizing them.

By teaching them to regularize their food sources so that time was available to contemplate Christianity, missionaries helped Indians "improve." That improvement came through baptism and subsequent recitation of the *doctrina*. By use of interpreters and direct instruction either in the Indian tongue or in Spanish, Lasuén believed, the missionaries "well prepared" Indians to receive the sacrament. "It will happen but rarely," he wrote, "that anyone is baptized after no more than eight days of instruction. Fifteen, twenty, and thirty or more days are devoted to it" depending upon the missionary's determination of the Indian's aptitude for comprehension. Smarting under charges that a week to a month's instruction was insufficient for Indians to obtain "the necessary grasp of the articles of our holy religion," Lasuén countered, "let them [the accusers] keep in mind that there is a strong presumption in our favor when there is a question of observing an obligation so primary." This instruction preparatory for baptism was followed by twice daily recital of the doctrina in the church, alternating between Spanish and native language, for the remainder of the Indian's life at the mission. Children being catechized recited the doctrina twice more daily in front of the priests' quarters.[30]

Religious instruction and more efficient production of food at the missions

through sowing and harvesting of grain and cereals three times annually, however, did not fully satisfy Indians who yearned for their homelands, for visits to
relatives and friends, and for access to native foods. Missionaries had to make
adjustments to such Indian demands, and one way was by permitting them to
return for visits that totaled several weeks each year.[31] Yet the missionaries
feared that visits to the gentiles would prove near occasions of sin for their
neophytes, obligating the priests to venture into the forest to retrieve them. To
do so, and to carry out necessary missionary duties among Indians who were
sick or needed the sacraments while in a *ranchería,* the priests needed the
military protection of the guard. As Lasuén expressed this need to the governor, "Given this protection [the military guard], the missionary attends to his
duties with a greater sense of security. Without it, he risks his life."[32] The
notion that the Spanish military had sufficiently cowed the Indian population
so that the missionary could traverse 40 or 50 leagues (100 to 130 miles)
across gentile territory without a guard must be treated as Spanish propa-
ganda and considered yet another California mission myth.[33]

The Franciscan struggle in Lasuén's words to "gently withdraw [Indian]
hearts from their own way of living" did not proceed in any steady or even pace.
It proved an ongoing missionary challenge. A year after his thoroughgoing
defense of the missionaries and their tasks, Lasuén expressed his frustrations
to his superior. "What anxieties! What disappointments! What vigilance!
What anguish of mind! What labors day and night for the missionaries! What
liberties! What excesses! What irregularities! What ignorance! What disorders!" he wrote. "How," he wondered, "can Christian civilization and pagan
barbarity give way to one another in the same neophytes!" Based upon his
experience with Indians in both Californias he concluded, "Those of Lower
California are less intractable, more inclined to Christianity, and much easier
to detach from their old habits and pagan observances than are those of Upper
California."[34] Lasuén and his fellow missionaries failed to see that the majority of their neophytes despite baptism had *not* converted to Christianity and
continued actively to preserve as much of their culture inside the mission as
possible. The Indian struggle to endure culturally, despite population decline
and externally directed change, would persistently oppose Franciscan evangelization efforts throughout the mission era.

Lasuén's approach to mission building was cautious; he proceeded slowly and
deliberately in contrast to Serra's impetuosity. Serra goaded the military to
accelerate the pace of mission founding. Lasuén, in contrast, had to restrain a
military impatient to create more Indian settlements because each new mission
had to be supplied with surplus from other existing missions as opposed to

receiving supplies from the port of San Blas as Serra's missions had. Closing of the overland route via the Colorado River by the Quechan in 1781 and irregularities in ship supply from New Spain attending the twelve-year civil war that erupted in 1810 forced the missions to seek trade with outsiders. Over time Franciscans developed a clandestine trade in hides and tallow to secure from foreigners the commodities they could no longer obtain from Spanish-approved sources. Indians herded and slaughtered cattle, then tanned their hides and boiled the fat of the carcasses down for candle tallow. Deer tallow, however, provided the most lucrative trade element because its candles burned longer in the deep silver mines of Potosí in Upper Perú than did those made from cattle tallow. In exchange, missionaries received iron and metal, tobacco, rope, clothing, and, most dearly sought after, chocolate.[35] Through the hide and tallow trade, the products of California Indian labor entered the international economy.

Lasuén took a practical approach toward educating Indians, deepening their religious instruction in an effort to effect permanent change. Under Serra, the Indians watched and imitated the actions of Spanish sailors and soldiers he had persuaded to help him build his missions, had taught Indians to clear and hoe fields, sow and harvest grain, cart produce, and make adobe bricks. Serra would rely on a soldier appointed as *mayordomo* to live at the missions who could teach more specialized tasks such as tanning and shoemaking. Lasuén, wishing to alter that dependence, cooperated with Governors Fages and Borica to request and then bring artisans from Mexico to teach trades, skills, and artistic decoration to California mission Indians. Among the twenty who actually came for a four- or five-year contract were carpenters, smiths, stonecutters, masons, weavers, tailors, and one miller. At least six painters from New Spain came to teach decorative art for the churches. Lasuén's goal was to use these largely temporary migrants to teach young Indians at each mission their craft or skill so that they could in turn teach other Indians and the missions could remain more independent of the presidios and towns.[36]

The Franciscan tradition of creating schools to teach reading and writing — a more formal education — to their Indian charges was never pursued in California. The most promising of male children who could be useful to the priests, however, were taught to read and write. But, despite widespread Franciscan practice and the 1793 royal edict that Indian languages were to be suppressed and all instruction conducted in Spanish, priests in California did not and could not extend that instruction to all neophytes. The reasons lay in the nature of the missionary division of labor and in their opinion of their Indian wards.

Prevailing Franciscan practice divided missionary work into two categories, internal and external relations. The senior priest generally took responsibility for the maintenance of religious life within the mission, and the junior priest worked with the Indians in completing their tasks outside the church and in dealing with settlers and soldiers. Both priests said the Mass and heard confessions and their daily lives were full. In 1806, for example, eight of the nineteen missions counted Indian populations in excess of one thousand, with four additional numbering nine hundred or more. Multiple Indian languages at the same mission challenged the priests to learn Indian tongues and forced them to employ interpreters to communicate with their neophytes.[37] With daily Indian spiritual duties of attending the Mass and two recitations of the doctrina in addition to their work assignments, scant time remained for further lessons. Any surplus time the senior priest generally devoted to cultivating the choir. These Indian men chosen by the priest for their ability to replicate European sound in song were among those who did receive instruction in Spanish. To Franciscans Indian choristers constituted the most important group within the missions.

Missionary assessment of Indian intellectual abilities added to the reasons for Franciscan neglect of their formal education. Neophytes "owing to the dullness of their mental facilities, their inherent indolence, their lack of will-power and their want of self-reliance, save in a small number," wrote a Franciscan historian, meant that "they failed to emerge from the apprenticeship in either religious, civil, or social matters. In spite of all missionary efforts, they remained children."[38] Such negative attitudes reinforced a priestly disinclination to institute schools for Indians in an already busy mission environment.

Yet despite any Franciscan-perceived neophyte mental limitations, missionaries like Lasuén made concerted efforts to deepen the Indian understanding of Christianity. The tools employed were the catechism and the confessional aid, or *confesionario*. Catechisms were books of religious instruction designed to impart Christian beliefs to newcomers. In Indian California, as elsewhere in the New World, catechisms sought to teach Indians Christian/Spanish hierarchy beginning, as Lasuén's did, with the question of "How many gods are there?" combined with the correct reply, "There is only one true God." The very first question, written in Spanish with Esselen and Rumsen translations to convey the material in the major languages of Carmel mission, directly assaulted the Indian's sense of community and his role in it as a communicator with many Gods. Lasuén as linguist had prepared this guide for himself and the priests at the mission to enable them to probe the Indian mind, seeking to subordinate Indian feeling to Europeanized reasoning. The questions and responses continued through the mystery of the Trinity—three distinct persons in only one God—through the role of Mary in the birth of Jesus as the Son of

God. To the query "Why was the Son of God made man?" the reply was, "To cleanse our souls of our sins and later to take us to Heaven."[39] Further didactic questions informed the Indian that good Christians, upon their deaths, go to Heaven because they have kept God's commandments. The summary prepared the Indians for confession by admonishing them to "think first of our sins, then tell all the big ones to the priest; feel in our hearts that we have not obeyed God's commandments, vow in our souls that we will not tell lies anymore." Lasuén's catechetical guide closed with an exhortation that identified the Indian's role and place in the new order: we must "keep God's commandments, those of the Holy Mother the Church, and comply with the obligations of our status (*nuestro estado*)."

Lasuén's catechism conformed to the norms for such aids generated in New Spain and applied to local missionary situations. Other priests created them as well along with confesionarios. One of them, Padre Mariano Payeras at mission La Purísima,[40] wrote his in Purisimeño Chumash. Catechisms and confesionarios were vital elements in mission Indian religious life and would have been used at all establishments although few examples adapted by missionaries for California use have survived. The confesionario took the Indian through the Ten Commandments, creating a detailed examination of behaviors. Priests paid special attention to sexual sins. If abortion were suspected or coitus interruptus had been practiced, such behavior was confessed under the Fifth Commandment; such behaviors as fornication, masturbation, adultery, sodomy, incest, and intercourse with animals all were interrogated under the Six and Ninth Commandments. A missionary at Santa Barbara, in the Chumash territory as was La Purísima, conducted his interrogation in Barbareño. In addition to the questions just given he inquired about the relationship to the confessant of those with whom the Indian had sinned. Under the First Commandment he asked his confessants if they had scattered seeds in the field, believed in dreams, believed in the power of one who claimed to cure by the use of water or the acorn, believed in the owl. Such regionally specific questions posed in native language reflected a progressively growing priestly awareness of Indian culture and a more direct missionary interrogation designed to elicit knowledge of Indian behavior and to instill a sense of guilt on the part of the interrogated.[41]

Together the catechism and the confesionario assaulted Indian culture. The first sought to undermine the Indian inclination to submerge the individual within the group, by teaching a strict hierarchy with a defined subordinate Indian position. Simultaneously, the second sought to instill within the Indian the value of personal responsibility as more important than a sense of group identity. Potentially the confesionario could be more damaging or effective from either an Indian or Franciscan perspective. Consider sexuality. Christian interrogation classified sexual acts under three categories of abstraction, categories Indians had to learn before reflecting upon their personal behavior. Indian sexuality did not make the distinctions that Christians did, and learning the new ways of thinking, combined with newly prescribed prohibitions or taboos against formerly common behavior, created stress and consternation among the neophytes.

As powerful a weapon as the confesionario could be in evangelization, its potential was restricted by the time it took for missionaries to learn local languages to create them and by the priestly power available to use them. Confession could not be administered as frequently as the missionaries desired once the congregation reached a size where only the annual confession required of Easter Duty, performed during the forty days preceding Easter, could be accomplished. Among other factors influencing the uprising, refusal to perform that Easter Duty contributed to the timing of the 1824 Chumash revolt.[42]

The catechism, part of the daily routine of the doctrina for more advanced neophytes, perhaps had a more immediate impact on Indians' lives. This is because patriarchy, with God the Father at the top, served as the foundation for the new sense of hierarchy it taught. Priests also taught Indian men that as heads of new Christian families, they were now superior to Indian women. Indian women henceforth were to be subservient to their Christian husbands. Such patriarchy, however, violated the California Indian sense of social order and gender relations among men and women. If in their gentile state women could be chiefs or shamans like Toypurina, they could not continue such roles within the mission compound. Thus Indian women lost status and power in the Franciscan and Hispanic world, all the while being admonished to accept and internalize their new, subordinate roles.

7

Evangelization in Serra's Shadow

Missionaries concentrated on enforced behavioral modification over instruction for women neophytes probably because they thought women less capable than men of grasping religious thought. Certainly that was Padre Mariano Payeras's thinking in writing to his superior that after years of working with interpreters he had finally written "a long catechism which [in addition to the standard materials] included the Acts of Faith, Hope, and Charity; [and] another concerning matters necessary for our salvation." Payeras observed or imposed gender difference. "By great patience, we have succeeded in having nearly all the men learn both catechisms," he continued; however, "with the women, since after all they are only women, instruction is not so advanced."[1] Franciscan attitudes toward Indian women reflected the medieval expression that sin entered the world through a woman and the world would find salvation through the Virgin. Franciscans devoted themselves to the perfect woman in the form of Mary Most Holy even as they discounted and sought to control her profane sisters.

As Christians, Indian women were to restrict their sexual activity to marriage and to preserve their chastity until they entered that estate. To enforce these values unmarried women over the age of seven were kept under lock at night in a single room known as the *monjerío*, sometimes written as *monjería*, both terms meaning "nunnery." To keep women busy and unavailable for

Figure 9. An Esselen or Rumsen woman, drawn at Mission Carmel or Monterey in 1791 by José Cardero, an artist with the Spanish voyage of discovery commanded by Alejandro Malaspina. The woman holds a basket in her hands and wears the traditional dress of braided-tule front skirt, buckskin rear skirt, and sea-otter-skin robe. Even more than men, native women suffered within the confines of the mission compound, the sad rhythm of their lives shaped by inflexible medieval European concepts of sexual roles and behavior that were strikingly different from those of the California Indians. Courtesy Museo Naval, Madrid. Photograph Courtesy Iris Engstrand.

sexual activity, priests assigned them to various tasks beyond gathering wood, cooking, cleaning, and child care — group activities such as weaving on looms and roasting and grinding corn for flour. Tortilla and bread preparation illustrates Franciscan deliberateness in keeping women's hands from becoming idle. During the visit of Jean François de La Pérouse in 1786, two years after Serra's death, the Frenchman found himself distressed by the "tedious and laborious grinding of corn" women did by rolling a stone (*mano*) over a slab of volcanic rock (*metate*). One of his associates gave the missionaries a pocket mill. In La Pérouse's words, "It was difficult to have rendered them a greater service, since four women will now do the work of a hundred," freeing the women's time for other activity.[2] As a Frenchman of the Enlightenment, La Pérouse believed that his contribution to female efficiency in grinding corn, a model for a simple flourmill, represented a solution to an obvious problem.

Twenty years later the German George von Langsdorff, accompanying a Russian sailing visit to San Francisco, remarked that the flour, although "very white," produced bread that was "heavy and hard." He had read La Pérouse's account and knew that the Frenchman had left the missionaries a hand-mill. However, "It was not in existence at the time of our visit, neither had it been used as a model for the manufacture of others." Given the history of windmills in Spain and the excellence of Spanish bread, Langsdorff could not fathom why something so useful had not been created in California. He inquired into the matter and learned from the missionaries "that in preferring the poorly ground flour produced by the methods just described [they] . . . are really actuated by economic motives." Langsdorff recorded that "as they [the missionaries] have more Indians of both sexes under their care than they can keep constantly employed the whole year, they fear that the introduction of mills would only be productive of idleness, whereas under the present system the *neofitos* can be kept busy making flour during the periods of unemployment."[3] In this operation Indian men using donkey power to turn grinding stones performed the initial cracking of the grain and Indian women did the finishing work more slowly by the traditional methods.[4] Missionaries resisted efficiency and abandoned the taste of better bread to keep Indians busy; priests hoped that busyness would keep Indians from idleness and succumbing to the lure of the forest, prevent them from succumbing to the near occasion of sin.

Priestly imposed division of labor usually kept Indian women inside the mission compound where they could be more closely watched. Since women could not be *vaqueros,* or field hands, they had fewer reasons to leave the mission, which doubtless contributed to the lower rates of fugitivism by women neophytes, especially those with children.[5] If a female neophyte's sins required punishment, being placed in shackles was most common. Flogging, when

Franciscans deemed it necessary, was done in private and administered by another woman for the sake of modesty.[6] La Pérouse, no friend of the missions, thought that Indian women were flogged in the *monjerío* so that Indian men would not hear their cries and be enflamed against the missionaries.[7]

Procreation was critical to mission success. Since deaths routinely exceeded births, Indian women suspected of aborting a fetus, voluntarily or involuntarily, suffered particularly severe punishments. The suspected abortionist's head was shaved, she was flogged for up to fifteen consecutive days, a shackle was placed upon her legs for up to three months, she was forced to wear sackcloth, to rub her face with ashes, and to carry with her at all times a wooden effigy of a child, painted red. On Sundays she had to stand with the doll at the entrance to the church and receive the jeers and verbal abuse of her fellow congregants. Franciscans visited these punishments upon women, most of them administered in the medieval tradition of the public humiliation of sinners, throughout the mission system.[8] Given what neophyte women had to endure and the loss of status they incurred in the process of missionization, their stereotyping by Franciscans as "often fall[ing] into the weakness of ingratitude" should not be surprising.

Returning neophyte runaways became a more important Franciscan responsibility as mission populations increased in size after 1800 as a result of intensified recruitment of gentiles in the interior, which Spaniards called the *tulares* (place of reeds). Priestly responsibility flowed from the Franciscans' need as spiritual fathers to protect their children from the temptations of bad companionship, from the lure of sinful activities that came from letting their charges be exposed to the near occasion of sin.[9] Since military support for such expeditions proved erratic, Franciscans had to develop their own Indian police force, called *auxiliares,* to forcibly return fugitives. Whenever possible such an expedition was accompanied by a Spanish soldier or two. These paramilitary ventures went to gentile and neophyte *rancherías* to bring back to the mission those neophytes who had fled. Theologically Franciscans could not acknowledge Indian apostasy or outright rejection of Christianity and permit absconded neophytes to remain free. As long as Indians rejected baptism they could remain gentiles, a condition the priests had to accept until they could accommodate Indians either at the missions or in an arrangement like San Diego or San Luis Rey where most of the baptized population still lived in their native villages.

Once Indians had accepted baptism, however, they became neophytes and they no longer had the freedom to reject Christianity. Baptism to Franciscans meant an irrevocable commitment to a Christian life, not a temporary accommodation to a more powerful culture. When Indians fled the mission they returned to their gentile communities, and as long as they lived there they exposed themselves to the near occasion of sin, something the priests could not allow. Hence the forcible return of neophyte runaways. Skirmishes frequently ensued during the course of such forays, and sometimes gentiles were captured for alleged crimes against neophytes or the *gente de razón* who had accompanied them. On such occasions the expedition brought captured gentiles back to the mission for punishment. There was, however, no forced recruitment of gentiles for missionization, no rounding up of pagans and driving them into the missions for compulsory baptism as one sometimes encounters in the literature on the missions. Such charges of "forced conversion" of Indians made against the Franciscans in California episodically from the 1820s onward are nonsensical within the framework of Franciscan theology; they are also without historical proof and should be dismissed as yet another mission myth.[10]

Training auxiliares took an unanticipated turn after 1818 under the threat and subsequent invasion of parts of the California coast by the French-born Argentine privateer, Hippolyte Bouchard. Championing the cause of New Spain's independence, Bouchard sailed two black-painted warships into Monterey Bay on November 20, 1818, and after seizing the town stayed a week to ransack whatever he could find. Bouchard caused Governor Pablo Vicente de Solá and others to flee to the hills. Bouchard then sailed south, landing in the Santa Barbara area where he raided ranchos and then on to San Juan Capistrano, which he looted in late December before sailing out to sea.[11]

Rumor of Bouchard's preparations and approach preceded him and had prompted Spanish authorities to augment their military forces with armed and trained Indian auxiliaries. In June Governor Solá issued orders to each presidio to resist to the last drop of blood and sent copies to each mission. Within a week each mission responded by preparing fifteen to twenty vaqueros armed with *riatas* (lariats), ready to ride to the nearest presidio as soon as called. Indians with ropes, however, would be of limited value against Europeans with firearms and so, within a month, the governor sought Indian archers as well, calling for 600 of them. Most missions met their quota, and these auxiliares received some instruction and drill in European military methods. In 1820 Solá renewed the earlier measures for defense. At Santa Barbara, Padre Antonio Ripoll's response proved astonishing. He assembled and trained a company of 180 Indians composed of 100 archers reinforced by 50 more armed with machetes and a cavalry of another 30 lancers. Ripoll let them choose their corporals and sergeants, but he had the commanding officer at the nearby presidio select the company commander. Such arming of Indians for colonial defense had unintended long-term consequences. Unbeknown to soldiers and missionaries, they had prepared mission Indians to contend with Spanish military power, something Mexican authorities would learn to their dismay four years later in the Chumash uprising.[12]

The need to cooperate for common defense endeared Payeras, now father president of the missions, to the local military commander at presidio Santa Barbara, José Guerra. At one point Payeras wrote to him, "I agree, of course, that those Indians of La Purísima are at your disposal, since as the representative of the higher voice of government of the province, you will know how and in what way to use them." Such words coming from Serra would have been unthinkable. Moreover, Payeras permitted Guerra to use the Indians to build huts for the soldiers and to perform any other work the commander deemed reasonable, affirming that "you can count on my approval without consulting me."[13] Franciscan attitudes toward the military had softened since the days of Serra and Lasuén. When Bouchard's forces pillaged Santa Barbara — area ranchos, Payeras wrote Governor Solá that the insurgents encountered the defenders and were losing ground to the Spanish military and their Indian auxiliares. Payeras noted movingly, "It would cause me joy if you could see the preparation and enthusiasm of these Indians" for the military service they provided.[14]

Payeras's and, by extension, Franciscan cooperation in the matter of Indian auxiliares may have been a tactical response seeking to mitigate the effects of intensified demands to secularize the missions. The civil complaint came in the traditional form of demanding that the priests make Indian labor available to presidios and towns. In June 1821 Solá proposed to emancipate the "useful Indians" — those who, in Payeras's words, were the "right hand of the father missionaries and who with their [the "useful Indians'"] help rule and maintain these missions in the good condition in which they are found." Solá sought to release selected artisans and assign these skilled neophytes to work in towns and presidios far removed from their missions, a tactic that Payeras feared might be a prelude to the full secularization he felt the neophytes were still unprepared to handle.[15]

Payeras proved right. A decree of the Spanish Cortes in 1813 had required missionaries to relinquish control over Indian property and administration. Bickering delayed that law from reaching California until 1820.[16] A year later when the College of San Fernando, following Spanish directives, ordered Payeras to surrender his missions, he so notified the governor and his fellow missionaries.[17] According to Spanish law secularization remained a religious matter, with the missionaries giving over their establishments to a bishop who was then responsible for assigning priests to the newly created parishes while the apostolic missionaries sought new work among unconverted Indians. Conditions in California did not permit civil authorities to enjoy their victory or clerics to implement it. By May 1822, California was a province of newly independent Mexico, and the bishop of Sonora to whom Payeras had surrendered his missions "did not accept the offer." "To the contrary," Payeras wrote his college, the bishop invited the Franciscans "to continue administering this spiritual field with full authority as has been the case up to now."[18] The bishop had no priests to send to replace the Franciscans. While good fortune or Divine Providence had stalled the move to secularization, it was a reprieve and not a pardon as the growing Enlightenment idea of freeing the individual from any external restraint gained ground in the political arena, and Mexico, not Spain, ultimately determined the new direction.

In the midst of the turmoil occasioned by the need to defend the province against Bouchard, the disruption of the civil war then raging in New Spain, and the renewed pressure for secularization, Payeras undertook a remarkable self-examination of the missions. From his headquarters at mission La Purísima, the fifth father president wrote a thoughtful and disturbing letter to his superiors in Mexico City early in 1820. "Every thoughtful missionary," he began, "has noted that while gentiles procreate easily and are healthy and robust (though errant) in the wilds . . . as soon as they commit themselves to a sociable and Christian life, they become extremely feeble, lose weight, get sick, and die. This plague affects the women particularly, especially those who have recently become pregnant." Payeras noted that earlier missionaries had believed that the children born in the missions would recover their natural health. "However," he continued, "the sad experience of fifty-one years [since the beginning in 1769] has showed us all too well that we too have erred in our calculation. Having already seen two generations in the missions, we sadly observe that the mission native dies equally, and perhaps more so than the Indians of the sierra." Payeras and his colleagues knew that recruitment of gentiles rather than natural reproduction was all that kept mission populations from showing greater decline. Payeras saw a grim future, writing, "I fear that a few years hence on seeing Alta California deserted and depopulated of Indians within a century of its discovery and conquest by the Spaniards, it will be asked where is the numerous heathendom that used to populate it?" The answer Payeras understood would be this: "The missionary priest baptized them, administered the Sacraments to them, and buried them." Payeras asked his superiors to take actions which "would free us for all time from undeserved reproach."[19]

Payeras after much thought and following countless conversations with his fellow priests had come to question the very approach Serra had employed in

California. Payeras received no answer. Perhaps those at the College of San Fernando could not engage the question, arising as it did from what appeared to be the most successful of all their missionary enterprises. Payeras's superiors, doubtless beset by the vicissitudes of the civil war, seem to have let that excuse serve as a reply. The turmoil that produced Mexico terminated Spanish rule within two years and rendered moot both a reexamination of the missionary efforts and of the success of Spanish attempts at social control. Mexico then sought to impose its own ideas of social control.

Mexican representatives arrived in California in October 1822 and convened with Franciscans and local military commanders to decide, in Payeras's words, "the fate of our Indians." The Plan of Iguala, under which Agustín Iturbide had won power in Mexico, conferred citizenship upon all Indians.[20] The central question Payeras expressed clearly was: "Whether the new citizen as a free man, according to the law, should emancipate himself from the jurisdiction of his Father Minister [sic], the Missionary [sic]." After much discussion it was concluded that since the majority of the neophytes could not live on their own they should remain subject to the missionaries. The man who could live on his own, however, with the permission of the local military commander and the missionary, might take his family and the mission property to which he was entitled and move to a pueblo or other appropriate location.[21] Solá's plan to remove the "useful Indians" from the mission was to become a reality. The conference of October 1822 succeeded in driving the wedge of separation between neophyte and missionary deep into the fabric of mission society. Mexican law now recognized all Indians as adult citizens, meaning mission Indians no longer would be considered adult children. This shift meant that secularization and full emancipation had become inevitable, subject to a political rather than a religious timetable. The decade-long turmoil that had given birth to Mexico, followed by a tumultuous period of internal strife, however, combined to temporarily defer the matter of Indian emancipation.

For the Spanish and Mexican governments, the term "emancipation" derived from Roman and civil law, in which the term meant "termination of parental control over someone"—in this case, termination of the missionary role of father over what he regarded as his adult children. In the United States the term "emancipation," on the other hand, has been invariably linked to chattel slavery. This coincidence of American usage coupled with descriptions by mission critics of neophytes being treated like slaves has produced a serious misunderstanding over the Indian's status in the mission. Governor Neve seems to have been the first to make a comparison to slavery when he alleged that "the Indian's fate [was] worse than that of slaves."[22] Neve's metaphor was an exaggeration, since he knew that Spanish society had slaves and legal codes for them just as there were legal codes for mission Indians, and neophytes assuredly were not slaves. The first foreign visitor to the missions, La Pérouse, sided with his country's "rights of man" against Franciscan theology and wished that the neophytes could be considered as citizens according to the Enlightenment thinking that had prevailed in France. From his experience visiting the French territories in the Caribbean he wrote that the state of the California mission Indian "scarcely differs from that of the Negro inhabitants of our colonies, at least in those plantations which are governed with most mildness and humanity."[23]

Such comparisons between the treatment of Indians and slaves and between the missions and plantations have established, at least in the minds of some American scholars, an image of missions and their Indian laborers that fully resonates with the high-performance, socially insensitive, profit-driven plantation systems of the Caribbean and the Old South. Such comparisons are unfair. The purpose of a mission was to organize a religious community in isolation that could nourish itself physically and spiritually. Surplus production was to feed other missions and local towns and presidios. Profit was never a consideration, unlike plantations, where profit was the purpose and reason for their creation. Plantations employed large, usually overwhelmingly male labor forces to produce cash crops such as sugar, tobacco, and cotton for the international market. Punishments were typically inflicted on workers whose insufficient or decreased production hurt owner profits. Moreover, chattel slavery meant the owner could buy his property from and sell it to another, something that no Franciscan father could do to his son or daughter.

Yet to some Americans the analogy of the missions to slavery remains powerful. Because missionaries had Indians punished for what priests deemed to be infractions and refused to allow Indians to change their minds after having accepted baptism; because missionaries sent out expeditions to return neophyte runaways analogous to those slave hunters who pursued runaways in the Old South; and because missionaries used force to keep Indians at the missions, there are those who agree with the argument that "the result in many cases was slavery in fact although not in intent."[24] Perhaps this thinking derives from an incomplete sense of the American past. Metaphors can be too persuasive, and here the remark from Abraham Lincoln's celebrated 1858 "House Divided" speech — in which he argued that the country could not "endure, permanently half *slave* and half *free*" — may be the culprit.[25] Lincoln misstated the case. Labor was not *either* free or slave, because other unfree labor systems had been and still were being used in America as he spoke.

Indentured servitude, voluntarily surrendering freedom for a fixed amount of time to a person who provided passage to the British colonies, had been an early source of immigration on the Eastern Seaboard. When Lincoln spoke, another kind of unfree labor existed in America in the recently admitted State of California, where former mission Indians worked for rancho owners in a Spanish-derived form of wage labor called "debt peonage."[26] In that system, workers were bound to their employer by advances of food, money, or goods. Under Spanish law, workers could not leave their employer until they had retired their debt. The American legal terms "peon" and "peonage" derive from this Spanish practice.[27]

Mission Indian labor resembled peonage more than slavery. Indians could leave the mission for five to six weeks annually to visit relatives and friends and to hunt and gather wild foods.[28] They were not free, however, to come and go as they pleased. In voluntarily accepting baptism, whether they knew it or not at the time, they gave up the freedom of their former life for a new one that constrained their freedom. This new life had religious and work demands associated with it, and neophytes were bound to both. In Catholic theology one of the consequences of sin is the temporal punishment that must be served in Purgatory that accompanies the forgiveness of each sinful act. Confession and absolution together do not leave the sinner with a clean balance sheet before God. There exists a further debt the sinner must repay, and temporal punishment is a type of residue that remains even after the sin has been forgiven. Despite the penance assigned by the priest after confession and performed in this life, the sinner also has a debt to be paid in the afterlife. Measured in terms of days, this debt accumulates over the course of each communicant's life. Securing indulgences granted by the pope that forgive the spiritual debt a person has been accumulating can erase some or all of that temporal punishment.[29] Such erasures, however, can be only temporary because it is human to sin so therefore the cycle repeats and the obligation is rarely or never retired. Because the neophyte had voluntarily forsaken part of his freedom in return for the spiritual salvation promised by the Christian God, the terms "spiritual debt peonage" and "spiritual debt peon" also describe the status of the baptized Indian within the mission system. Once baptized the Indian was free to be a Christian bound to the mission spiritually and physically and not free to be a pagan.

Secularization operated in a climate of anti-Spanish hostility within Mexico that had its counterpart in California. By late 1827 the Mexican government decreed that peninsular Spaniards, with a few exceptions, had to leave the country. In California the Spanish missionaries from the College of San Fernando, called Fernandinos, were required to swear absolute allegiance to the Mexican Constitution of 1824. When they refused, Governor José María de

Echeandía explained to the Mexican president that without replacements he could not deport the Fernandinos because the missions would collapse. The taxes they paid were crucial for maintenance of presidios and settlements. The Mexican government therefore sought to reduce California's dependency upon Spanish missionaries by turning to the Franciscan college of Our Lady of Guadalupe in Zacatecas, which was staffed exclusively by Mexican clergy, to send priests to California. In early 1833 the Zacatecans took over the six missions from San Francisco Solano in present-day Sonoma down to San Carlos and the Fernandinos, under the leadership of Padre Narciso Durán as father president and commissary general retained control of the fifteen missions from Carmel to San Diego. Durán made his new headquarters at mission Santa Barbara.[30]

Fernandinos stridently opposed secularization, claiming that their neophytes were unprepared for pueblo life. In many instances the priests were right. In part the Fernandinos' apprehension was rooted in their knowledge that many of their charges, despite the age of the missions, were new Christians, gentiles only recently brought to baptism and with only a rudimentary knowledge of Spanish language and customs. Indian life beyond the missions seemed unrealistic to the priests. Durán, however, knew that he could not resist the coming change and instead hoped to shape it to the benefit of the neophytes.

Three conflicting ideas for the missions and their wards contended for adoption. One sought to convert the missions to parish churches and create Indians pueblos, *pueblos de indios* in Spanish law, in which Indians received the mission lands and administered their own affairs under the guidance of a civil administrator. In 1833 Governor José Figueroa tried this approach and created one pueblo de indios from the lands of San Juan Capistrano mission he secularized, a property in excess of 50 square leagues, or more than twelve times the size of a typical Spanish pueblo or presidio.[31] San Juan Capistrano's pasturage comprised 338 square miles, or 224,000 square acres.[32] Indians freed from caring Franciscan paternalism, however, found themselves subject to a new and uncaring paternalism as they were forced to work for the administrator on his property; the civil appointee also sold much of their lands to settlers. Within seven years only a hundred Indians lived at the pueblo. The experiment had failed.[33] Mexican colonizers had a different view of the secularization process. Colonists wanted the government to create parishes from the missions and turn the lands over to civil administrators who then would convert the vast non-Indian allotments into the public domain where they could be made available to the gente de razón in land grants given by the governor.[34] The *Californios* — those gente de razón already living in California, the majority of whom had been born there—also wanted the mission lands administered by civil authorities but sought to privilege their position against any newcomers.[35] The Californios wanted first access to any newly public lands.

Against all three plans, Durán insisted that nearly all the land belonged to the Indians and that the Franciscans, as their guardians, must hold it in trust for them and see it allocated fairly. Durán entered into "cautious cooperation" with the governors, vainly trying to make the Indians the beneficiaries of secularization while seeking to make the civil administrators work with the priests against settlers and colonizers. He, too, failed.[36]

Secularization undid the missions. At the beginning of the 1830s the mission Indian population numbered 18,000; by 1839 fewer than 1,000 remained.[37] Released from their enforced residence, Indians returned to their homelands, drifted into towns and pueblos, joined the labor forces of newly emerging ranchos, or joined the bands that began raiding the herds of missions and ranchos. The spiritual bond to the Christian way of life seems not to have been as strong as the military coercion that had assured the Indians continued physical presence during the main period of mission life. Emancipation meant physical as well as religious freedom from spiritual debt peonage.

Mission wealth measured in land, herds, and assets dwindled from the 1830s to the 1840s. The value of mission estates at San Carlos, La Purísima, Santa Cruz, Soledad, San Juan Bautista, San Miguel, San Fernando, and Santa Inés, for example, stood at 548,100 pesos at secularization and at only 73,755 pesos in 1845, a decline of 86 percent. Cattle herds and flocks of sheep for thirteen of the twenty-one missions dropped 74 percent from 1834 to 1839,[38] most of those animals becoming the property of Californio rancheros. The mid-1830s marked the end of the California mission system as begun by Junípero Serra in 1769.

8

"The Only Heritage Their Parents Gave Them"
Syphilis, Gonorrhea, and Other Diseases

Indians died in the missions in numbers that appalled Franciscans. Many of the priests, however, thought they knew why. As Ramón Olbés wrote from mission Santa Bárbara late in 1813, twenty-seven years after its founding, "The most pernicious [disease] and the one that has afflicted them most here for some years is syphilis. All are infected with it." Olbés described its effect succinctly by noting, "As a result births are few and deaths are many."[1]

How could syphilis contribute significantly to, if not be responsible for, the high death rates? When Spaniards in various stages of exploration and expansion entered into territory unacquainted with disease, they unwittingly unleashed disease microbes into what demographers call "virgin soil." The resulting wildfire-like spread of contagion, called "virgin soil epidemics," decimated unprotected American Indian populations by the millions.[2] In California, such epidemics intensified human destruction in a nearly incalculable way because of the further ravages of epidemic syphilis. Venereal disease among Alta California Indians, once mistakenly thought to be endemic but only now perceived as introduced by colonization, constitutes one of the previously underappreciated factors contributing to the process of precipitous native population decline.[3]

"Venereal disease," as opposed to the contemporary medical literature's preference for "sexually transmitted disease" (STD),[4] is used here because "venereal" carries the primary, but not the exclusive, means by which the diseases of syphilis and gonorrhea are spread as well as the judgment at that time that such actions are sinful. STD carries with it the contemporary notion of "no-fault," a concept that would be historically incorrect.[5] Using the more historically accurate term "venereal disease" is also consistent with the argument advanced by the French historian of thought and science Claude Quétel, that since the seventeenth-century secular and religious authorities have developed a progressively greater need to name sex and sexual activities defined as sinful in order to control behavior. In California can be seen the encounter between two conflicting attitudes toward sexual pleasure as argued by Michel Foucault: the *ars erotica* of the various Indian societies and the *scientia sexualis* of Europe. For Foucault the epitome of the ethos of scientia sexualis was found in confession, and for priests the primary sins among the Indians in need of confession were sexual.[6]

Spaniards first recorded that *they* introduced syphilis to California native peoples when Franciscans José de Miguel and José María Zalvidea at Mission San Gabriel claimed that the "putrid and contagious disease had its beginnings with the time Don Juan Bautista de Anza stopped at the Mission San Gabriel with his expedition [in 1777]."[7] A twentieth-century physiologist and student of Indian–white contact, Sherburne F. Cook, pointed out that Anza's soldiers were not the only source of the disease. Cook asserted that the "expeditionary forces of [Gaspar de] Portolá in 1769 and other troops entering the country were without doubt heavily infected, not to speak of the early civilian settlers."[8]

Attention focused upon the soldiers, since they were men without women, were highly mobile, and possessed force superior to get what they wanted. While the missionaries with their Eurocentric bias lamented the Indian openness to sexuality—what the priests termed immorality or licentiousness—Indian women did not always go voluntarily with the Spaniards. When Indian women resisted, they were raped. Those crimes frequently angered Indian men as well, causing tension and hostility between Indian communities and Spanish troops.[9] "Since there were soldiers stationed at every mission, since the troops were continually moving around from one place to another, and since this military group was itself generously infected," the physiologist argued, "the introduction [of syphilis] may be regarded as wholesale and substantially universal."[10]

Generally overlooked as carriers at the time were Indians from Mexico the Spanish had infected, especially those from Baja California, and those whom the Spanish brought with them to help colonize the northern province.[11] An anthropologist observed that syphilis was "blamed for a large portion of the mortality in every medical report from Alta California since 1791, the year in which [Governor] Pedro Fages noted its spread from the Baja California missions."[12] There is, then, no debate over the role the Spanish played in introducing syphilis to Alta California.

In order to appreciate better syphilis's impact upon California Indians, however, we need to consider how the disease affected another population in which it was introduced. The one area in which extensive description does exist from the time syphilis first appeared as an epidemic late in the fifteenth century until it settled into the population to become endemic by the mid-sixteenth century lies in Europe. But one cannot mention syphilis in Europe without some discussion of the deep and persistent controversy over syphilis's origins.

Where did syphilis originate? This question has produced a vast literature varying in approach from the anecdotal to the highly technical. A historical biologist, Alfred L. Crosby, reviewed this literature in a lively and cogent essay written thirty years ago, and it remains the best place to begin an inquiry.[13] There are three answers to the question of origin: (1) the New World, where Columbus brought it back from his earliest explorations; (2) Europe, where it had been spread since biblical times but had gone unrecognized before the outbreak; (3) neither of the above because it is a single disease present world-wide that happened to mutate in Europe late in the fifteenth century and became syphilis. These three schools of thought have been termed the Columbian, the anti-Columbian, and the Unitarian theories, respectively.

Crosby discusses each theory carefully, focusing upon the Columbian (introduced *from* the New World) and Unitarian (present in the Old World and mutated) arguments as the most plausible and important. He finds testimony from early Spanish writers concerning the American origins of syphilis particularly compelling. Among these writers are: Columbus's son Ferdinand; conquistador turned cleric and chronicler Bartolomé de las Casas; court intimate Gonzalo Fernández de Oviedo y Valdés; and physician Ruy Díaz de Isla, who treated some of Columbus's crew and described the disease they contracted in the New World.

Crosby, however, considers the evidence that *Treponema pallidum* (syphilis), a spiral-shaped (spirochetal) bacterium, has left in skeletal remains in Europe and America. He finds it ambiguous. Bone lesions caused by treponematosis had been found in New World skeletons — and not in remains from the Old World — at the time of his writing. If the treponemas were widespread, however, it would only be a matter of time until they were discovered. The validity of the Unitarian theory, therefore, was questionable. Crosby concludes that the Columbian theory is viable and "allows the American Indians and Columbus the dubious honor of incubating and transporting venereal syphilis."

Since Crosby's research, many new studies have been done on skeletal evidence of treponematosis in America and, to a lesser degree, in Europe. A thoroughgoing review of the skeletal evidence using the latest scanning devices — permitting more accurate paleopathological assessment of the presence of treponemas — has led a team of anthropologists to conclude that "treponematosis is a relatively new disease that originated in the tropical or temperate zone of the Americas and was spread by casual contact. This nonvenereal infection is the disease that was initially contracted by Columbus's crew, but social and environmental conditions in Europe at that time were conducive to its spread in urban areas."[14] Thus the biological evidence, complementing the historical testimony of Spaniards at the time, now seems to leave the Unitarian case disproved and affirms the Columbian argument.

If syphilis originated in the New World, would not the peoples there have some knowledge of it and perhaps immunity? The answer lies in two parts. Native peoples who had the nonvenereal *Treponema* knew and described the disease. The treponemas causing syphilis (*T. pallidum*), yaws (*T. pertenue*), and pinta (*T. carateum*) are undistinguishable under a microscope, meaning that the microorganisms are highly unstable. Historically and today, in developing areas where yaws is present in a population some immunity against syphilis is conferred.[15]

The study of skeletal lesions tells us that the nonvenereal treponemas (*T. pertenue* and *carateum*) were found in the West Indies, South America, and much of North America, but *not* among the California Indians subjected to missionization. Thus, when *Treponema pallidum* became venereal in Europe, it could be *reintroduced* to the New World among those populations with no previous history of *Treponema* exposure. Such was the case of the Indians of both Baja and Alta California. The epidemic spread of syphilis in Europe from its first appearance in 1494 to the point at which it became endemic, about 1560, provides a basis for thinking about what happened in California from establishment of the first mission in 1769 to mission secularization from 1834 to 1836. In both instances "virgin soil" epidemics erupted.

As Crosby notes, the first epidemic of syphilis in Europe erupted in Italy in 1494 among the multinational troops of Charles VII. The first description of the disease dates from the battle of Fornovo, July 5, 1495. A doctor with the army combating the troops of Charles VII observed footsoldiers with "pustules on their faces and all over their bodies . . . and usually appeared on the outer surface of the foreskin, or on the glans, accompanied by a mild pruritis [itching]. . . . Some days later the sufferers were driven to distraction by the pains they experienced in their arms, legs and feet and by eruption of large pustules (which) lasted . . . for a year or more, if left untreated."[16]

This first description contains elements important to the history of syphilis. The disease most obviously manifested itself in genital ulcers, which were more readily visible on men than on women, who, as medical inquiry would much later reveal, frequently manifest their infections in chancres inside the cervix. Itching characterized syphilis in a world where unsanitary conditions made itching from lice, fleas, and other irritants commonplace. Pain associated with syphilis proved debilitating; soon Europeans would conclude that the disease led to death.

Treatment, such as it was, with sweat baths, mercury, or other concoctions, amounted to no treatment at all. No effective cure for syphilis appeared until the discovery of salvarsan, an arsenic-based compound that proved successful around 1910.[17]

The writings of Jean Astruc, a man described by Crosby as "probably the greatest venerologist who ever lived," divided the natural history of syphilis into several stages—from the outbreak of the epidemic to the point where it became endemic. Four of these stages pertain to our inquiry. In the first twenty-two years of its existence in Europe, 1494–1516, in addition to the symptoms described above of genital ulcer followed by rash, the spread of the disease through the body frequently destroyed the victim's throat. Large, gummy sores appeared on the surface of the skin, frequently opening to the bone; pain in bones and joints worsened at night. Physical deterioration commonly led to early death.

In the following decade bone inflammation sometimes led to degradation of both the bone and its marrow; some of the genital pustules became hardened. From 1526 to 1540 the malignancy of the disease began to diminish. In the ensuing twenty years the more dramatic manifestations of bodily deterioration declined sharply so that by the end of this period it had become an endemic part of the quotidian struggle. In this period, however, gonorrhea became misidentified as the first stage of syphilis, a confusion that would not be rectified until the two diseases were clearly differentiated in 1860.[18] Regardless of the misidentification, gonorrhea had been identified as accompanying syphilis.

Applying the phases of the natural history of syphilis to California mission history it is evident that the total episode lasted the entire life of the missions (see Table 1). Hence missionization occurred within the epidemiological context of virulent, debilitating infection and adjustment. This context made

Table 1. Alta California Missions Founded during the Four Phases of Epidemic Syphilis, 1769–1835

Phase 1, 1769–1791	Phase 2, 1792–1801
San Diego de Alcalá (1769)	San José de Guadalupe (1797)
San Carlos Borromeo (1770)	San Juan Bautista (1797)
San Antonio de Padua (1771)	San Miguel Arcángel (1797)
San Gabriel Arcángel (1771)	San Fernando Rey España (1797)
San Luis Obispo de Tolusa (1772)	San Luis Rey de Francia (1798)
San Francisco de Asís (1776)	Subtotal: 5 (24%)
San Juan Capistrano (1776)	Phase 3, 1802–1815
Santa Clara de Asís (1777)	Santa Inés (1804)
San Buenaventura (1782)	Subtotal: 1 (4%)
Santa Barbara (1786)	Phase 4, 1816–1835
La Purísima Concepción (1786)	San Rafael Arcángel (1817)
Santa Cruz (1791)	San Francisco Solano (1823)
Soledad (1791)	Subtotal: 2 (10%)
Subtotal: 13 (62%)	Total: 21 missions (100%)

Indians weak and highly susceptible to other nonvenereal infections. The cumulative effect dramatically reduced Indian numbers and caused profound psychological and emotional damage, especially to women. To understand how this happened requires reconsidering the spread and consequences of syphilitic infection first in Europe, then in California.

While Europeans recognized the importance of coitus in the transmission of syphilis early on, poor sanitation and then prevalent healing practices contributed to what the medical literature calls extragenital syphilis. Today medical authorities think that any nonsexual transmission of the disease must be congenital. Historically, however, especially in the epidemic stage, syphilis spread by direct contact through the medical and sociocultural practices of midwifery, wet-nursing, tattooing, and circumcision.[19] Syphilis could also spread indirectly, although rarely, by an uninfected person sleeping on the sheets of a person infected with weeping sores or by wearing the trousers or clothing of such a person.

Syphilis proved a baffling disease — its epidemiology requires modern microscopes and lengthy clinical observations to track.[20] *T. pallidum* invades the host at a cut or tear in the flesh or the mucous membrane. The resultant initial chancre at the site of infection, at least now, is rarely painful and can easily go unnoticed. But in this, the primary stage of syphilis, the victim is infectious as the spirochetes invade deeply the tissue of the entire body. From ten to forty days after infection the initial chancre disappears, even without treatment. That disappearance, a natural course of the disease trajectory, was the visible sign that allowed the various "cures" to be promoted and people deceived for centuries.

From two to six months after the primary sore disappears, the secondary stage begins; secondary syphilis can last up to two years. A rash is the most obvious sign, and narrow white mucous sores can appear in the lining of the mouth, throat, and rectum as well as the genitalia. Syphilis is highly contagious at this point because there are literally millions of spirochetes in the bloodstream, a condition called spirochetemia, and any contact with infected blood by an uninfected person with even a slight tear in the flesh or mucous membrane usually brings infection. If the sufferer has mouth sores, then kissing can spread the disease.

At this point hair may fall out, pain may be felt in joints and bones, and fever and headache can set in along with a general feeling of illness. And secondary syphilis, just like its primary stage, will disappear of its own accord within three to twelve weeks, only to return if it is left untreated. Such are the symptoms now, when the disease has long been endemic. During the epidemic stage, however, these symptoms would have been more intense. The quack cures common in earlier times were administered, but without any beneficial effects.

Late-stage syphilis, also called tertiary syphilis, can come shortly after the secondary symptoms have disappeared or it can lie dormant in a body for from five to fifteen years before returning to wreak its havoc. Late syphilis is far less contagious than its earlier manifestations, but it is far more devastating to its host. Skin ulcers recur, only usually thicker and dry. Spirochetes again attack the bones and the cardiovascular as well as the central nervous system. A variety of organs can be affected, ranging from the liver, stomach, heart, and brain to the optic nerve; late syphilis can cause blindness, crippling arthritis, an erratic, foot-slapping gait, memory loss, insanity, and burst aorta. Dementia characterized by delusional conversation is also common.

A surviving child of a mother who has primary or secondary syphilis in her last trimester has a high probability of being born with syphilis. The infant thus afflicted is often born deformed, with a macerated skull, and can manifest the symptoms of tertiary syphilis within her or his first few years, followed by early death. A baby with congenital syphilis can infect a wet nurse through contact between a nipple lesion, caused by nursing, and white mucous sores in the infant's mouth. This pattern of transmission was known in Europe as "syphilis of the innocents."[21]

The best natural protection against syphilis is an intact skin and intact mucous membranes. Many European medical and sociocultural practices analogous to those practiced by California Indians included puncturing the skin and mucous membranes, thus facilitating extragenital transmission of the disease.[22]

California Indians had what the Franciscans contemptuously called "sucking doctors," shamans who cured by sucking from the wound of the afflicted whatever evil lay inside the body. The priests thought the shamans nothing but tricksters, and at mission San Diego the following practice was described: "He [the shaman] places a stone, a piece of wood, or hair in his own mouth then puts his mouth to the affected part and begins to draw or suck on that part. When he withdraws he shows the patient what he had placed in his mouth and convinces [the patient] that this was the object causing him harm."[23] Whatever the priests may have thought of the shamans' curative powers, it is certain that such practices spread syphilis. So too did practices such as licking the eyes or kissing.[24]

The report cited from mission San Diego was but one in a series of replies to a detailed questionnaire (*interrogatorio*) sent from Spain in 1812 and answered in Alta California between 1813 and 1815. Responses were collected from eighteen of the then nineteen missions, lacking only those from La Purísima. The data from this questionnaire provide limited but valuable insights into the venereal health of the colony late in the third stage of the syphilis epidemic. These responses explain which native practices contributed to the extragenital spread of venereal disease.

The subject of the "sucking doctor" arose within a question about native medical practices, a question that sought to learn whether or not Indians employed "bloodletting," a term that some Europeans interpreted in such a narrow way as to miss the significance of Indian practice. Missions Santa Barbara, Santa Inés, and Santa Cruz returned no comments; San Diego, San Luis Rey, and San Juan Capistrano mentioned only sucking.

Yet other European missionaries at thirteen disparate sites saw clearly the connection between bloodletting and native practices. At San Gabriel the priests observed "some sort of bloodletting. It consists of cutting oneself with a sharp stone." At San Fernando, Indians "when they feel oppressed . . . bleed themselves with a flint." At San Buenaventura the priest recorded that "they have the equivalent of bloodletting in cutting themselves with a sharp stone and sucking the blood." From San Luis Obispo: "With a flint they scarify any part that aches. Then by forcibly sucking with the mouth the scarified spot they extract a considerable portion of blood."[25]

These practices extended the length of Alta California, as reports from other missions attest. At San Miguel, Indians "employ[ed] bloodletting by scarifying the affected part with a small, sharp stone. They then suck the wound." The priest at San Antonio observed, "They [Indians] also have recourse to bloodletting. This they do by scarifying with a flint the aching part (however it may be even in the very eyelids). Then they suck and suck, in general a poor curative method, because by such sucking they increase tumors with bad effects following particularly in the eyes and other delicate parts."[26] At Soledad the priest attempted some historical perspective. "In their pagan state . . . they had their healers who cured them . . . with sharp stones with which they bled the affected parts. Even now as Christians they customarily apply their native remedies." From San Carlos: "For bloodletting, a frequent practice, they gather very jagged flints; with these they puncture the aching part, be it head, body, abdomen, chest, etc., and they continue to scrape the wound so that much blood comes forth."[27] Terse padre responses to the type of Indian curing practices at missions San Juan Bautista, Santa Clara, and San José still underscored scarification of the afflicted part followed by sucking. At San Francisco the priest added opinion to his observation: "They scarify with a pointed stone and suck the blood. More often than not this does them more harm than good because they scarify abundantly and this irritates affected parts."[28]

Scarification and sucking have particular significance for the spread of syphilis in its early, epidemic stage. Sharp flints cut two ways, both into the flesh of the patient and into the fingers of the caregiver. Mixing blood of the infected with the uninfected facilitated disease spread during periods of spirochetemia. Moreover, any rupture of the mucous membranes within the mouth would have provided yet another avenue for receiving or depositing *T. pallidum.*

As in sixteenth-century Europe, social customs in California complemented medical practice in contributing to the extragenital transmission of syphilis. Scarification for purposes of tattooing, for both beautification and status designation, offered another occasion for disease transmission. Mission Indian women served as needed as midwives and wet-nurses for settlers at the presidios, and mission Indian girls acted as baby-sitters for the same group.[29] Since the settlers were already heavily infected, their nonsexual contact with mission Indians provided another avenue of infection. Children in the missions usually slept with their parents, where they were exposed directly via touch to any open sores or indirectly through contact with clothing that had been so exposed. Since the mission environment congregated people, the mere fact of proximity increased risk of infection. The priests took pains to keep all unmarried females over the age of seven locked in a closed room — a *mon-jerío*, or nunnery — at night. They did so, however, to limit male sexual access to them.

Priests were deeply concerned about Indian sexuality. From the Franciscan perspective, Indians were libidinous because they cheerfully, and apparently frequently, engaged in premarital and extramarital sex without guilt. Priests wanted to control that behavior and to instill the guilt they thought necessary to teach Indians self-control.

Franciscan knowledge of Indian sexual activity is reflected in answers cited to the questionnaire of 1812. To the query about the principal vices among the Indians at their missions, fifteen (83 percent) of the priests' replies emphasized sex. The majority called it "unchastity"; others used such terms as "impurity," "incontinence," "immorality," "intemperance," "fornication," and "lust."[30] Some priests expanded their commentary and revealed clinical familiarity with disease. At San Gabriel, the response noted that unchastity "has perme-ated them to the very marrow with venereal diseases to such an extent that many children at birth give evidence immediately of the only heritage their parents give them. As a result," the report continued, "of every four children born, three die in their first or second year, while of those who survive the majority do not reach the age of twenty-five." From San Luis Obispo the priests noted that "lust . . . soon puts an end to men as well as women. If no steps are taken to check these effects this [spiritual] conquest will soon come to an end." At San Antonio the padres wrote, "Unchastity is the prevailing vice in both sexes and this it is that is carrying them to the grave. They know this well enough and realize it but lack understanding."

In reply to the question about disease prevalence among the Indians, thir-teen of the eighteen respondents (72 percent) placed syphilis/venereal disease (*gálico, morvo venéreo*) high on their lists.[31] Some of the priests' comments reflected surprising insight and sensitivity for the time. As earlier mentioned at Santa Barbara, the respondent noted that "the most pernicious [disease] and the one that has afflicted them most here for some years is syphilis. All are infected with it for they see no objection to marrying another infected with it. As a result, births are few and deaths are many." At San Luis Obispo the Indians generally made "use of hot baths [*temescales*, or sweathouses] to cure the itch and venereal epidemics, an infirmity with which generally all Indians are infected to such an extent that any other illness during the various stages of the year kills them." At San Francisco the priest went into more detail. "The dominant disease among them is syphilis," he wrote, "but it is quite hidden and from it arises a great number of illnesses. Some are covered with sores. These live longer although they do not easily recover. In others it strikes

internally and they die sooner. Others succumb more slowly." In a final remark the padre noted that "the climate possibly acts unfavorably to this disease since it is cold and damp [here]."

Observers from outside the missions confirmed and elaborated upon these
Franciscan perceptions. A French physician in 1786, during his ten-day stay in
Monterey and environs, "examined a great many individuals (Indians) of both
sexes." Pertinent to the extragenital means of syphilis transmission, he noted
that Indians "pierce their ears" and "sleep all in a heap, without distinction of
age or sex, on some skins which they spread around a fire." He saw pox or
syphilis as a common malady that, he was told, the Spanish had introduced.
Regardless of source, he wrote, "It causes the same ravage . . . as among us.
Buboes, chancres, tumors, gonorrhea, etc. are its usual characteristics." He
further noted Indian women, "subject to the special disorder of their sex,"
frequently suffered uterine hemorrhaging following childbirth.[32]

Six years later the Englishman George Vancouver discreetly made no mention of pox during the course of his visits. He did, however, offer descriptions
of Indian lethargy, very likely reflecting the impact of the disease upon its
hosts. At mission San Francisco he regarded the Indian faces as "ugly, presenting a dull, heavy, and stupid countenance, devoid of sensibility or the least
expression. One of their greatest aversions is cleanliness." Later, in southern
California, Vancouver encountered nonmissionized Chumash who seemed to
him "to possess great sensibility and much vivacity, yet they conducted themselves with the most perfect decorum and good order, very unlike that inanimate stupidity that marked the character of most of the Indians we had seen
under Spanish jurisdiction at St. Francisco and Monterrey [sic]."[33]

Vancouver's observations, like many others, mistook the impact of venereal
disease for the natural condition of the California Indian. Observers then did
not know that in addition to painful bone inflammation, cranial palsies, and
damage to liver, spleen, lungs, stomach, pancreas, and kidneys, eight out of
nine children born with congenital syphilis would also have suffered from
anemia, and six would have had jaundice; anemia and jaundice would have
produced weakness, lassitude, and loss of appetite.[34] Thus the alleged indolence of California Indians noted by Spanish and foreign observers probably
had its roots in newly introduced venereal disease.

In early 1805, the Spanish surgeon general of California, stationed in Monterey, made the first medical survey of the province. The primary disease
among Indians was "syphilis or the French malady (morbo gálico)." He visited
the northern missions of San Francisco, Soledad, and San Juan Bautista, then
traveled as far south as San Antonio, San Luis Obispo, and San Miguel. He
identified the causes as "impure relations on an excessive scale, the great

filthiness of their bodies and villages, direct and indirect contact, the sick sleeping with the healthy ones, [and] the custom of frequently exchanging clothes." In visiting missionized Indian villages he learned that the inhabitants scorned priestly help and his, noting that "they doctor themselves by washing their sores or wounds and scarifying themselves with flints, even to the eyelids, whatever the sickness is."[35] Scarification spread disease.

In 1806, a German naturalist visiting San Francisco reported that "[Indian] tattooing is a common practice, but principally among the women." He recognized the prevalence of venereal disease among them and described the consequences: "Spots upon the skin, hard swellings, pains in the bones, inflammations of the throat, loss of the nose, consumption, and death."[36] Ten years later, a Frenchman in the company of a Russian expedition visited San Francisco and also was struck by Indians' lethargy. He accepted the priests' descriptions of the people as "lazy" and "stupid" and observed, "I have never seen one laugh. I have never seen one look one in the face. They look as though they were interested in nothing."[37] He did not remark upon venereal disease and may have been unaware that he saw its impact in the demeanor of those Indians. Over the three decades of outside visitors, the missionized Indians of San Francisco had passed through the first three phases of the syphilis epidemic. (See Table 1.)

Before considering the sexual means of transmission of venereal disease among the Indians, it is necessary to address the question: Could priests have contracted syphilis? Priests were European and so were familiar with bloodletting as a medical cure. They employed it in California. Mariano Payeras wrote in 1812 that although he had enjoyed good health for twenty years, "Recently I had two blood lettings in order to reduce the sluggishness caused by excessive weight."[38] A male Indian assistant performing a bloodletting with a cut on his fingers or hand, while suffering from spirochetemia, could have inadvertently transmitted the disease to the padre.[39]

Seriously overweight priests who may have tried this approach would have made themselves vulnerable to infection. Such corpulent friars as Fermín Francisco de Lasuén, Antonio Tomás de la Peña, Catarino Rodríguez, and Narciso Durán could have been so exposed.[40] While there is no direct evidence that any of these men suffered from syphilis, the possibility of infection by extragenital means must be considered real. So also would be possible infection from Indian servants treating the self-imposed priestly lacerations on the back caused by using the *disciplina,* or short whip, with which fervent padres would scourge themselves in imitation of Jesus's suffering.[41]

Father José Maria Zalvidea suffered from dementia late in his life, partly characterized by conversations with the Devil, that could have been caused by

lith par Marlet.

habitants de Californie.

des.t par L.

Figure 10. Habitants de Californie, a lithograph derived from a watercolor made in 1816 by Louis Choris, depicts five native men at Mission Dolores, two of whom have facial tattoos. A common practice among many California Indians, tattooing was one of the avenues for the transmission of syphilis, which was pandemic through the native population following Spanish colonization, and may have contributed to the lassitude observed among the neophytes by Choris, an artist with the Russian exploring expedition commanded by Otto von Kotzebue. "I have never seen one laugh," Choris wrote. "I have never seen one look one in the face. They look as though they were interested in nothing." From Louis Choris, *Voyage pittoresque autour du monde,* 1822. Courtesy California Historical Society, Templeton Crocker Collection, FN-30510.

third-stage syphilis. Father Luis Gil y Taboada had a reputation as a surgeon specializing in delivering children via cesarian section.[42] This practice would have put him at high risk for exposure and infection. If infected, then at times when he suffered from spirochetemia and performed such an operation on an uninfected Indian woman, he undoubtedly would have transmitted the disease to her and likely to her newborn child.

Men with a vow of celibacy would have been less likely than those not so self-limited to contract syphilis via sexual union. But one priest, Blas Ordaz, had a reputation for sexual promiscuity that led to charges that he had two if not three children by Indian women. It would be difficult to imagine that he, at least, was not infected. Mariano Rubí, another priest, was removed from

California for his peculiar behavior, and Franciscans in Mexico later concluded that he was infected with syphilis.[43] Thus priests in Alta California were exposed to syphilis both by venereal and extragenital contact and a small but undetermined number probably contracted it.

Syphilis spread among Indians primarily by vaginal but also by oral and anal contact. As the medical literature laconically notes, "The penis is an efficient fomite," meaning that it readily transfers bacteria from one orifice to another.[44] Since gonorrhea accompanied syphilis it is the combined effects of both that are important. In an environment in which it was unknown to wash the genitals with soap after sex, physical conditions facilitated disease transmission and disease could be spread by heterosexual as well as homosexual and bisexual practices.[45] Since missionized Indian cultures had homosexuals whom they revered, men whom the Spanish derisively called "jewels,"[46] same-sex as well as different-sex possibilities existed for disease spread.

Syphilis and gonorrhea, in addition to their debilitating impacts on individuals, also affect the reprodutive *ability* of a population, its fecundity. According to the medical literature, however, venereal disease affects fecundity indirectly, through subfecundity, the diminished *capacity* to reproduce, by impairing any or all of the three major biological aspects of reproduction — coitus, conception, and carrying the conceived to live birth.[47] While both men and women endure the pain of venereal diseases, one of the subfecundity factors — birth — affects only women and they primarily are affected by difficulties in conception. This means that women suffer disproportionately in two of the three critical areas of population reproduction. That suffering is both physical and emotional.

Venereal disease affects each subfecundity factor differently. Gonorrhea causes men temporary, sometimes long-term, painful ejaculation which can lead to impotence. When coitus is achieved, the resultant sperm may not be viable, contributing to conceptive failure. Women suffer from scarification of their fallopian tubes as a consequence of venereal diseases, and that scarification can partially or totally block those tubes. Total blockage means failure to conceive. Partial blockage, however, means that the fertilized egg will not be transported through the tube to the uterus but instead will become implanted within the tube. Successful live births then become problematic and frequently require cesarian section. Gonorrhea also can deform the pelvis and consequently alter blood supply and diminish ability to fight further infection.[48]

Pregnancies among syphilitics, however, nearly always result in spontaneous abortions, especially among recently infected mothers. Women contracting syphilis within two years of their first pregnancy — that is, during the first, second, and early latent third stages of syphilis—almost invariably miscarry, have stillbirths, or give birth to infants with syphilis. A study conducted in the early twentieth century, several centuries after syphilis had become endemic, nonetheless found that "seventy-five percent of children born to syphilitic parents would be [spontaneously] aborted, stillborn, or die of congenital syphilis before their first birthday."[49] Historically, the rates must have been higher in colonial California.

Neither Franciscans nor Indians knew this medical information. Franciscans, however, saw no distinction between involuntary abortions—miscarriages—and voluntary abortions; both were against God's will in Franciscan eyes and they treated females harshly for either.[50] They generally blamed women for reduced population caused by venereal disease, adding insult to their injuries. An Indian historical memory from Mission Santa Cruz about Padre Ramón Olbés, sometime between 1818 and 1821, reveals an Indian perception of Franciscan response to conceptive failure.

Learning that a couple had failed to conceive, Olbés brought them one at a time to a room, along with an interpreter, to determine the reason. Olbés first asked the husband if he slept with his wife and the Indian answered affirmatively. Why, then, asked Olbés, did they not have children? "Ask God," the man replied. Olbés then decided to inspect the Indian's penis to determine if it were impaired; he sent the Indian to the guardhouse and then summoned the Indian's wife. Olbés asked, "Why don't you bear children?" to which she answered, "Who knows?" When Olbés then tried to inspect her vagina, the woman resisted and tried to bite him. The narrative continues, "Then Olbés ordered that they take her and give her fifty lashes. After the fifty lashes, he ordered that she be shackled and locked in the nunnery. Finishing this, Padre Olbés ordered that a wooden doll be made, like a recently born child. He took the doll to the whipped woman and ordered her to take that doll for her child, and to carry it in front of all the people for nine days. He obligated her to present herself in front of the church with that doll as if it were her child for nine days." Indians understood the larger point Olbés made as the story concludes, "With all these things, the women who were sterile became very alarmed."[51] Women crippled by venereal diseases could not control their bodies the way Franciscans wanted, and some outside observers recognized that fact.[52] Within the mission world, however, mitigating circumstances for this human distress hardly mattered and contemplating that the finger shaken in condemnation at the Indian may have come from a syphilitic priestly hand was not an irony for their times.

Three powerful forces contended for Indian women's bodies in missionized California: invading venereal diseases, Franciscan expectations for appropriate maternal behavior, and Indian women's frustrated desires to recover their health and to produce healthy children. No one can imagine the anxiety of Indian mothers as they beheld their children born sickly and weak. Some babies and children had collapsed skulls and potbellies. Others had inflammation of the mucous lining inside the eyelid that made their eyes swell nearly shut and occasionally resulted in blindness. Yet others suffered from severe infections of the nasal cavity, causing the "snuffles," a dry almost soundless (aphonic) cry; in extreme cases, these infections made the nose collapse.[53]

In a population with a high rate of infection, syphilis per se would not have caused childlessness or depopulation, but it would have depressed fertility rates because of increased rates of pregnancy loss.[54] Determining exactly how those fertility rates were depressed in the California missions is nearly impossible because measures of fertility normally refer only to live births and do not account for miscarriages. Establishing a miscarriage rate per woman cannot be done with existing data because priests recorded only live births or those who could be baptized.[55] The best that can be approximated at this time is a net rate of reproduction (NRR), an estimate of the average number of daughters born to a group (birth cohort) of women during their lifetime. Given mortality rates and disease, this calculation is only approximate. A value of 1.0 for the NRR would signify that fertility and mortality of a population are such that the population exactly replaces itself; a higher value indicates growth, and a lower value shows decline.[56] Estimates to date indicate an NRR of 0.5 or less for much of the mission era, meaning that the population declined by half or more from its previous level, beginning a movement upward to only 1.0 and then slightly exceeding it toward the end of the period.[57]

Syphilis affected the mortality rate of the population but, again, in ways difficult to detect. Without the benefit of modern autopsy, determining death by syphilis is haphazard at best. One study found that clinical observation had undercounted syphilis-caused deaths by 26 percent.[58] In long-term studies of untreated syphilis in a population in which the disease was endemic, autopsy revealed about 23 percent mortality.[59] The rate would have been higher in colonial California, but no one knows how much higher.

Mortality rates in the missions, the Crude Death Rate (CDR), yield general rather than specific causes of death. The physiologist who did the greatest amount of work on the California Indian population posited a CDR of 50 per 1,000 persons among the total aboriginal population prior to contact. He calculated a rate of 70 per 1,000 during the first decade of missionization (1770–1780), rising to 85 per 1,000 by 1800 and declining thereafter. But within that figure a much higher rate prevailed for children, one that approached 170 per 1,000 in the decade prior to 1800. Measles, the worst nonvenereal epidemic to strike this virgin soil, took one-third of the children under 5 years of age in 1806. After 1810 the average mortality rate among children declined so that at the end of the mission era it stood at 110 per thousand.[60] The other serious study of the mission population confirms these findings.[61] Mission San Miguel, a relatively healthy mission, meaning that its population declined 69 percent over a generation, had an average life expectancy for newborns of 10.2 years. Life expectancy of a non-Indian child born at a presidio, however, where conditions and diet more closely resembled those of the missions, was three times longer, for an average of 31.4 years.[62] The congenital syphilis that killed young Indian children stalks these figures, but in incalculable ways.

Once syphilis became endemic, toward the end of the mission era, the effects of syphilis on childbirth would have been less devastating. A pregnancy history from the first quarter of the twentieth century, when syphilis was endemic in the American population, is suggestive of California Indian women's pregnancy histories once the disease became endemic in the missions. In one case, an immigrant woman uninfected with venereal disease married a syphilitic immigrant man. He infected her and she remained untreated until her children were identified with the symptoms of congenital syphilis. Over thirteen years she had five pregnancies producing eight children. Her first pregnancy resulted in a stillbirth at seven months; the second, a full-term male with congenital syphilis; the third, full-term triplets, two with congenital syphilis; the fourth, full-term twins, one with congenital syphilis; and the fifth, a full-term female, uninfected.[63] In the last pregnancy she had replaced herself (NRR = 1.0), and three of her eight children had been born syphilis-free. The other five, however, showed "the only heritage their parents gave them," to recall the phrase from mission San Gabriel in response to the 1812 questionnaire.

Missionization in California occurred within the epidemiological context of an acute syphilitic epidemic and concluded with the disease becoming chronic and endemic. Such a pattern repeated itself in other parts of the world where syphilis had been unknown. Care must be taken then in any area studied to observe and calculate the three stages of epidemic syphilis and their consequences. The spread of syphilis and civilization — "syphilization" — among the indigenous population wrought profound consequences for Native American life.[64] In California, Indians as girls and women suffered disproportionately more than men from the new diseases. Female Indians bore the brunt of the colonial experience, while children simultaneously suffered the greatest fatality rates in the missions. Then or now, without a careful consideration of syphilis no one will recognize the children's aphonic cries.

9

Music and Conversion

"He who sings prays twice!" In my memory from five decades back, at a
time when the pronoun was understood to represent all humankind, I
can still hear the stentorian voice of Monsignor Francis Xavier Singleton
declaiming to the congregation on Sunday, his voice reverberating off
the walls of Saint John's cathedral in Fresno, California: "He who sings,
prays twice!" Although he made this invocation several times a year,
singing was always part of the Sunday ritual whether the Mass was
High — sung throughout, primarily by the choir — or Low — with songs
generally at the end by the congregation. And Monsignor never intoned
it once but several times then called the assembled to their feet, the
faithful symbolically joined together in the Mystical Body of Christ, to
raise their collective voices, no matter how meager the individual talent,
in sung praise to the Almighty. "He who sings prays twice! Now all join
me in the Salve Regina."

— JS

Materialist interpretations of the California missions have rightly directed attention to the contributions Indians made and the price they paid in
building and maintaining these institutions. In their exclusive focus on the
exploitation of Indian labor, however, these interpretations overlook the spiri-

tual dimension of Spanish colonization and the Franciscan attempt to transform Indian hearts and minds as well as Indian behavior. Franciscan-oriented
considerations of California mission history, alternatively, have accepted the
priestly calculus that receipt of the sacrament of Baptism equaled conversion
and so have spent little time considering exactly how conversion occurred.

If, however, conversion generally was a process of some indeterminate
length subsequent to rather than symbolized by baptism, how then was conversion achieved? How, and to what extent, were those Indian hearts and
minds transformed? One answer to that troubling question, an answer essential to a more balanced appreciation of Franciscan-Indian interaction in the
missions, can be found by studying European church music. Within the context of the Roman Catholic liturgy, scholars must consider Franciscan approaches to teaching Indians music, Indian responses, and the effect such
teaching would have had upon Indians in light of current research on music
learning and its impact on other areas of human life.

Music has had an ancient role in the Roman Catholic Church. For those
spreading the Church's teachings in the eighteenth century, music held special
missiological as well as liturgical value. Following the medieval adage that
"He who does not sing is only half a priest,"[1] missionaries to Alta California
came prepared to sing, even if they individually possessed minimal musical
aptitude. As missionaries charged to bring their God's word to those who had
not yet heard it, many of the Franciscans who came to California were accomplished vocalists and some were accomplished musicians as well. Spanish
Franciscans brought a particular Spanish musical practice with them. They
began the day with an *alabado* (*alabanza* in Spanish), a simple Hymn of Divine
Praise, which they introduced into the New World in their missions in Texas
and California.[2] Although their initial chronicler, Fray Francisco Palóu, com-
mented only occasionally on music while describing Franciscan evangelization, his writings reveal glimpses illustrating that music characterized Franciscan interactions with Indians from contact.

The first father president of the missions, Junípero Serra, had a sonorous
voice, loved singing, and first taught Indian children to sing Spanish hymns at
San Diego. Serra favored beginning with morning songs, such as the alabanza,
imparting some Spanish in the process, or a Marian hymn (dedicated to Mary,
Mother of Jesus) such as the *Salve Regina,* simultaneously introducing some
Latin.[3] Serra continued that activity wherever he went and later created choirs
at his headquarters at Mission San Carlos from among those he had taught.

Palóu, who had a fine voice, regarded Serra as exceptional in this area, a
fitting attribute for one devoted to Saint Francis Solano, who frequently was
depicted in paintings holding a violin.[4] Serra, Palóu, and other Franciscans

taught Indian children to sing wherever they went. On one occasion, Palóu recalled that while traveling from mission San Diego to San Gabriel, at a *ranchería* about two leagues (5 miles) north of San Diego, he and his companions encountered fifteen Indians whom he and Padre José Murgía had baptized three weeks earlier. The Indians greeted the priests by kneeling in the road and singing an alabanza. The Franciscans responded with tears of joy and gave the Indians some pinole and a few rosaries before continuing their journey.[5]

Serra's commitment to song is reflected both in his beginnings in California and in his death there. José de Gálvez's expedition to Upper California in 1769, which included Serra, had been dedicated to the protection of Saint Joseph as its patron. When hardships confronting the expedition became so desperate that all seemed lost, the relief ship was sighted at San Diego on March 19, the patron's feast day. To honor and thank Saint Joseph, Serra decreed that a High Mass would be celebrated on the nineteenth of every month as long as he lived. In August 1784, while weak and dying, Serra had Palóu sing the High Mass on the nineteenth; the father president sang also. A few days later Serra died, shortly after singing the *Tantum ergo Sacramentum,* "with tears in his eyes," and after receiving the Holy Viaticum in the ceremonies of the last rites.[6] Thus music was important to the Franciscan effort in Alta California from the beginning, and in his fifteen-year tenure as chief administrator, Serra instilled a musical tradition in the missions that far outlived him.

Music played an important, but heretofore largely overlooked, role in converting California Indians to Roman Catholicism. Music's importance lay in its centrality to the Mass, and the Mass, in turn, lay at the religious center of the Franciscan mission. The Mass had a powerful social function inextricably linked to its religious purpose. The Church intended music to involve people in the Mass through singing, and by singing psalmody ordinary folk, as well as the more specialized choir, joined the priest in celebrating the Mass. The Mass performed the ongoing function of integrating, or attempting to integrate, participants of the Mass into the Church and thereby into the Mystical Body of Christ to which all baptized members of the faith automatically belonged.[7] Song involved the congregation and the choir directly in this integrative act.

Sin alienated people from that automatic right conferred by the sacrament of Baptism, and so reconciliation to the Mystical Body of Christ became an important act that the Mass symbolized and made possible. Low Mass, accompanied by song, was said every day, and High Mass was sung on Sundays. Thus the Mass constituted the single most important religious ritual for neophytes — one which could be experienced daily. Music, whether in the simple accompaniment of Low Mass or in the elaborately orchestrated High Mass, was supposed to arouse the emotions of the congregation and to move their collective spirits into harmony with Jesus Christ.

The structure of the Mass is linked to religious texts. Texts that are fixed and unchanging belong to the Ordinary of the Mass, and those that change according to the individual feast day belong to the Proper. Although within the liturgy texts of the Proper rank above those of the Ordinary, both are required for the Mass and their *functions* remain unchanged regardless of season.[8] The division of the Mass into these two parts reflects theological and historical thinking. The Ordinary is the oldest section of the ritual and is rooted in the antiquity of the Church. The Proper illustrates that Church ritual branches from its roots and changes both with the seasons (i.e., Lent, Advent) and grows over time to incorporate new saints (those confirmed by the Church to be in Heaven) whose feast days must be celebrated.

The Proper, with variable text anchored in the psalms, gave rise to psalmody, which led to the intricate elaboration of plainchant. This music, commonly known as Gregorian Chant, was named for Pope Gregory the Great (590–604), who had them written down. Polyphonic versions of these texts — many voices singing independent melodic lines but in contrapuntal harmony — were performed long before Franciscans came to California.

The Proper provided occasion for singing three types of psalmody: direct, responsorial, and antiphonal. In direct psalmody, part or the whole of the psalm is sung syllabically, usually by the priest, alternating with either the congregation or the choir. Antiphonal psalmody derived from direct psalmody. In this the priest sings or intones only one phrase at a time, to which the others respond in unison. Antiphonal psalmody became popular perhaps because the singers found it easy to know when to come in with their part. The response and antiphon begin or end on the same pitch. In responsorial psalmody a soloist usually initiates a chant and is answered by the choir. Originally, responses were short, consisting of a word or brief phrase, and sung by the congregation. But as the melodies for the text became more complex, the tasks of singing responsorial psalmody increasingly fell upon the trained choir.

In syllabic melody (singing the syllables) the chanted words these syllables assemble are more important than the melody or melodic setting. It is the case in almost all of the Mass that text is heard clearly and delivered syllable after syllable. In the Alleluia, the opposite prevails. The Alleluia is melismatic chant, with long vocal flourishes on a single syllable, designed to express intense religious joy. It is the only part of the Mass wherein the joy of singing for its own sake is indulged, providing the vocalist with a respite from the controlled chant. During Lent or during the performance of a Requiem Mass, however, the Alleluia is omitted.

Other parts of the Mass developed differently. The Introit and Communion are antiphonal and somewhat stylistically similar; the Gradual and Offertory are responsorial. Singing of the Ordinary (roots) evolved into its standard form between the seventh and eleventh centuries. Alternation in singing constituted the guiding principle and could be taught more easily to a congregation because it is not complex and strict in response patterns as the direct, responsorial, and antiphonal psalmody required of the Proper (branches).

Even though choirs began to displace congregational singing in Europe as the music became more complex, the more traditional approach, with its inclusion of all Mass participants, had value, especially with new Christian communities. Consider the Kyrie, a ninefold supplication to Christ for mercy. One of the very few vestigial remnants of Greek in the Mass, it is explicitly designed to incorporate the congregation in song by intoning each phrase three times. Musically this can be done most simply by alternating two melodies in a variety of ways. For example, the priest can sing a line of "Kyrie eleison" and the congregation responds, or the choir can take one or two repetitions of the phrase and the full assembly can vocalize the third. Numerous variations are possible, and variety provides interest and differing levels of congregational participation. Each part of the Mass beyond the Kyrie has its own musical pattern.[9] Throughout the Proper and the Ordinary, music is essential to the High Mass. In California, group vocal participation by Indians, whether by the relatively untrained congregation or by the carefully tutored choir, was as important to celebrating the Mass as priestly singing.

Teaching Indians to sing Low and High Mass constituted important priestly work. In California, Franciscans found people with a musical background that could be shaped to European ends, even though the padres wrongly thought that Indians in their aboriginal state had no music.[10] California Indians shared an ancient musical tradition apparently common to all North American Indians, a musical repertoire consisting of "animal songs." These were incantations, simple and repetitive, with one or more short melodic phrases repeated as frequently as a particular culture or the individual singer wished. Europeans thought such incantations speech-like, with the words — often from foreign or forgotten languages — syllabized, usually imitating or describing what an animal or spirit person did in mythic times before humans existed.[11]

The narrow melodic range of a fifth or less, occasionally stretching to an octave, often followed a melodic contour, which was either level or undulating, measured by Europeans in 2/4 or 3/4 time. A characteristic particular to some California Indian songs, called "the rise," identifies a melodic pattern in which incantations are sung at a higher pitch than the opening phrases of the song. While most songs were sung in unison, with all singing the same melody when groups participated, in the phrase known as "the rise" some complexity, such as paired melodic repetitions, could be found.[12] Such paired melodic repetitions were similar to the European-introduced chant of the Mass Kyrie, for example, and "the rise" converged nicely with the pitch changes in much of Catholic plainsong.

Franciscans approached their musical tasks with a determination reinforced by a pedagogical understanding of education's purpose; they also had a practical sense of how to teach music to novices. Plainsong combines sacred text — words — with melody. The man responsible for devising a musical notation system that made writing it down possible, Guido D'Arezzo (ca. 995), loomed large in Franciscan thinking about music.

D'Arezzo, a Benedictine monk and musical theorist as well as extraordinary teacher, sought to achieve the concept of harmoniousness, in which as one scholars puts it, "The significance of the words and the significance of the music are the same — they both manifest *musica,* 'realize' its truth in sounds."[13] Melody should be so fitted to the words being conveyed that spiritual awareness may be heightened and the soul, upon singing or hearing this music, may be moved by its emotive power to right behavior. As a Benedictine monk observed, "in the mystical tradition" that informed Gregorian Chant, "the groups of notes were believed to resonate with the human soul."[14]

D'Arezzo's thinking about the emotive effect of music both anticipated and reflected that of other church luminaries. Johannes de Grocheo (ca. 1300), for example, wanted the Kyrie sung slowly, in "perfect longs . . . in order to move the hearts of the congregation to devotion."[15] Aurelian of Réôme's (ca. 850), commenting on the Agnus Dei, sung just before receiving the Eucharist, wanted music such "that all the faithful communicating on the body and blood of the Lord may drink with the melody of the singing Him whom they receive by mouth; that is to say, within themselves may contemplate, crucified, dead and buried, Him whom they taste."[16]

While it may be doubted that such complex emotive states automatically were produced among California Indians, or among European congregations, the Franciscans nevertheless desired that goal. Although mission Indians apparently received the Eucharist much less frequently than did the *gente de razón* (Spanish/Mexican military and civilian settlers), the padres encouraged/required participation for all neophytes at Mass.[17]

To achieve an emotive state and to praise God in song required teaching plainsong to the uninitiated, and no one had succeeded like D'Arezzo. He created a method of solmization — of singing musical pitches with special syllables. He derived these syllables from his version of a well-known hymn to John the Baptist, "Sanctes Johannes."[18] That hymn began with the Latin phrase "Ut queant laxis." To the opening syllable of each of its first six phrases Guido assigned scale pitches in ascending order. He instructed his pupils to sing them to notes. D'Arezzo's syllables then could represent pitches of a six-note scale, known as the "natural hexachord."

To facilitate memorizing the melody to "Sanctes Johannes" and its hexachord, D'Arezzo devised yet another aid for instructing the choir: the Guidonian Hand. He mapped the method on an open left hand, beginning at the tip of the thumb. The syllables, representing pitches, encompassed the scale and charted the ascents and descents in a manner designed to impress both the student's eye and ear. The choir master would point to these syllables as their pitches were to be sung by the choir. D'Arezzo went further, transferring his simple teaching method of precise pitch notation to the drawn musical staff of lines and intervals and to the drawn staff carrying a musical sign designating pitch, known as the clef. Both the staff and the clef made it possible for singers to perform music at sight.[19] This brilliant monk devised a method for teaching illiterate Italian boys, in his words, "to sing an unknown melody before the third day, which by other methods would not have been possible in many weeks."[20] He succeeded in teaching his pupils to sing new music by "combining thought, memory and musical ear, in a practical manner."[21]

D'Arezzo's importance in the musical instruction of California Indians cannot be overstated. His method of notation, with modification — printed in the surviving mission songbooks — was used throughout the mission system. Teaching via the hand would have preceded sight-reading from notation. Even Protestants adopted his methods and his hexachords and taught them in British North American colonies.[22]

Serra and his confreres began instructing California Indians according to the method effectively codified nearly eight centuries earlier. That the Indians knew no Spanish or Latin made no difference, just as illiteracy made no difference to D'Arezzo's Italian students. Pitches, intervals, rhythms, and text were taught by imitation and pointing to hand positions, all of which was visual and did not necessitate reading from a printed score in a book. Pitches, intervals, rhythms, and text were to be Indian clues to Christian religious experience.

Over time, Franciscans hoped that they would unlock the code to the emotive effect of Christian liturgical music.

Priests started musical instruction by teaching boys and girls how to sing prayers. They instructed the children in the proper form of address to their new God. First they taught the "Pater Noster," or the Lord's Prayer, chanted to a single note without variation for an entire sentence, followed by a change in each successive sentence. Since this was usually done to a Psalm chant, the incipient congregation was already learning its responsorial role for upcoming masses.

Invariably "Ave Maria" became the second song taught. Set to a lyrical Spanish melody, according to one Franciscan historian, it "became the most popular hymn. It could be heard at the homes, at work, at the plays of the children, on the march, and above all in the church and in the popular [religious] processions." When the children had learned their prayers they were brought into the church where they sang, alternately, before the Blessed Sacrament on the main altar, and before a side altar containing an image of the Blessed Virgin. This act reinforced the reason for their practicing and linked singing to the new celestial beings that these Indians now ought to venerate. Afterward, and outside the church, the priests rewarded the children with candies and fruits.[23]

Through this approach the Franciscans could teach children to sing the principal hymns in a few days, and children learned them very well in a few weeks. Adults were encouraged by the singing of their children both at home and in church. Standard Franciscan practice required all neophytes to recite their prayers and sing them daily at morning Mass and at evening services; they repeated this again at Sunday Mass.[24] Thus, over time, the congregation learned to sing and to assume its role at Mass.

An individual mission could remain at this level of musical instruction indefinitely, depending upon the abilities and desires of the missionaries. A further goal of musical instruction at nearly all missions, however, was to create a male choir to sing the Gregorian plainchant, which the Franciscans wanted to employ to celebrate High Mass.

Their efforts to teach music were not uniform. Padre Narciso Durán, who arrived at Mission San José in 1806, nine years after the founding of that establishment and thirty-seven years after Serra had begun the mission system,[25] is the only Franciscan choir organizer whose musical notes and advice have survived. By his own admission, Durán had no formal training in music. He was not a music teacher, but he was "cursed" with perfect pitch. At San José he found "the Ecclesiastical Chant was so faulty that the one song the boys knew, the 'Asperges' [a Psalm], . . . seemed like a howl rather than a song.

Figure 11. Father Narciso Durán offers a piece of fruit to an Indian child, a customary practice among the California missionaries for rewarding improvement in singing. Durán, who served at Mission San José from 1806 until 1833, was among the most capable and devoted of the missionaries, achieving his greatest success as a music teacher and choirmaster. Though lacking formal training himself, he devised innovative methods for instructing neophytes, who learned to play violin, violoncello, flute, and drum and to accompany themselves while singing the Mass. In 1812 he wrote with great pride of the performance of his choristers that here "the feasts of the Church are celebrated with a decency and a majesty superior to anything which the land seemed to promise." From Eugène Duflot de Mofras, *Exploration,* 1844. Courtesy Bancroft Library.

And let us not speak of the Masses, for in telling you, scarcely without exaggeration, that they did not know how to respond 'Amen,' you can judge the rest for yourself."

Given the myriad difficulties of ministering to a relatively new mission, Durán chose not to avail his neophytes of the "singing [that] was being organized at some of the missions." But, he continued, "As I did not deem it necessary to send the boys elsewhere to learn, and as I did not hasten to teach them myself, things remained the same." For a time Durán stayed content with the general Spanish assumption that Indians were intellectually inferior. He was convinced "that the boys did not possess the ability to take up singing." Offenses against his sense of pitch progressively grated.

Durán began to question his own assumptions about innate Indian abilities, however, when he observed boys from a nearby mission playing European instruments. He decided to send some of his young neophytes to study the rudiments of music with Padre José Viader at mission Santa Clara. To Durán, "The results exceeded my first hopes and now the sacred functions were carried out with a fitness more than mediocre."

Yet he remained troubled by the impermanence of the arrangement. He thought that the improvement would last only as long as some friar who knew music could be found in the area to continue instruction. If such a talented priest left, all would fall again into disarray. Durán began to believe that choristers could learn two or three complete masses, but he remarked that from his group of eight or ten, only two or three "really knew the masses, so that if these were missing there could be no High Mass." The problem, as he identified it, lay in trying to get the boys to learn to sing from memory, at which they generally failed, "and not by rule and principle."

He realized that Indian choristers would have to learn to read music and that he would have to teach them to do it. "[W]hat is most necessary at a mission," he wrote, "is to teach the boys the Sacred Chant according to rules or principles so that they will not have to trust everything to memory, but will be able to read notes and sing by themselves whatever is plainly written; and this not only two or three among ten or twelve, but all, or the greater number of them." Durán, who saw himself as a musical iconoclast because he questioned the applicability of musical "masters" to help solve his problems, claimed to have made up a system that would work. He wanted a simpler, uncluttered chant to replace the elaborate practices that had crept into the liturgy in his day. He wanted "not to lose sight of the spirit of the Church, striving to conform the beat of the Chant upon the ear to the beat of the word upon the heart."

Durán reinvented the music teaching methods of D'Arezzo, from the Benedictine's theory to his practice. Durán went further, further even than the expectations of the Council of Trent (1545–1563), in his insistence that his singers also play instruments and accompany themselves while singing the Mass. "Between musicians and singers (*entre músicos y cantores*)," he wrote emphatically, "there can be no difference (*que unos mismos canten y toquen*)." This practice directly correlated to D'Arezzo's notion of harmoniousness, in which the significance of the words would become one with the music if singer and player were also one. To ensure that the solemnity of the service would not be broken by musical errors, Durán also specified that two violins play accompaniment at each Requiem Mass.

In addition to learning to play the violin, his choristers learned flutes and trumpets to keep them on pitch and learned drums to keep their rhythm. Since California Indians had no similar drum, and their flute traversed a narrow range, they had limited instrumental training to apply to their new performing tasks. Yet, by all accounts, they learned European instruments quickly and played them well. Durán insisted upon his instrumental approach for two reasons: "First, to firmly sustain the voices of the boys, not permitting them to go flat or sharp, as regularly happens without this precaution. Second, that seeing the distances between notes on the instruments, due to the various finger positions, the boys might gain some idea of the same intervals in singing, modulating their voices accordingly."

Durán simplified the melodic contours of several Mass parts to enhance his singers' accomplishments. All Introits and Communions, for example, he set to the same scale. As Indians developed greater familiarity with European scales, they also became more adept at replicating them. This gave rise to polyphony, in which one half of the choir took the same melody and sang it lower or higher against the other half, or each half sang a different melody simultaneously. To perform these complex masses, Durán encouraged part-singing and facilitated it by using colored notes in his songbooks to differenti-ate the soprano, alto, tenor, and bass of three- and four-part music.[26]

The degree to which Durán's work was strictly original or represented the application of ideas formed at his Apostolic College in Mexico is moot. Durán popularized the "Misa de Cataluña" and the "Misa Viscaína." Judging from extant copies of the former, found in the archives of missions Santa Barbara, Santa Inés, and San Juan Bautista, the "Misa de Cataluña" was widely per-formed in California.[27]

It has been said about Durán's liturgical music that its "hauntingly sad or melancholy overall atmosphere are thought to represent Durán's attempt to capture and express this quality of native California Indian music — a quality that was repeatedly noticed and mentioned by European visitors to Spanish California."[28] If true, then the social context in which Durán composed di-rectly influenced Church music in California and made it, if not exactly a shared musical liturgy, then one which was at least significantly influenced by those being missionized. There can be no doubt, however, that Durán changed his opinion about Indian intellectual ability. Students taught the teacher in a context of reciprocity.

After six years at mission San José, Durán wrote his thoughts about teach-ing music as a "Prologue" to his songbook.[29] He did so to aid any successor and to advise priests who were confronting similar problems elsewhere. Sing-ing the Mass was too important to him to allow leaving musical instruction to a missionary who might have formal music training and reject his model or who might rely on the whims of rote memorization. Durán's zealous proselytizing about and practice of music instruction continued for more than twenty years.

In 1831, Alfred Robinson visited Durán at San José and heard the neophytes sing a Mass. The choir and orchestra of thirty had practiced for two months to perform this particular piece; "so acute was the ear of the priest [Durán]," Robinson wrote, "that he would detect a wrong note on the part of either instantly, and chide the erring performer." Robinson concluded his recollection by observing, "I have often seen the old gentleman, bareheaded, in the large square of the Mission beating time against one of the pillars of the corridor, whilst his music was in rehearsal."[30] Subsequent testimony indicates that his musical legacy at mission San José endured to the end of the mission era.[31]

In 1833, Durán was transferred to mission Santa Barbara where he continued his musical teaching. A story about him from this era has clear antecedents at San José. When acting as celebrant of a High Mass, which required him to face the altar with his back both to the congregation and to the choir in the loft above the entrance, Durán nevertheless continued to direct his musicians. When seated during the Gloria and Credo, with his hands upon his knees as behavior prescribed, the singers watched the forefinger of his left hand; by slight movement he directed them. Although regarded as a special Durán code,[32] it was a conducting technique indicating tempo of his own improvisation, perhaps, on the master teacher of Arezzo.

While we know more about Durán than about other music teachers because his memoir has survived, abundant evidence exists to demonstrate that his efforts and successes can be seen as part of a larger context of Franciscan musical accomplishments with California Indians.[33] Padre Viader's renowned skill at training the choir at Santa Clara and its subsequent influence upon Durán have already been mentioned. At mission La Purísima, Padre Mariano Payeras in early 1810 wrote feelingly about the Indians, "We hear them pray, sing (this year another beautiful Mass with much music was created) and play, as proficient musicians and singers."[34]

The two men who became the second and third father president of the missions following Serra continued the Mallorcan's musical precedent. Fermín Francisco Lasuén, father president from 1785 to 1803, for example, endured in Indian memory at Santa Inés as the authority to correct any dispute in their singing.[35] Padre Estevan Tapis, father president from 1803 to 1812, went to San Juan Bautista after leaving office and created one of the finest musical groups in the mission system. Tapis composed several Mass songbooks, which he also embellished with artistic drawings, and he used the same staff and clef as Durán, as well as a similar color code to differentiate voices for part-singing.[36]

Tapis's success at San Juan Bautista was linked with his fellow missionary there, Felipe Arroyo de la Cuesta. A man of extraordinary linguistic as well as musical talents, Arroyo de la Cuesta, according to local lore, preached in thirteen Indian dialects during his twenty-five years at the mission. Evidence, rather than lore, attests to his composing a Mitsun language grammar, his setting some Mitsun words to common mission melodies, and his writing several masses and hymns.[37] Arroyo de la Cuesta also played and helped to teach the secular music that came with the mechanical barrel organ originally given to Lasuén and eventually lodged at San Juan Bautista. Neophyte accomplishments in playing popular music for parties and fiestas of the gente de razón in the area undoubtedly stemmed from their learning from this device, which contained over thirty songs, and from the encouragement of this priest.[38]

At mission San Antonio two friars, Pedro Cabot, a linguist, and Juan Sancho, a musicologist, combined their talents to persuade Indians to accept Christianity and perform music at a level that few other choirs in Alta California ever achieved. A representative artifact from their era has survived. It is a prayer/songboard containing inscriptions in Spanish and Salinan; the song board is large enough to be seen by the congregation, facing the altar during Mass.

The board front contains prayers in both languages, including the "Brief Act of Contrition" and the "Acts of Faith, Hope and Love." The back of the board has two brief prayers and a musical inscription for two psalms below, with directions to the priest for informing the choir. The two psalms, antiphons, are "Asperges Me" (Sprinkle Me, O Lord) and "Vidi Aquam" (Water of Life), and the music is figured and colored for part-singing as well as chant. At the bottom of each sheet is the inscription "1817, P. Cabot." No doubt Sancho, rather than Cabot, wrote the musical notations.[39]

Prayer and songboards were used at all the missions. The prayer/songboard is an important example of how the Franciscans taught neophytes significant elements of European culture and religion. These instructional devices could be carried in religious procession, hung upon a wall or tree, or inserted into a music stand inside the church. Priests led their "charges" reciting and singing their daily prayers with such boards. They used them as a prompting aid for congregational and choral singing during Sunday Mass.[40]

Padre Sancho's contributions to music education came from his background as choirmaster in his native Mallorca, but perhaps his most significant offering was his introduction of the music of Ignacio de Jerusalem to Alta California. De Jerusalem, an Italian violinist and composer, came to Mexico City where he became choirmaster in 1749. He held this post until his death twenty years later, the year Serra led his Franciscans into Alta California. De Jerusalem composed masses of remarkable beauty.[41]

De Jerusalem's masses were in the handwriting of Sancho, himself a choir director, who had heard them in Mexico City. Sancho transcribed them and brought them with him when he came to Alta California in 1804. Because Sancho had enlarged and perfected his choir and had continued musical education at mission San Antonio, music of de Jerusalem's complexity could be played there as well as at missions Santa Clara, San José, Santa Barbara, and probably several others. This recent discovery points to a previously unappreciated high level of musical performance by California Indians, along with new evidence of priestly musical sophistication.

Sancho's confrere at nearby mission Soledad, Padre Florencio Ibáñez, also had been a choir organizer. He eventually assumed that post at the Franciscan College of San Fernando in Mexico City. An accomplished artist as well as musician, Ibáñez illuminated and transcribed four large songbooks, in this case *antiphonaria*, while at the college. He came to the California missions, where his musical service at Soledad distinguished his choir. He once greeted the governor of California, José Joaquín Arrillaga, with a performance of musical selections he had written for his choir. Ibáñez also composed and had performed a *pastorela* — a Christmas play consisting of song and verse detailing the travails besetting the shepherds who first learn of Christ's birth. Because St. Francis, founder of the Franciscans, had been the first to secure papal permission to depict the manger at Christmastime, accompanying pastorelas became a significant Franciscan devotional innovation.[42]

Mission choirs, as distinct from mission congregations, consisted of from thirty to forty men and boys, many of them musicians as well as singers. The padres distinguished these choristers from other Indians.[43] By first choosing these Indians for their ability to replicate European musical sounds and then giving them special musical training, distinct clothing, and select work assignments, the priests created a new class of high-status Indian in the mission community. This new class of ascribed status derived strictly from priestly determined individual Indian abilities, rather than from hereditary lineage or Indian custom. Indians took pride in this new status and work. Individual Indian craftsmanship, invested in personal musical instruments, has come down to us in two artifacts. At mission San Juan Bautista, an Indian-made wooden violin has survived, its tailpiece made of bone and its neckpiece elaborately carved in the form of an animal, possibly a pre-mission religious symbol. The time-consuming, nonfunctional decoration of the violin suggests the emotional attachment of the carver to the instrument. In a faded photograph of choristers at mission San Buenaventura, an Indian can be seen playing a flute cleverly made from an old rifle barrel.[44] In both cases Indian pride in workmanship and in the role of musician/chorister is evident.

This corps of elite men and boys performed a special role on Sundays and feast days. Wherever possible on these occasions, the priests dressed them differently from the rest of the congregation. Eugéne Duflot de Mofras, a French diplomat and commercial agent, described Viader's choir at Santa Clara in 1841 as wearing French uniforms, consisting of blue pants with a red stripe running the outside trouser length and red caps adorned with a tassel.[45] The shirt, presumably, was of standard mission issue white wool, but, unlike other mission Indian males, choristers abandoned the conventional white woolen pants for the uniform trousers on special occasions. Similar uniforms, perhaps identical, were worn by Indian musicians at missions Santa Barbara, San Jose, and San Buenaventura.[46]

Mission Indian *alcaldes* (overseers), typically numbering two and serving for one-year terms, wore a red sash to distinguish their superior rank, and the alcaldes generally came from Indian high-status or chiefly families. The mission choir of thirty to forty men created significant social mobility for those Indians who wished to rise in the mission hierarchy but who lacked status in native culture.[47]

Franciscans rewarded their choristers with what priests thought were better jobs, placing the Indians closer to themselves. Durán put it most succinctly in his advice on music training. "If he [the priest reading Durán's instruction] keeps things as they are now, he will have to do nothing more than introduce boys as novices, permitting them to grow up at the side of the older singers, and when they marry let him give them domestic employment, such as weaving, shoemaking or blacksmithing, in order to have them always on hand when there is singing or playing to be done."[48] Choristers, then, occupied an elevated position within the mission social structure; this was further reinforced by their professions.

Joining the choir, moreover, became a way for Indians to achieve within the mission the high status accorded in native culture to membership in a secret society. Like those secret societies that incorporated only select individuals, becoming a chorister meant learning a separate and secret language for ritual (Latin), playing a significant role in ritual observance (the Mass), and wearing special ceremonial clothing (the uniform).[49] The Franciscans probably did not know of this powerful incentive from within the Indian community to become choristers.

As one aged Californio woman, Guadalupe Vallejo, remembered: "Many young Indians had good voices, and these were selected with great care to be trained in singing for the church choir. It was thought such an honor to sing in church that the Indian families were all very anxious to be represented. Every prominent mission had fathers who paid great attention to training the Indians in music."[50]

Indian choristers had more and different contact with the gente de razón from other mission Indians. Because of their musical training and their familiarity with secular as well as religious music, Indian musicians frequently played at weddings, receptions, fiestas, and all-night fandangos. Prominent Californio Juan B. Alvarado recalled, "The same Indians who had assisted in the Mass of the morning and the bull and the bear fight of the afternoon furnished the music for the dances; and they did it well, being much more accustomed even for their church music to lively and inspiriting operatic airs and dancing tunes than to slow and lugubrious elegies and dirges. The program consisted of contradanzes, minuets, Aragonese jotas, and various other dances usual among the Spanish population."[51]

Foreign visitors to the missions remarked on the quality of the music, both secular and religious, they heard there. During 1826–1827, several men of different nationalities and religions witnessed musical activity in California missions. In November 1826, Harrison Rogers, an American and a "stalwart Calvinist," accompanied fur trader and explorer Jedediah Smith into southern California and to Mission San Gabriel, where Rogers and companions enjoyed priestly hospitality for nearly two months. For religious reasons Rogers refused to listen to "Romish" Church music, but he nevertheless observed Indian musicians. On one occasion he went to a reception following a wedding: "Then the musick commenced serranading, the soldiers firing etc.; about 7 o'clock tea [chocolate] was served, and about 11 o'clock, dinner and musick." In his diary entry more than a month later, Rogers wrote: "The band of musick consists of two violins, one bass violin, a trumpet and triangle was played for two hours in the evening before the priests' door by the Indians. They made tolerable good musick, the most in imitation to white that [I] ever heard."[52] Rogers did not complain of repetition.

Sometime later the Englishman Frederick Beechey visited mission San José. Although a Protestant, he did attend a High Mass. Given what Durán had achieved there, Beechey's comments would appear to understate the level of Indian musical accomplishments. The choir, remarked Beechey, consisted "of several Indian musicians, who performed very well indeed on various instruments, and sang the *Te Deum* in a very passable manner. The congregation was very attentive, but" Beechey noted with his Protestant sensibilities, "the gratification they appeared to derive from the music furnished another proof of the strong hold this portion of the Romish church takes upon uninformed minds."[53]

About the same time Rogers was at San Gabriel, the intrepid French visitor Auguste Duhaut-Cilly came to mission Santa Barbara for Palm Sunday Mass. Because of the solemnity of the Lenten season, Padre Antonio Ripoll limited the repertoire of his Indian choristers inside the church, then took his musicians outside to entertain further. According to Duhaut-Cilly, Ripoll's "Indians rendered some songs with much taste and a delightful harmony, singing Spanish and Latin words to pretty Italian airs. After Mass we retired to the padre's parlor, and there heard a serenade to the commandant-general. The musicians were many and all in uniform. Although they rendered passably several French and Italian pieces, I judged that they had succeeded better with the [earlier] songs."[54] Duhaut-Cilly observed another aspect of Durán's practical musical education: secular song. Durán's choristers performed outside the church because this was not liturgical music; it was the music his choristers would make for the presidial soldiers or settlers for their entertainments and fiestas. Clearly Durán both instructed his musicians in such music and gave them time to practice it. In this way he provided them yet another reason to stay at the mission and earn income to supplement their mission allotment.

Many of Duhaut-Cilly's men were Roman Catholic, and so their familiarity with Church music, more so than with secular music, made their observations more pertinent to understanding neophyte accomplishment. Lieutenant Edmond Le Netrel recorded that at a Sunday Mass at mission San Francisco, "The Captain [Duhaut-Cilly], another member of the crew, and I went to the mission and assisted at the Mass. . . . The Indians of both sexes sang canticles. Although their voices were a little raucous there was much harmony in their chants."[55]

Pablo Emilio Botta, Duhaut-Cilly's ship's doctor, left a particularly well-informed observation: "I shall say that it seems to me," Botta wrote, "that the most outstanding trait of these Indians is their inclination for music. In the missions they learn soon and easily to play the violin, the cello, etc., and to sing together in such a manner that they can perform the music for the Mass of a very complicated harmony, certainly better than the peasants of our lands would be able to after [years of study.]"[56] That Botta heard elaborately sung masses is clear; perhaps the choir performed a de Jerusalem composition.

Because of their skills as professional craftsmen — such as blacksmiths, weavers, and cobblers — these same Indian choristers worked for the Spanish/Mexican settlers in capacities different from those mission Indians who labored on public works projects or in private fields. These Indian musicians also possessed greater familiarity with the Spanish language than did other mission Indians, an advantage that facilitated their interaction with the Californios.

Franciscan musical training wrought profound change in mission Indian intellectual, religious, and cultural life. Some of these changes the priests intended, such as increased religious devotion. Other changes, such as improved Spanish language facility and increased European-defined skills, the priests did not recognize as following upon their musical instruction. Until recently, the prevailing view of human learning held that the left hemisphere (lh) of the brain was dominant — later elaborated into dominant for language — and the right hemisphere (rh) lacked special competence and handled such artistic tasks as music. According to this theory, music learning and language learning were mutually exclusive intellectual activities. Recent neurological research has demonstrated the inaccuracy of such concepts and simultaneously revealed a much more complex processing of music in the brain.[57] The critical role in musical perception lies in how the brain constructs pitch in the auditory cortex.[58]

Pitch is the basis for music perception. A musical melody consists of a total pattern of pitches in a sequence; melody contour comprises the patterns of ascending and descending pitch. Adults and children perceive and retain a melody by remembering its contour. Research shows that infants eight to eleven months old, like adults, listen to global pitch relationships rather than to individual notes. Thus infants, like adults, listen for contour and remember in "chunks" (musical phrases), which is the way Western composers have organized their music, for example, in clearly marked phrases.[59] Plainchant, with its narrow range of pitch changes, is more easily "chunked" and remembered than, say, a Mozart piece. Both hemispheres of the brain are involved, coordinated by the auditory cortex.[60] Franciscan musical instruction, then, engaged and taught California Indians at the most fundamental level of musical cognition.

Studies among children reveal several influences that affect their musical preference. Children who are repeatedly exposed to a particular type of music, no matter how different from their existing musical diet, will come to prefer the new type over time. This tendency toward preference, or preference change, is increased if adults or authority figures also prefer the style being taught. Repetition increases preference even in a passive listening, as opposed to an active listening, situation.[61] Since children, the first targets of Franciscan musical instruction, could most easily be persuaded to imitate the new sounds, boys and girls became initial conveyers of European music to their parents. From childhood through adolescence to adulthood, individual experience, age, and intelligence "combine to increase a person's ability to discriminate rhythmic patterns, pitch, and tonal sequences."[62] Franciscans consciously taught those discrimination skills to their Indian choirs. The entire family repeated the music in priestly directed congregational singing.

One reason repetition increases preference in an active listening or performance setting is thought to lie in the notion of "well formedness" in music. The more familiar a listener/performer is with a certain musical style, the greater that person's ability will be to accept new songs based upon the learned expectations of pitch, rhythmic groupings, and beat patterns. Such a person is engaged in responding to the music.[63] "Well formedness," sometimes expressed as the music's inherent qualities, is quickly grasped in plainchant, and, following mastery of the basics of the form, additional song or chants can be learned easily because the singer's memory and anticipation of the next element in the new song conform readily to pre-set expectations. Church music teachers before D'Arrezo and after Durán have understood this facility for grasping new songs in plainchant.[64]

Studies show that while musical aptitude remains constant over time, musical achievement — demonstrated ability — improves with practice, experience, and training, as does mastering one's sense of pitch. As Durán knew, playing a musical instrument would enhance the player's sense of pitch and rhythm. He and other Franciscans taught the Indians to play instruments. Performance on a musical instrument depends upon practice, and practice requires time. Practicing is a motor skill that affects, among other things, hand–eye coordination and speed and range of movement; these functions also will improve over time. Girls tend to do better than boys in these areas,[65] but in colonial California the patriarchal traditions dictated a preference for male-only choirs and musicians. The most talented pool of potential students to make church music — girls — was not utilized.

Evaluating the impact of music on intelligence — a culturally defined construct — is difficult. A modern widely reported and controversial study found that students performed significantly higher on the spatial reasoning portion of a standard intelligence test after listening to ten minutes of Mozart's sonata for two pianos in D major, K488. The same students then took the same test after listening to a relaxation tape for ten minutes or after experiencing ten minutes of silence. Listening to Mozart improved the scores by eight to nine points over the other conditions.[66]

Although California mission Indians never heard Mozart or listened to a piano, they repeatedly performed music and played musical instruments, which probably enhanced their spatial reasoning ability. California mission Indians listened to church music in an engaged rather than a passive state, and they performed it, according to the informed observations of foreign visitors, in a manner comparable to anything heard in Europe.

The occupations of Durán's choristers — weavers, shoemakers, blacksmiths

—required spatial reasoning abilities beyond those needed by field hands or herdsmen. Music improved those spatial reasoning abilities, enhanced choristers' "intelligence" in the European culturally defined use of the term, and contributed substantially to California Indians' learning European religion and ways of prayer. Perhaps European tools and worldview initially disoriented Indians. Such disorientation, however, would have been temporary. As one historian explains, claiming that "Indian laborers suffered [permanent] psychological disorientation when they tried to reconcile Spanish tools, technologies and schedules with their own world views," denies the Indian ability "to incorporate aspects of it selectively into their own lives."[67] Music training would have facilitated that Indian incorporation of European technologies both directly and indirectly.

Music learning can enhance language learning. This phenomenon can be explored by considering the way Franciscans used music to teach the *doctrina* and prayers.[68] In the California missions the initial teaching by song was followed by recitation twice daily—once in the dominant Indian dialect and once in Spanish—and at that time instruction became rote memorization.[69] In the early stages of missionization, however, when Durán and other Franciscans functioned as music educators, they told children about the correct forms for addressing God the Father (Pater Noster, Padre Nuestro) and Mary (Ave Maria, Salve Regina), the general confession made daily at Mass in the *confiteor,* the Ten Commandments, and the other items included in the doctrina. The priests conveyed this information through song. Those structural prompts also had significant impact in teaching Indian choristers the Spanish language.

Children learn a new language in "chunks," just as they learn music. Initially, children try to replicate the sounds they hear for correctness but, since the information they receive is vast and complex, they speak with limited comprehension. As they are given more instruction, their formulaic utterances, based solely on memorization, give way to incorrect speaking or seeming disarray. Given enough exposure they then eventually formulate novel speech in the new language.[70] Music instruction in the California missions took the choristers far beyond the rote language memorization of other mission Indians because language learning is facilitated when it is associated with or accompanied by music instruction.

Franciscans recognized that the Indians who sang in the choir, served the Mass, and led other Indians in reciting the doctrina had a better command of Spanish than did others. The popular view that Indians did not learn Spanish stems from misreading the padres' responses to the famous questionnaire of 1812, in which the priests complained that adult and aged Indians entering the missions learned Spanish slowly or not at all. Children, the priests avowed, learned Spanish quite rapidly, even though a school for Indians existed only at mission San Luis Rey.[71] The scarcity of first-language Spanish speakers at each mission — customarily consisting of two priests, a mayordomo, and three or four soldiers as guard — meant that musicians had the greatest access to priests and thus greater exposure to the Spanish language than did other Indians. Music instruction, rather than formal education, had been the aide for language adoption.

Were these simply the "best and brightest" from the Indian communities missionized? Were they no more than a talented tenth that chose to adopt the colonizer's ways? The answer is no. Although these Indians had a missionary-prized ability to replicate European musical sounds, ability was not enough — achievement counted for more with the priests. Achievement required work and diligent musical practice in addition to learning a vocational skill. Indians who became choristers developed a European work ethic to implement their musical abilities, along with their profession, or they were passed over in favor of those Indians who would develop one.

What did the neophytes learn? Crucial to attempting an answer is an awareness both of how teacher and pupil generate, share, and control meaning, and of how a grammar of the musical system itself can communicate content.[72] Music events, like speech events, involve an addresser contacting an addressee through the medium of song or speech, for the purpose of conveying a message. These events occur in a context that influences the communication outcome.[73] Religious ritual in the California missions came in the contexts of both practice and performance, in both an informal and a formal setting, customarily located within the church. The site of the event contributed to the meaning of the activity by reinforcing the idea that music's purpose and the purpose of those who sang it was to give glory and honor to the Christian God. External Indian conduct during these events reflected the priestly desired attitude of respect. This Indian behavior suggests one aspect of how both addresser (priest) and addressee (Indian) shared the meaning of their act.

While the priest imposed his will upon his pupils and they responded submissively to his will,[74] the relationship was reciprocal because the priest needed the Indians to perform in a certain way and they had the power to resist if they chose. By joining the choir, Indians had chosen to learn the new music and to learn enough Spanish to cooperate with the priest in their joint venture. Although Indians learned from the priest, they also shared their talents with him. Reciprocity, rather than simple dominance, characterized these clerical events.

Priests used language, song, sheet music, and prayer/songboard to communicate both the sounds and the meaning those sounds were to convey to the singers and to their audience. Plainchant had its distinctive grammar, and the Mass had its sequences with the fixed or rooted music of the Ordinary and the varied or branching music of the Proper. Practice followed practice, leading to performance, but the variety in song assured by the Mass meant that learning new works always fell within the comfortable and recognizable parameters of "well formedness." Variety also forestalled boredom.

In the late twentieth century "extensive" music instruction was defined as training schoolchildren for forty minutes a day, five days a week, for seven months.[75] Choristers rehearsed twice a day, at about an hour at a time, usually six days a week, to perform High Mass on Sundays, Holy Days of Obligation, and feast days. The training and practicing continued for life. In addition to the fifty-two Sundays, the annual liturgical calendar of that time stipulated thirty-four more days of musical celebration,[76] meaning that an average of one day in every four found Indian choirs performing a High Mass. Repetition as reinforcement mapped the Franciscan meaning onto the words and music, creating a code that Indian singers, over time, came to share.

Forging this shared code, priest and singers created the new religious and social conventions of conversion. Indians did not renounce their aboriginal mores and beliefs as the priests intended; rather, Indians allowed the new material to coexist with the old and only allowed the new to become dominant as their beliefs in it became more confident — and confidence led to change. Choristers were in the forefront, then, of those Indians who, in Indians ways, converted.

Conversion was not, however, a straightforward process. Indian singers, like Indian non-singers, resisted Spanish and Mexican colonialism. Choristers participated in the largest uprising in Mission history, the Chumash revolt of 1824, which involved Indians from missions La Purísima, Santa Inés, and Santa Barbara. Chumash made a bold try for freedom with some fleeing to the Channel Islands, some making a military stand at La Purísima and the majority escaping into the *tulares* of the great Central Valley. Indians neither harmed nor killed priests but did kill or wound about seven Mexicans. The resolution of this conflict came when Indians who had fled to the tulares decided to accept the governor's pardon and return with the priests and soldiers.

The feasts of both Trinity Sunday and Corpus Christi (Christ the King) fell during the return, and Indians cleared a space and built an arbor for a temporary chapel so that the priests could celebrate these feast days properly. In the wilderness, the Indians joined the priests in singing the High Masses and then returned to Santa Barbara, signaling the end of the rebellion. Chorister attitudes had been crucial in resolving the uprising, since choir leader Jaime had been "one of the first to have taken part in the uprising" and later, after reconsidering, led the Indians back.[77]

Eighty years after the uprising and long after the missions had been secularized and fallen into decay, a priest appeared at mission Santa Inés to minister to whatever slight congregation there might be in that remote spot. As Holy Week approached, an Indian appeared and offered to act as server for the Easter Mass. Slowly, over the course of that week, Indians came in increasing numbers for the services. The old church, full at Easter, contained Indian singers who helped celebrate the Mass.[78]

Teaching sacred music carries with it the possibility that the pupil will use it in profane ways.[79] Choirs developed their own distinctive personalities since they sang together, took professional pride in their abilities, wore distinctive clothing, and held good jobs in the missions. Duflot de Mofras recalled that the choir from mission Santa Clara, visiting at mission Santa Cruz to celebrate the feast of the Holy Cross in 1841, sang "La Marseillaise" in the church as the congregation rose, and escorted the religious procession singing "Vive Henri Quatre."[80] Not only was the insertion of secular music in a religious service a shock to the faithful, but the content of the French anthem celebrated individual liberty, an objective that Mexican secularization had intended and which the Indian choir may have applauded. Since this and similar examples from other missions reveal Indians performing secular music within the church at the end of the mission era, while the missions were still under priestly supervision, direct Indian agency as opposed to clerical agency in these activities is difficult to discern.[81]

Despite their resistance, however, most choristers persevered in practicing their new religion and remained loyal to the missions even after freed by secularization. The return of Indians, including singers, to mission Santa Inés eighty years after the uprising is one of many examples that occurred throughout the system. A photograph from the turn of the century depicts Indian musicians accompanying a priest celebrating Mass in the ruins of the sanctuary at mission San Antonio, the former home of Padre Juan Sancho, the Franciscan who had brought de Jerusalem's masses to California.[82]

By repeating the rituals they enjoyed long after they had been released from the obligation to do so, choristers testified that they had retained their musical interest and skill. But was that all? Some visitors thought that music had helped make Indians Catholics. Robert Louis Stevenson, visiting the headquarters mission of Serra, San Carlos Borromeo, in 1879, attended a Mass celebrated in the only room that still had a roof. "An Indian, stone-blind and about eighty years of age conducts the singing," Stevenson wrote. "Other

Figure 12. Father Angelo Casanova leads a group of worshippers, including an aged Indian choirmaster, toward the sacristy of the old mission church of San Carlos Borromeo for a celebration of the Mass on November 4, 1879, the anniversary of the founding. Joseph Strong, the artist of the work, was a friend of the writer Robert Louis Stevenson, who also attended Mass that day. The young Scot movingly recalled that he had "never seen faces more vividly lit up with joy than the faces of these Indian singers," declaring that "here was an old, medieval civilization, and your old primeval barbarian, hand-in-hand, the one devoutly following the other." *Courtesy California Historical Society, FN-08402.*

Indians compose the choir," he continued, "yet they have the Gregorian music at their finger ends and pronounce Latin so correctly that I could follow the meaning as they sang."[83]

Helen Hunt Jackson was in California about the time of Stevenson's visit, and her ethnographic fieldwork informed her celebrated novel *Ramona*. In that story the Indian protagonist, Alessandro, is invited to the Moreno house to minister to the ill scion, Felipe. Alessandro is widely known for his violin playing, the sweetness of which is supposed to cure Felipe's ills. Alessandro is such a fine violinist because he received his musical instruction from Father Antonio Peyri at mission San Luis Rey.

It should not be surprising, then, that the "voices" of mission Indian males that have survived belong to musicians/singers. Both Pablo Tac, the first California Indian to write a history of the missionization of his people, and Julio César were choristers at mission San Luis Rey. Lorenzo Assisara, born at mission Santa Cruz, joined the choir early, became a flutist, and, when he was thirteen years old, Padre Antonio Real sent him to Monterey to learn the clarinet. Fernando Librado was a chorister and musician at mission Santa Inés and knew other Indian musician/singers at missions San Buenaventura and Santa Barbara. Rogerio Rocha, a musician and chorister as his father had been, obtained a Mexican land grant following his release from mission San Fernando. Acú, the celebrated bell-ringer at mission San Juan Capistrano, also earned fame for his ability to play a variety of musical instruments. It was said that he followed in his father's footsteps.[84] Through the training begun by D'Arrezo, continued and modified by the structural prompts of Padre Durán, these native Californians acquired a European musical voice and, through the Spanish language, conveyed their complex views about mission life to us.

In the attempt to win Indian hearts and minds, the Franciscans possessed a powerful tactic in musical instruction. Priests wanted ritual song to move Indians emotionally and stir their souls. Priestly ability to relate plainchant to neophyte life, whether as members of the congregation or the choir, intentionally sought to transform the baptized into practicing true believers. How well Franciscans accomplished this task is difficult to calculate. Choristers numbered from thirty to forty at each mission, a tiny percentage of the total neophyte population. If, however, we consider the number of people these men and boys affected simply within their families and fictive kinship groups of godparents and confirmation sponsors, then a larger number emerges. I estimate conservatively that 10 percent of the mission Indian population was directly affected by the choir members and that they formed the nucleus of converts.[85]

The missionaries, in addition to their intended consequences, produced unintended results with music. Indians who joined the choir and persevered in the practice that the role required gained enormously from the mission. They learned the language of the colonizers better than other Indians did, which helped them learn tasks for which there was better compensation than for tending herds, sowing fields, clearing, planting and picking the fruit from orchards, making adobes, or constructing buildings. They learned skills that could be sold to settlers in addition to the money they made playing secular music at settlers' fiestas. These Indians became a significant, albeit legally inferior, part of frontier Spanish society.

Chorister/musicians and their families remained loyal to the mission community, of which they had been a part long after the buildings had fallen away.

How else can we explain that loyalty except as testimony to the fact that they had converted? Certainly it is equally absurd to claim that no Indians genuinely converted or that all did since in both instances an Indian sense of volition and humanity is denied. For those who did convert, the emotional power of singing together, whether in choir or congregation, provided at the very least a sense of belonging, if not pride in belonging, to an institution (the Church) and a ritual (the Mass) that endured beyond hunger, disease, and death. These subjective feelings, difficult to define and impossible to quantify, are at the core of conversion and have been left unexplored by those who consider only the material culture side of mission history.

Indian Resistance to Missionization

Resistance to authority, unless expressed in a bloody uprising, is often subtle. In a colonial encounter the need for the colonizer to impose order, usually in a new language, further obscures detection of opposition by the colonized. Accounts of colonization from the perspective of native peoples are frequently revealing. California Indians had no written language, yet Indian views of their mission experiences have been preserved. One of these is the only known example of a Native American's written history of the missionization of his people in California. Pablo Tac, born at mission San Luis Rey and educated there in Spanish by the Franciscans, was sent to Europe to further his studies and to become a priest. He died young, but, at about age thirteen he wrote an account of the arrival of the Spanish among his people, whom the Europeans called Luiseños, and of the missionary activities of the Franciscan priests known as Fernandinos.[1]

Because his command of Spanish grammar was weak and because the priests undoubtedly made him write the account, it would be easy to dismiss Tac's document as immature and reflecting only Christophilic Triumphalism. This approach, however, would miss the evidence of resistance to Spanish invasion that Tac included in his version of events. Describing the first contact between a Fernandino and a chief of the *Quechnajuichom,* as Tac called his people in his native tongue, the Indian declared in his dialect, "What is it you seek here? Get out of our country!" Tac concludes his narrative with an encounter between an armed Spanish soldier, seeking to restore order after participants in a ballgame between Luiseños and Indians from mission San Juan Capistrano had become unruly, in which a Luiseño man challenges the Spaniard by saying, "Raise your saber and I will eat you." Both of these encounters, Tac tells us, are related in the original language of *Quechla,* his Indian territory, meaning that the Spanish could not understand them.[2]

Tac's account, however, is more revealing to our generation. Tac reflects a Native American tradition of shifting to Indian language to convey an authentic feeling that cannot be expressed in the dominant language shared by Indian and non-Indian groups.[3] Tac's narrative discloses, albeit discreetly, the powerful opposition to the Spanish invasion Luiseños communicated both at initial contact and in late mission times. In recounting daily life at the mission, he also inserted a trickster tale involving a mission Indian boy who enters the Fernandino's forbidden garden to eat figs, is discovered by the Indian gardener, and then transforms himself into a raven, an enforcer of the moral code of Chinigchinich, a Luiseño God.[4] Whatever else may have happened to Tac in the course of his European education begun in California, continued in Mexico, and ended in Italy, where he wrote his history, he had lost neither his Indian identity nor his sense of outrage at Spanish occupation. In this more carefully controlled public tale of evangelization among the heathen, related by a missionized Indian at the behest of the Franciscan missionaries, Tac's account manages to communicate neophyte resistance. Tac's work, seemingly telling one story while actually relating another, illustrates the difficulty in analyzing Indian resistance in the missions.

Consider two other instances of Indian resistance. A thirty-five-year-old unidentified Christian Indian at mission San Juan Capistrano (Juaneño), for example, dying of a European disease, renounced his baptism and Christian religion on his deathbed. Padre Gerónimo Boscana asked the neophyte to confess his sins before meeting his God. "I will not," replied the Indian. "If I have been deceived whilst living," he continued, "I do not wish to die in the delusion!"[5] To Boscana, this was the action of an apostate. In another example, during the Chumash uprising in 1824, an unnamed neophyte caught in a chapel surrounded by armed Spaniards firing upon it spied a crucifix. Disregarding the Spanish-taught polite speech, the *usted* form, to be used by Indians in addressing their superiors, including the Christian God, this neophyte used the familiar *tu* form, and spoke to God on the crucifix as an equal. "Now I will know if you are God Almighty as the padre says. Carrying you completely hidden so that no one will see you, I am going alone to fight against all of the soldiers. If they don't kill me or shoot me, I will serve you well until I die."[6] The armed Indian concealed the crucifix under his shirt, then fled the church. Once outside, he emptied his quiver at the soldiers and returned, walking at a normal pace, to the chapel. Despite the shots fired at him he remained untouched. Afterward he fulfilled his vow, working as sacristan at the mission until he died. This instance of Indian self-shaping occurred during the largest rebellion in California mission history, one in which Indians from missions La Purísima, Santa Inés, and Santa Barbara challenged Spanish and Franciscan authority. This individual incident within the collective experience underscores the diversity of Indian resistance to the missions.

Over the past twenty years scholars have focused on overt Indian resistance to the California missions but have had difficulty clarifying the more subtle forms of resistance that undergirded overt violence.[7] This anomaly is perhaps due to the tendency of recent mission critics to focus almost exclusively on the exploitation of the Indian at the expense of the Christianization and civilization components of the Franciscan goal. Such a focus omits such stories as those of Tac, the Juaneño, and the Chumash. To correct this anomaly, the original intention of colonization must be recalled.

The Spanish sovereigns' intentions toward the Indian were, as the dean of borderlands historians wrote, "to convert him, to civilize [sic] him, and to exploit him. . . . It was soon found that if the savage [sic] were to be converted, or disciplined, or exploited, he must be put under control."[8] Hence Indians became neophytes and worked at priestly assigned tasks. Some Indians did so through genuine transformation, but others did so grudgingly and only temporarily.

Relationships between neophytes and gentiles, the unbaptized Indians still in the wild, were always complex. These relationships changed over time when new Indian groups became the targets of missionization as older groups either became incorporated or died. Neophytes confronted two constellations of conflicting motives, the desire to leave the mission and the desire to stay. Reasons to leave included a longing to see and be with family and friends, to live in the culture in which they had been reared, and to associate with people of their own kind. Such motives intensified if gentile family or friends became ill or if new people, not of the neophytes' own kind, perhaps even their enemies, became incorporated into their mission. Sorrow and shock from the deaths at the mission could impel neophytes to flee. Freedom in all its multiple guises—freedom from abuse by Indian *alcaldes* (overseers), freedom from priestly ordered punishment, freedom from forced social change, from new ritual, from Europeanized ideas of work—served to increase the powerful allure to return to previous ways.

Yet as time passed, those previous ways changed, as did neophyte access to them. Gradually or quickly, family, friends, and kinship groups became part of the mission and those who were the neophyte's people no longer lived in the wild. The longer one lived in the mission, the more atrophied became the knowledge of how to live outside it. This became especially true after a generation or more of mission life. Over time neophytes came to adopt mission food, to adapt to new work habits, and to adjust to or embrace new ritual and life ways. Simply put, some Indians came to accept the mission. Yet even those who acquiesced and benefited from it often engaged in nonmilitant resistance to the perceived exploitation of everyday life.

Within a context of spiritual, cultural, and material change a new approach to resistance appeared. Anthropologist James C. Scott, studying colonized peoples, proposes to "privilege the issues of dignity and autonomy, which have typically been seen as secondary to material exploitation."[9] In a situation of dominance, he argues that elites create a public transcript of apparent dominant unanimity. This public transcript comprises a domain of material appropriation (labor), a domain of public mastery and subordination (rituals of hierarchy, deference, speech, punishment, and humiliation), and a domain of ideological justification for inequalities (elite religious and political worldview). Spanish colonization and dominance over native peoples of Alta California exemplify many of Scott's insights.

An uprising, such as the 1824 Chumash rebellion, is viewed as aberrant by the public transcript because it challenges the notion of smooth Spanish control of the colony and its people. Since elites leave the written records of their transcript and tend to present the public record of subordinates, when it appears at all, within the dominant tale, the elite view is often mistaken for the totality of others' experience. From the elite perspective only bloody, violent acts constitute resistance, and because such acts are allegedly rare they constitute the only real but infrequent opposition to foreign power.

Scott contends, to the contrary, that subordinate groups respond to the public transcript of elites by creating a hidden transcript of their own. Since many subordinate groups, however, lack a written language and many are illiterate in the dominant tongue, and since their acts must be conducted in secrecy, it is difficult for the outside observer to detect the hidden transcript. Moreover, according to Scott, the creation of the hidden transcript is site-specific, meaning that in California one would need to study carefully the elite written documents and histories of all twenty-one missions to develop it. In the California missions, however, it is not difficult to detect Indian resistance because critical reading of the public transcript reveals it. That Franciscans read Tac's manuscript superficially does not preclude others from recognizing the subtext.

The hidden transcript, Scott argues, is present in the public transcript but in disguised form. Yet critical reading quickly penetrates any disguise, and the public transcript discloses Indian agency. For example, the Spanish branded as criminals any Indians who shot arrows into cattle, mules, and horses. The Spanish remained oblivious to the fact that when they turned these newly introduced European animals into native fields they disrupted Indian patterns of seed and grass cultivation with a resultant loss of food for Indians. From the Indian perspective the Spaniards were thieves because this trespass violated long-standing cultivation practices and the offenders offered no recompense.[10] The Indian response perfectly suited the Spanish crime. Yet in the Spanish public transcript the colonizer is innocent of any wrongdoing and it is the Indians who are perverse and criminal.

The hidden transcript is also conveyed in rumors, folktales, trickster stories, wish fulfillment, gossip, and a host of other indicators of opposition. Thus from the hidden transcript, contained within the public transcript, one can see the wish fulfilling language of the original Luiseños in Tac's history of their missionization and the transformation of the neophyte trickster who became a raven — points missed by the Franciscans. In the Juaneño neophyte renunciation of his baptism one can see the hidden transcript affirmation of Indian culture which the priest who told the tale saw as Indian apostasy. And in the Chumash neophyte disregarding foreign-imposed polite speech, and the asymmetrical power relationship it entailed, one can see a deal-maker negotiating with the Christian God as an equal, rather than a divine act of intervention to help sustain the mission system.

An intriguing incident from Mission Santa Cruz, the alleged murder of missionary Andrés Quintana by neophytes, exposes the range of rumor, folktale, wish fulfillment, and gossip present in the contest between the public and the hidden transcript. It also reveals oral history as a source for the hidden transcript. The story's significance lies more in the interpretations put on it by both missionaries and Indians than in whether it happened as told.

For the Spanish, the importance of the story began one day in 1814 when mission mayordomo (Spanish administrator) Carlos Castro, a man fluent in the prevailing Indian dialects, on his return to the midday meal overheard two Indian women behind a fence squabbling over money. He heard one accuse the other's husband of having murdered "the Father," Padre Quintana, who had died suddenly two years earlier. Although an investigation had been conducted at the time, Quintana's death was determined to have resulted from illness rather than from violence.

With the new information, however, came renewed inquiry and subsequently a conspiracy was uncovered involving more than ten neophytes, all of whom were charged with conspiring to murder the priest. They had deceived him into leaving his residence and, once he was outside the mission and unguarded, the Indians had killed him. Five neophytes were found guilty and punished with 200 lashes each and sent to work in chains at Santa Barbara for periods ranging from two to ten years. Officials in Mexico City reviewing the case and assigning punishment believed Indian testimony that they had murdered the priest because of his cruel treatment of them including beating two neophytes nearly to death. Alta California governor Pablo Vicente de Solá, however, responded with a vigorous defense of Quintana and the missionaries claiming that if there were any overreaction on their part it was in the direction of mercy and leniency in dealing with their charges.[11] In the public transcript of Quintana's murder there would be no missionary cruelty against neophytes.

An Indian witness to the conspiracy, Venancio, gave a first-person account to his son Lorenzo Asisara, who in turn told it to a Spanish-speaking interviewer in 1877. In this telling the Indian perspective offers a different story. Indian conspirators included gardeners and pages, neophytes trusted by the priest but who were afraid of his punishments. The decision to act came from Quintana's threatened introduction of a new metal-tipped whip with which to cut the flesh of those being flogged. The night before the Sunday on which the new device, the *cuarta de hierro,* would be inaugurated, Julian, one of the gardeners, pretended to be ill so that the priest could be summoned. Others waited outside his hut to seize Quintana when he approached. Three times this happened and each time the collaborators were too frightened to apprehend the priest, although Julian feigned his worsened condition even to the point of receiving the holy oil of Last Rites. The priest told Julian's wife that he would return one last time, and when he did the conspirators sprang into action and brought him down. There was no alternative but to kill him despite his pleas for mercy, his apology for making the cuarta de hierro, and his promise to leave the mission. They killed him by simultaneously smothering him and cutting off a testicle; they then undressed him and put him to bed so that he would appear to have died in his sleep. Then they liberated the unmarried women from the *monjerío* (nunnery) and the unmarried men from their quarters and all frolicked in the orchard away from the view of whites and other Indians until early in the morning. They also divided up gold and silver coins they had found in the priest's room. The conspirators were able to set out Quintana's breviary as though he had read it before retiring, and they managed to lock the door from the inside. On Sunday morning when the priest did not command the page to ring the bells, the Spaniards discovered that the padre had died. But they had his stomach cut open anyway to ensure that he had not been poisoned; then they buried him. The Spanish discovered the conspiracy only later when the mayordomo overheard the women quarreling over the money that had been discovered and taken from Quintana's room.[12]

The Indian version reveals wish fulfillment in terms of Indian victories over the priest. In forcing him to plead for their mercy, in his promising to leave the mission, in his apologizing for the wire-tipped whip, in taking his wealth, in covering up his murder, or in the actual murder itself—the Indians were victorious. In the Indian view the world had been turned upside down: they were the masters and the priest was their ward. They liberated Indian women and socialized as they saw fit. And Indian women were important actors in the story, for it was Julian's wife who suggested he feign illness and who threatened to expose the conspiracy if they did not seize the priest when she summoned him one last time. Women arguing led to discovery of the plot. The power of rumor, gossip, and folklore can be found in the Indian ability to play on Spanish fears of being poisoned by their neophytes, in the Indian claim that the priest had been killed by removing his manhood (castration), and in the ability of the conspirators to conceal their acts. Whether or not the conspirators killed Quintana in the manner described, whether they killed him at all, the Spanish believed that they had. They also believed that neophytes had murdered the priest in secret. Despite the public transcript, both missionaries and settlers must have been appalled—a missionary had been murdered by those he trusted at an established mission—frightened of what they did not know and did not want to suspect about "their" Indians. Fear among the Hispanic population must have been a major consequence of this incident, making more tenuous, at least at mission Santa Cruz and at the nearby pueblo of Villa Branciforte, Spanish colonial rule.

That the hidden transcript of mission Indian resistance is thick is not surprising given the anomalous position of Indians within that institution. Proselytized by missionaries offering gifts of beads and, later, food, with the threat of Spanish arms nearby, and beset by new diseases their shamans or doctors could not heal, California Indians faced a bewildering offering of European spiritual and material culture and were torn between trying to sustain existing Indian ways and joining the new.

"Most [Indian] individuals," one anthropologist wrote in an important study of the San Francisco Bay Area missions with applicability to the entire system, "struggled with mixed feelings, hatred and respect, in a terrible, internally destructive attempt to cope with external change beyond their control. . . . Day in day out . . . ambivalent people struggled with a choice to join the mission. They could make the choice to reject the mission life ways a thousand days in a row, but they were allowed to make the choice to join a mission community only once."[13]

When Indians voluntarily joined the mission as symbolized by baptism following eight or more days of religious instruction,[14] they were not permitted to change their minds. Baptized Indians became legal wards, children, subservient to their priests/fathers at the mission to which they were assigned. Mission Indians lost personal freedom and could travel about only with a pass, resulting in a kind of "churchly captivity."[15] Indians most commonly responded to that captivity by running away.

Franciscans learned early on, however, that they needed to allow neophytes to visit their gentile families, gather seeds, and to hunt and fish, if the neophytes were to remain loyal to the mission. Priests furloughed mission Indians, mainly men, on pass for up to two months annually. Some of those chose not to return. Others simply left without permission. Since prolonged absence adversely affected mission harvest and labor programs, priests sent neophyte auxiliaries, frequently accompanied and commanded by Spanish/Mexican soldiers, to capture and return neophyte runaways.

A poignant example of the Indian view can be found in the reasons twelve fugitive neophytes gave for departing from mission San Francisco on their return in July 1797: Tiburcio had been flogged five times by Padre Antonio Danti "for crying at the death of his wife and child"; Magin had been "put in the stocks while ill"; Tarazon overstayed his pass; Claudio had been "beaten by the alcalde with a stick and forced to work while ill"; José Manuel had been "struck by a bludgeon" by Raymundo, leader of the neophyte auxiliaries; Liberato "ran away to escape dying of hunger as his mother, two brothers, and three nephews had done"; Otolon had been "flogged for not caring for his wife after she had sinned with the vaquero"; Milan had to work "with no food for his family and was flogged after going after clams"; Pato "had lost his family and there was no one to take care of him"; Orencio's "niece died of hunger"; Toribio was "always hungry"; Magno "received no ration because, occupied in tending his sick son, he could not work."[16]

The father president of the missions, however, denied all Indian reasons for flight except the ravages of disease.[17] But in this he was being disingenuous. Junípero Serra, the first father president, early noted the reasons for neophyte departure: "It will happen that one day, because they are punished or reprimanded, another day, because they fear punishment, yet another day because they have friends over there [in the wild], little by little they will flee there and it will multiply our enemies."[18] As will be recalled, returned runaways, unless charged with a more serious offense, were routinely flogged or placed in stocks

Figure 13. Two Northern Valley Yokuts hunt the shore of San Francisco Bay in the autumn of 1816. From time to time the Franciscans allowed neophytes to visit their native villages, and periodically, particularly during droughts and bad harvests, they found it necessary to release them from the missions to gather plants and hunt game. Once reunited with their extended family and old companions, or under the influence of other pagan Indians, some chose not to return. From Louis Choris, *Voyage pittoresque autour du monde*, 1822. Courtesy California Historical Society, Templeton Crocker Collection, FN-30511.

as punishment, which could again initiate the cycle. Throughout the mission era fugitivism ebbed and flowed, with Indians trickling or occasionally streaming out and back as runaways returned voluntarily or involuntarily. Approximately 10 percent stayed away permanently.[19]

Pursuing runaways could be dangerous as well as self-defeating. In January 1806, Padre Pedro de la Cueva, newly arrived in California and posted to mission San José, set out in the company of a Spanish majordomo, two soldiers, and a few Indians to visit some ill neophytes in a mission *ranchería* fifteen miles distant. Whether through overzealousness on Cueva's part because he wanted to proselytize gentiles or treachery by the neophyte guide, Cueva and his party arrived in a gentile (Luecha) village rather than a neophyte (Asirin) ranchería as he was told. The gentiles attacked, killing the

Spaniard and three Indians and wounding Cueva with an arrow in the eye. Such an affront to Spanish control — murder of a member of the *gente de razón,* wounding of a missionary — called for reprisal. A punitive expedition was dispatched that killed eleven Luecha, took four prisoners, and brought back twenty-five gentile Luecha children and women as hostages against future bad behavior by those in the wild. Order had been restored. But in the aftermath the soldiers blamed the missionary and the father president blamed the guide.[20] Franciscans had encountered resistance from both outside and inside the mission, occurrences that proved commonplace and made the perpetrators difficult to identify.

From 1776 to 1782, three times Indians set on fire mission San Luis Obispo. In 1776 gentiles sent burning arrows into the reed roofs, destroying the buildings and implements but leaving intact the church and the granary. Making the best of the situation the Franciscans decided to use rounded tile for roofing material, at least for the churches. Two subsequent fires — whether set by neophytes, gentiles, or both — contributed to making the roof tiles universal in the missions.[21] But a latecomer to the tile program, mission San Miguel, experienced a fire in 1806 that destroyed most of the buildings used for manufacturing, all the work implements, hides, cloths, 6,000 bushels of wheat, and part of the church roof.[22] While destruction of food seems inadvertent, elimination of the work area and its tools smacks of neophyte arson from the hidden transcript of that mission.

Rumors offer another insight into the hidden transcript. Reported plots against a particular mission, such as alleged conspiracies by neighboring rancherías to rise against priest and neophytes, occurred throughout the mission era. So too did suspicious stomach disorders experienced by Franciscans raise fears that neophytes were poisoning the priests' food or drink — poisoning that may have caused Franciscan deaths.[23] Although such reports proved mainly to be rumors initiated by disgruntled neophytes and spread by the gullible — whether Indian, settler, soldier, or priest — they disrupted normal activity because they raised apprehensions and increased tension in mission life. These rumors, like folktales, gambling, shirking work, clandestinely perpetuating native customs, and other activities, all originate in the world of gossip and covert activities known as "infra-politics." Infra-politics, like infra-rays, which are just beyond the range of visible light, are those acts that fall just short of political rebellion but that nonetheless exist as forms of resistance.

Indian resistance also included exploiting the opportunities available in mission life for personal advantage. Indian cultivators dropped the tip of the plow deeply into the soil only when they passed in front of a priest. Otherwise, according to one visitor who observed it, the plowmen barely scratched the ground's surface despite the presence of overseers whose job it was to see that they did. While such shirking reduced the overall amount of grain that could be harvested that year it was sufficient for most needs. The priests did not seem to mind the practice, since it kept a large number of men and oxen busy at the plow.[24]

Healthy Indians feigned illness knowing that even if the priests suspected malingering they would still likely exempt the neophyte from a work assignment. That Indian would frequently then leave the mission clandestinely to go to the nearby presidio or pueblo to exchange labor or sexual favors for food, a piece of leather, glass beads, or other goods. Indian absence meant diminished work accomplished at the mission. When missionaries discovered such activity, the Indian would be punished and the soldier or settler verbally chastised. But the practice continued.[25]

Because of their legal relationship to the Franciscans as children, when Indians engaged in serious crimes against the Spanish or Mexican authorities they knew that they could count on the missionaries, in most cases, to ameliorate the punishments of civil authorities. This protection had begun with Serra, who had urged pardon and clemency even for those who had attacked mission San Diego and murdered Padre Luís Jayme in 1775.[26] Conversely, Indians displeased with a missionary could complain to civil authorities who, eager to have more Indian labor which they thought the Franciscans kept too much to themselves, would frequently take the Indian's side against a priest.[27] Although such controversies, some quite protracted, invariably ended with exoneration of the missionary they injected further tension into mission life and civil-military-mission relations.

In the public transcript priests equated baptism with conversion and viewed moral backsliding—like fugitivism, along with the failure of many neophytes to learn Spanish—as indications of the innately limited moral and intellectual capacity of their charges.[28] Viewed from our perspective outside the missions, however, conversion was a process of some indeterminate length subsequent to, rather than signified by, baptism.[29] This process consisted of tension over time. The tension between nominal and effective conversion—if effective conversion occurred at all—can be glimpsed through the priestly concern over sin.[30]

Viewed from the perspective of the hidden transcript, Indian "sin" constituted resistance. Sin affirmed Indian culture through reiteration of Indian social and sexual practices that the priests proscribed as sinful and for which observed sinners were physically corrected. These corrections included discipline by flogging, by being hobbled with irons, or by being placed in stocks. In convincing themselves that the Indian sinned excessively, priests blinded themselves to Indian resistance and to continuation of Indian culture within the mission compound.

Indians learned to camouflage their resistance. An art historian has contended that graffiti, unauthorized graphic works by Indians in the missions that he calls "abusive," must have been "found in most, if not all, of the missions." He found them only at five missions because of the priests' tendency to whitewash them when discovered. Yet he has found Indian symbols at the earliest level of whitewash, indicating that this form of resistance began at the earliest stages of church building.[31] No amount of erasing by whitewash stopped the Indians from drawing.

"These abusive drawings are either painted or scratched," and, according to this art historian, they are the equivalents, on mission walls, of pictographs and petroglyphs of which they are really a continuation." While all the symbols cannot be deciphered, at mission San Juan Capistrano there appear to be at least two depictions of the Tobet, a human figure wearing a headdress and a skirt, the primary Juaneño god.[32] Did Juaneños continue to practice their religion in the Christian compound and, if so, when or did they stop?

At mission San Miguel Indian graffiti entered the church proper, where "The number of scratched designs is enormous. . . . Presumably, all the Indian ones were done while seated on the floor, quite possibly during mass. Most are concentrated in the area of the choir loft itself, the area beneath it, and surprisingly, opposite the pulpit."[33] Even if these inscriptions were no more than doodling, which seems doubtful, they suggest that the Indian churchgoers did not always focus their attention on the Christian ritual.

Emphasizing exploitation of Indians has meant subtly accepting at face value the Franciscan account of what happened, of uncritically accepting the public transcript. Certainly the missionaries wanted to accept Indians at roughly the same rate that they could feed their new charges, but such was not always the case.[34] When Indians chose to enter the missions in large numbers, such as the Miwok and Costanoan (Oholone) of the Bay Area in 1794–1795 and the Chumash of the Central Coast in 1803–1804, the priests were overwhelmed by what they took to be the success of their preaching and the will of their God.

The Indian population of mission San Francisco increased by 75 percent from October 1794, to May 1795 (628 to 1,095), and at mission Santa Clara during the same period the Indian population grew by 83 percent (852 to 1,558).[35] A decade later, 25 percent of all Chumash baptized in the mission era entered the compounds of Santa Barbara, Santa Inés, and La Purísima.[36] In each case Indians made a tactical decision about coping with the Spanish by entering their missions, and in each case they disoriented their colonizers, who could neither feed nor manage their numbers for some months or years to come.

Such disorienting behavior testifies to the complexity of Indian response to the missions. Once inside the compound sheer Indian numbers ensured at least temporary cultural perpetuation. Priests would have to give them frequent passes to guarantee sufficient food. Simultaneously, however, the massing made Indians more susceptible to disease. At the crudest level, more, healthy Indians closer to the Spanish permitted greater Indian observation of and plotting against the colonizers.

Priests taught Indians patriarchy and, in the process, lowered the status of Indian women within Indian culture. Such devaluation was further compounded by the shameful raping of Indian women by Spanish soldiers and settlers. Angry Indian men were killed for their opposition to the rape of tribal women.[37] Partly to protect them from soldiers, priests in the missions had unmarried Indian females over the age of seven locked together at night in the monjerío to preserve their Spanish-valued chastity. Female separation from the extended family must have been emotionally painful. Female aggregation, morever, facilitated the spread of infectious disease, helping to make women more vulnerable to microbes than were the men. All these changes created tension and required personal adjustment — profound for some, less so for others.

Not surprisingly, then, women joined in conspiracies to overturn the missions. In 1785, in Gabrielino (Kumi·vit) territory, the gentile female shaman and leader Toypurina, under the leadership inside the mission of neophyte Nicolás José, joined a pan-tribal movement against mission San Gabriel designed to expel the Spanish and revive Gabrielino lifeways.[38] In 1801, before the dramatic Chumash influx and perhaps the cause of that influx, during the course of an epidemic of pneumonia and pleurisy, a female neophyte at mission Santa Barbara had a dream. In it, the Chumash god Chupu appeared to her with a warning: all gentiles must refuse baptism or they would die and all neophytes must renounce their baptism and give offerings to Chupu or they too would die. Neophytes were to wash their heads with a special water called "tears of the sun" to cancel the Christian holy water.

Almost all neophytes, including *alcaldes* (Indian officials and overseers), came to visit her, bringing beads and seeds as offerings and undergoing the new ritual. The conspiracy extended to all Chumash settlements of the channel and mountains before the priests discovered it. How they suppressed the movement is unknown, but certainly the female neophyte was made to recant publicly.[39] Nevertheless, this incident instilled suspicion and no little fear in

Franciscan hearts. In both instances it appears that women leaders saw more clearly than men exactly what their gender would lose in the new social order of Spanish "civilization" and sought to revitalize their cultures by a return to past ways.

Critical to issues of women's sensitivity to colonization are the issues of abortion and infanticide as acts of resistance. Spontaneous abortion involuntarily caused by disease has been noted. Abortion within the mission compound could have represented, however, as in the case of the Chumash, cultural continuation, since Chumash women regarded aborting the first child as necessary for continued fertility. Infanticide of unwanted children, usually those produced by rape, was a tragic act of resistance, which must have occurred at most missions but has been documented only at San Gabriel and San Diego.[40] Differentiating among voluntary and involuntary abortion and infanticide as expressions of resistance, cultural continuity, or victimization by disease is impossible.

Women resisted colonization by contributing to the continuation of Indian culture throughout missionization in two other important areas: magic and dance. Toypurina had been recruited by Nicolás José in 1785 both to rally her ranchería and its neighbors against the mission and to use her magic to kill the priests. She never had the opportunity to employ her magic. Part of the general Indian displeasure stemmed from the priestly prohibition against dances the Franciscans regarded as unchristian.[41] Gabrielino shamanism, however, continued within the mission after Toypurina's banishment. A *capitán* (Indian headman) at San Gabriel, fearing his enemies inside the mission, sought the aid of two sorcerers from Santa Catalina Island to perform magic to send sickness against his opponents at the mission. The two shamans worked their magic and an epidemic struck the mission between 1799 and 1805, but the capitán's daughter was accidentally killed in its wake.[42]

In an Ineseño woman's account of the 1824 Chumash revolt recorded ninety years after the event, magic figured prominently in the story. Some Indians believed they were medicine men and that the priests could not hurt them; others thought that only water would come out of the cannons and that bullets would not tear their flesh. Two Indian men entered a prison through a keyhole to free their fellows. Yet others divined their future or the location of lost children by using a string placed on the ground formed as a cross.[43] The oral tradition of magic indicates the persistence and modification of indigenous culture in its resistance to colonization.

Dancing, sometimes of a nature priests considered lascivious, also continued during missionization. Padre Boscana was appalled by a Juaneño puberty ceremony in which a young woman danced naked, hands under her breasts as though offering herself to the men, while naming her genitalia and that of the men. Boscana had supposed that Indians had abandoned such dances after becoming Christians, but disabused of that notion he expressed gratitude that "at least they do not execute them in public."[44]

Clandestine performance of native dances seems to have become a routine form of resistance. In the Chumash area several survived beyond mission times. One of the more important, the Coyote Dance, was performed for weddings and other fiestas. A singer followed by a man in a loincloth painted as a coyote, lamented the passing of coyote's magic; the singer also remarked on the accumulation of human dung on the ground, all of which the trickster coyote had produced. During the song the coyote player would try to get someone to lick his penis; if he found no one to do so, he would do it himself. Then he would end the performance by defecating on the ground. On one occasion a coyote dancer had sexual intercourse with a woman publicly and on another he had sex with two women, one at a time, while the other watched.[45] Such activity would have drawn the wrath of any priest who learned of it, but it also reaffirmed aspects of Chumash culture.

In the missions Indians learned a hierarchy and subordination of gender previously unknown. "In the Mission of San Luis Rey de Francia," Tac wrote, "the Fernandino Father is like a King, having his pages, Alcaldes, Mayordomos Musicians, [and] Soldiers."[46] Alcaldes had particular responsibility to overcome inertia and get other Indians to work, and these tasks ranged over every category of activity needed to sustain the mission such as farming, herding, gardening, adobe making, carpentry, blacksmithing, tallow making, hide skinning and tanning, weaving, corn grinding, and food preparation. Alcaldes were masters of the Spanish language and of the European sense of time, since with clock and sundial the daily tasks were announced by the sound of the bell. The bell tolled for religious and secular purposes, but each toll reinforced for the Indian a time consciousness and a sense of timely performance of duty unknown before colonization. As Tac described the activities at mission San Luis Rey, the alcaldes led the laborers to their tasks "to see how the work is done, to hurry them if they are lazy, so that they will finish soon what was ordered, and to punish the guilty or lazy one who leaves his plow and quits the field keeping on with his laziness."[47]

Women could not be alcaldes in the Franciscan missions, and this office became progressively more important as the missions persisted and grew. The alcalde position was anomalous, part Indian part Spaniard, with a wide degree of power over subordinates which could be used/abused for personal advantage. Beginning in Serra's time, some alcaldes favored action independent of priests. Baltazar used his appointment at mission San Carlos as an opportunity to practice polygamy, producing a child in the process, an Indian custom that Serra and his fellow Franciscans condemned. He also flogged a neophyte for obeying a priest's order rather than his own. Baltazar fled the mission for the hills, taking with him many followers, including, according to Serra, "those we most need, such as the blacksmith, a number of carpenters, and day workmen."[48] Because Baltazar had been an appointee of the governor, Serra took pains that in the future the Franciscans should carefully manage elections for such posts and keep them out of the hands of civil authority.

Conventional thinking has been that priests generally chose alcaldes, deliberately seeking to undermine traditional Indian village chiefly authority by choosing new men. Then other mission Indians voted the priestly ticket. These newly elected officials were rank accommodationists who gave little thought to the people from whom they had come. Alcaldes, in this view, represented a sharp break from the tribal kinship groups of pre-contact days.

A study of alcaldes at mission San Carlos Borromeo from 1770 to 1833 disputes the conventional view. It finds that the political accommodation at the mission depended not so much on personalities as on functions and that the duties of village chiefs resembled those of Indian officials. Both, for example, "performed police duties, were responsible for the economic stability of the Indian group, had proven military skills, and enjoyed similar advantages of office."[49]

A strong convergence, therefore, existed between Indian and Spanish office. Moreover, half of the Indian officials in the fifty years of study came from high-status Indian families, thus preserving some elements of traditional Indian leadership. Yet the remaining 50 percent of Indian officials whose extended families could not be found in the mission registers leaves room for the type of individuals described in the conventional view. Indian officials then were of two types, those with traditional ties to the Indians they served based upon kinship and status, and the new men. Both types could, and in some instances did, abuse their office, depending upon Spanish or Indian perspective. Alcaldes played it both ways, using priests against civil officials and vice versa.

Covert resistance, rooted in personal dissatisfaction and gratifying individual need, prepared the ground for overt and collective violence directed against the mission system. Alcaldes became increasingly involved in this transition as missionization spread toward the interior. From 1820 to 1823, a former San Rafael neophyte named Pomponio, rumored to have been an alcalde, fled the mission and began a series of raids against the missions and their rancherías in the bay area. He gathered a small group of followers, chief among them one named Gonzalo. Since his band preyed on mission sites he found both friends and enemies among the mission Indians he visited. But he drew fugitive followers from as far south as San Diego and he secured at least enough passive acceptance to remain at large for nearly four years. His movement all around the bay area, from as far southeast as Soledad and Santa Clara to his ultimate capture northwest near present-day Novato, gave rise to innumerable rumors, folktales, and gossip of his whereabouts, his next target, his last or next crime. When captured he was immediately tried by a military tribunal and sentenced to execution by firing squad. While incarcerated and awaiting death, the stories went, Gonzalo managed to escape from his shackles by cutting off his own heel! With Pomponio's execution in early January 1824, Padre Durán at mission San José wrote that the example had had a good effect on all mission neophytes.[50] A few weeks later, however, and unrelated to Pomponio, the Chumash of the Santa Barbara area launched the largest uprising in the history of the mission system.

During the 1824 Chumash uprising, alcaldes played significant insurgent roles. The Indians who occupied La Purísima for a month, reinforced by other neophyte fugitives and gentiles from the interior region (the *tulares*), sought an armed confrontation with the Spanish. Certainly the neophyte who struck a deal with the Christian god during the fight at La Purísima faced great odds with gritty determination. Spanish arms prevailed, however, reinforced with muskets clandestinely supplied by the Russians from their distant colony at Ross.[51] This proved the first instance in which competing imperial powers cooperated to vanquish native resistance in California, a resistance sustained and led by native mission officials.

Alcaldes from Santa Barbara took their followers to the tulares, where all reverted to Indian cultural practices and made camp with the interior Yokuts. Only after pursuit by Spanish soldiers, accompanied by Franciscans as peace-makers, and following several violent skirmishes, did these alcaldes shape-shift to accommodate a reality they could not change, and bring their people back.[52] Choristers choosing to rejoin the mission also proved decisive in persuading other Chumash to do likewise. Andrés Sagimomatsse had been the most prominent of the alcaldes, going from trusted aide of the Franciscans to Indian insurgent and back again, seeking to cope with the escalating pressures of his position.

The most dramatic of the insurgent alcaldes, and perhaps the most tragic, proved to be Estanislao of mission San José. Estanislao seems to have been born of high status among the Lakisamni Yokuts around 1800, and was brought to the mission for baptism at an early age. He rose in the mission hierarchy, where Padre Narciso Durán noticed his intelligence and leadership ability. Estanislao became a skilled horseman, or *vaquero,* and eventually an alcalde. With the release of selected married neophytes under the orders of Governor José María Echeandía in 1826, dissatisfaction among remaining Indians at mission San José mushroomed. In fall 1828 Estanislao and many of his tribe, while on a pass to visit relatives in the interior, simply stayed. Estanislao told the returning alcalde to inform Padre Durán that Estanislao and his people declared themselves in rebellion, that "they have no fear of the soldiers because they, the soldiers, are few in number, are very young, and do not shoot well."[53]

Neophyte fugitives from missions San Juan Bautista and Santa Cruz, the latter led by alcalde Cipriano, joined Estanislao at his cluster of Lakisamni villages along a tributary of the San Joaquin River. A pan-Indian movement of gentiles and neophytes of some magnitude now challenged Mexican authority. After the protracted conflict with him, the Spanish named the tributary for Estanislao.

Californios mounted two expeditions against Estanislao, and he defeated both. His villages lay in an extended, dense thicket and, by using breastworks and trenches covered with vines and trees, Estanislao denied Europeans the advantage of their muskets. Through taunts and challenges to their machismo, Estanislao lured the soldiers into his thicket for hand-to-hand combat. Mexican dead were mutilated and their body parts paraded in defiance. As Estanislao's reputation among Indians grew, his followers increased to nearly 1,000 ex-neophyte and gentile warriors. Since about 22,000 Indians remained in the missions and the white population numbered about 6,000, Estanislao's success and continued defiance aggravated white fear and demanded action.

In retaliation, in May 1829 the California government sent twenty-two-year-old Lieutenant Mariano G. Vallejo to attack Estanislao. Young Vallejo's force comprised 107 Californio soldiers, 50 Indian auxiliaries, 1 cannon, and more musket cartridges, 3,550, than had ever before been assembled for a military campaign in California. Once at Estanislao's stronghold, Vallejo discovered that the Indians had interconnected their trenches, permitting them to deploy warriors easily to any point along their line. Vallejo responded with cannon rounds that shattered the breastworks, wounding and killing defenders from the resulting wooden shrapnel; he also successfully set fire to the thicket, driving the Indians into Californio musket fire. After three days of relentless fighting, Vallejo had won. Estanislao, however, had disappeared into the smoke with many of his followers.

Despite atrocities committed by his soldiers and Indian auxiliaries seeking revenge against their enemies, Vallejo returned a hero because he had accomplished what no one else had. But Vallejo became frustrated and angry when he learned that Estanislao secretly had returned to mission San José and Padre

Durán had secured the governor's pardon for him. Franciscan intercession spared the insurgent the consequences of military or civil trial. Estanislao, upon his return, refashioned himself, becoming a skilled hunter of fugitive neophytes until smallpox killed him four years later.

Chumash flight to the interior during the 1824 uprising and Estanislao's rebellion in 1828 both reflected and contributed to a process of neophyte fugitivism and cooperation with gentiles that began to intensify from Pomponio's time in the early 1820s onward. The general purpose of such flight was not individual freedom per se but joint action, combining neophyte knowledge of the foreigners with gentile military force, to raid the Spanish/Mexican settlements for supplies and to revenge themselves upon the settlers.

Many factors contributed to this process, most notably the spread of a common language and the enlargement of market opportunities provided by other outsiders among interior Indians. Language learning had produced unanticipated consequences. Ironically for Franciscans who thought Indians unable to learn Spanish for purposes of their discourse, Spanish first gradually then rapidly spread as the common tongue, permitting Indians with mutually unintelligible dialects to communicate. This phenomenon coincided with political instability among the Spanish-speaking elites in California and was intensified by demands for Indian emancipation from the missions emanating from Mexico. Indians progressively used Spanish as their lingua franca for joint actions in both trading and raiding, while Californios, divided over political rule, presented a weakened common front against Indian depredations. This occurred at the very time that Indians began to be freed from the missions in a series of Mexican decisions in the 1820s that culminated in total neophyte emancipation through secularization of the missions from 1834 to 1836.[54]

Individual Indian resistance stood at the core of all opposition and lasted throughout the mission era, manifested in a nearly infinite variety of ways, practiced even by those who accepted the mission and its way of life but objected to individual tasks or personal abuse. Individual covert resistance prepared the way for overt group opposition. Group resistance, manifested in increasing incidents of physical violence, gradually grew after 1800 as Franciscans began actively to proselytize the interior of the great San Joaquin Valley to replace the populations dying off in the coastal establishments. After 1800 more disaffected mission Indian leaders, many of them alcaldes, fled to the interior and shared their Europeanized customs and knowledge with other Indians.

Shared language, knowledge of European ways, and interest in striking against a common religious and secular foe led to a series of violent eruptions in the 1820s that shook the missions from San Rafael in the north to San Buenaventura in the south. Such assaults subsided only as experiments with secularization begun in the mid-1820s continued to full emancipation a decade later. Collective Indian action contributed to the decline of the California missions.

In the history of the California missions Franciscans and Spanish-speaking elites encountered Indian resistance from first occupation in San Diego in 1769 until full secularization. But Indian resistance continued past 1836, directed against the secular Mexican and later American societies that replaced it. Indian resistance outlasted the missions because some Indians continued to oppose all attempts at domination.

Assessing California's Missions

Were the California missions a success? Such a question, characteristic of the twentieth century, prompted a ready answer from the founder of the Borderlands school of historical scholarship, Herbert Eugene Bolton. In 1917 he framed the answer for his students and for most of those who followed him. Bolton argued that the mission as pioneering institution had expanded the Spanish frontier in the Americas as had the conquistador with his retinue and the presidio. The mission, with the California example cited prominently as a success, testified to Spain's frontier "genius."[1] Bolton counted only physical success — size — of resident neophyte populations, of harvests and herds, of square leagues held, and he accepted unquestioningly the formula that baptism meant conversion. Bolton had so emphatically approved the Franciscan enterprise in California and extolled the virtues of its founder, Junípero Serra, that Bolton was asked to serve on the historical commission that prepared the brief for Serra's proposed canonization in the 1940s.[2] The Christophobic Nihilists opposed Bolton's Christophilic Triumphalism with a scathing condemnation of Franciscans as oppressors, missions as institutions that obliterated Native American culture, and Indians as victims. The question and the responses it elicited were moral rather than historical. Although they have protested to the contrary, students of material culture have generally been caught up in the moral debate and generally have sided with the Nihilists.[3]

A new generation of historians frequently questions the assumptions of earlier scholarship, and so it is with the California missions. In presenting the process of evangelization and Indian response to it, I intend to suggest that the question of success is irrelevant. Historical scholarship, however, has difficulty moving beyond recrimination because of the power of popular culture subtly to shape methodological approaches toward unintended ends. To move beyond the question of success I must first show why the question is historically irrelevant and then squarely address the issues within it that are historically germane to understanding evangelization.

Three different observations made by foreigners about the same mission, San Carlos (Carmel) illustrate the historical changes in the enterprise and the difficulty in forming any ready judgment of success or failure. In 1786 the Frenchman Jean François de La Pérouse wrote that upon their arrival he and his officers "were received like the lords of manors when they first take possession of their estates." They were greeted by Padre Fermín Francisco de Lasuén, father president of the missions, who met them at the church entrance "in the same manner as on the greatest feast days. He conducted us to the foot of the high altar, where he chanted the *Te Deum* in thanksgiving for the happy outcome of our voyage." They had passed through an assembly of most of the 700 Indians then resident at the mission.[4]

Fifty years later another French visitor familiar with La Pérouse's experience, Abel du Petit-Thouars, arrived in Monterey seeking supplies. To his surprise, he wrote, "I had assumed that I could supply myself more easily there [Monterey] but since the last revolution in November 1836 [mission secularization], San Carlos mission, completely abandoned by the Indians, no longer offers any resources and cannot supply the needs of visiting ships."[5] Petit-Thouars arrived a year after the Mexican government had permitted the Indians to leave the missions and were no longer being forcibly returned. It appeared that these religious enterprises had failed utterly.

Yet forty-four years later and less than a century after La Pérouse's arrival, author Robert Louis Stevenson, visiting Monterey in 1879, went to a Mass at what remained of the dilapidated Carmel mission. The priest had traveled overland to celebrate Mass in the "little sacristy, which is the only covered portion of the church." The ceiling timbers had been looted from the rest of the buildings and the roofs had fallen in. Nonetheless a small group of Indians gathered for religious services. In that strange place, Stevenson thought, "you may hear God served with perhaps more touching circumstances than in any other temple under heaven." An aged, blind Indian "conducts the singing; other Indians compose the choir; yet they have the Gregorian music at their finger ends, and pronounce the Latin so correctly that I could follow the

Figure 14. A man and two boys contemplate the romantic ruins of Mission San Luis Rey sometime in the early 1880s. Founded in 1798 by the great Franciscan Antonio Peyri, San Luis Rey became the largest and most populous in the mission chain, reaching its peak in the late 1820s, when the number of neophytes stood at nearly 2,900 and some 25,000 cattle roamed the ranges. Scholarly interest in the missions arose about the same time the famed California photographer Carleton E. Watkins made this picture, and over the course of more than a century it has continued unabated. Yet even today, despite the fiercely contentious debates of recent decades, a complete picture of mission life and the mission experience, with all its complexities and contradictions and nuances, has yet to emerge. Courtesy Bancroft Library.

meaning as they sang." Stevenson had been moved. "I have never seen faces more vividly lit up with joy than the faces of these Indian singers. It was to them not only the worship of God," he continued, "but was besides an exercise of culture, where all they knew of arts and letters was united and expressed."[6] Some Indians had converted, and they and their descendants had remained faithful to Christianity despite the passage of time.

To the question of whether the missions were a success, the response in light of these three experiences would seem to be yes, no, and maybe. Historical context prevents a glib answer. While my evidence shows missionization as a complex process in which all missionaries were not monsters and all Indians were not victims, to free future inquiry from past fetters demands that the old question be revisited. In posing the question of success, several perspectives must be considered to develop an answer. At a minimum the views of the

Franciscans and the Spanish and Mexican governments and settlers should be considered alongside those of the Indians missionized. Beyond those attitudes the treatment of the missions in popular culture and a brief comparison of mission to nonmission Indians should prove instructive. While these tasks seem straightforward, the complexity of the intertwined lived experience of Franciscans and neophytes in the past makes responding to clear analytical distinctions difficult in the present.

From the Franciscan perspective the missions were a qualified success. The large numbers of Indians baptized in less than seventy years, some 80,000, combined with the priestly formula that baptism equaled conversion, gave every justification for claiming the spiritual conquest of California a success. Yet even as the enterprises prospered with growing harvests of foodstuffs, expanding herds and flocks, and fluctuating, even expanding neophyte populations, many Franciscans knew that things were amiss. Father President Mariano Payeras may have put it in writing to the head of the College of San Fernando but his fellow Franciscans had known for some years that mission Indians sickened and died while their gentile counterparts lived. Mission populations were not viable — more Indians died than lived — and without gentile recruitment ever further into the interior the missions would collapse. If the enterprises had persisted longer, the neophyte populations doubtless would have recovered but the missions were secularized before that could happen.

Secularization — the plan to turn missions into parishes with secular clergy replacing the Franciscans, Indians emancipated, and the lands turned into pueblos in which settlers could claim plots — did not occur voluntarily. The mission, the frontier agency that Bolton had praised for its efficiency, was supposed to be temporary, lasting about ten years. In California, as elsewhere, it continued for decades. At secularization, eighteen of the twenty-one missions had been in existence from thirty-eight to sixty-seven years. Everywhere this was the case. California missions, coming late in the colonial period, had shorter lives than most. Spanish officials beginning with Felipe de Neve first brought pressure to bear for secularization ten years after Junípero Serra had begun; it would be a Mexican government six decades later that would achieve the goal. In failing to secularize their missions the Franciscans blamed the California Indians for being too slow and morally backward to take the personal responsibility that secularization demanded. They also argued that Indians needed protection from Spanish and Mexican rapaciousness.

Civil authorities, however, thought that the Franciscans — not the Indians or themselves — were to blame. They could not understand why the Franciscans could not educate the Indians to the point of self-sufficiency as they had elsewhere on the frontier. From the civil-military perspective, the missions in

California had prospered while the pueblos had faltered, the reverse of the desired outcome. In a relatively short time the missions became prosperous outposts in a poor province, and under Father President Francisco Lasuén they became rich. That anomaly could not persist indefinitely without governmental intervention on behalf of settlers and retired soldiers, in the name of liberating the Indians. When that intervention came and land was distributed, the era of the rancho of myth and reality came into being. As long as the missions remained intact, ranchos were but settlers' dreams and pueblos but a miserable collection of rude huts. From the governmental perspectives of Spain and Mexico the missions were successful only for the missionaries.

In assessing Franciscan accomplishments a series of interrelated questions about Indians must be addressed. Were the Indians slaves? As has been discussed, the answer is no: there was no sense of ownership of the Indian by the Franciscan. The Indian, once having accepted baptism, however, was not free to come and go as he pleased, was not free to resume or continue his native way of life. The Indian's new spiritual and physical obligations to the mission made him unfree but not a slave; the term "spiritual debt peon" more accurately describes neophyte status. To discipline neophytes, to reinforce Christian spiritual lessons violated by Indian behavior from their gentile life now deemed sinful, and to correct what the priests regarded as Indian shirking of mission labor, Franciscans employed a variety of corporal punishments.

Did Franciscans abuse Indians by the punishments they administered in the missions, specifically by flogging? The standards of the time for Spain, not England or some other country, and Indian standards must be considered. Spanish and Mexican civil-military officials' complaints may have been self-serving, designed to free Indian labor for civilian use. Some complaints, however, were justified. Fathers president of the missions Serra and Lasuén admitted that excesses had and would continue to occur. No record has been found of a priest being punished for it, and most Franciscan biographers have dismissed historical complaints against individual priests. Yet younger Franciscans of the mission era, influenced by Enlightenment thinking, knew a different reality. In 1833 the commissary prefect of the Zacatecan Franciscans — men born in New Spain, not Spain — Francisco García Diego y Moreno, ordered reduced corporal punishment for neophytes. He wrote to Governor José Figueroa concerning flogging, "My reason, my ideas, my feelings altogether are opposed to this custom of which I have never approved. Already in this mission under my charge [Santa Clara] such punishment as revolts my soul is being abolished."[7] To the Zacatecan Franciscan, the Fernandinos pursued punishment policies that he and his college abhorred. So, yes, by Spanish and

Mexican standards some missionary abuse of Indians did occur. Since Indians never punished their children or themselves that way, then from their perspective, as long as the native worldview persisted, flogging also was excessive.

Spanish colonization meant the unintended introduction of new diseases into California, resulting in "virgin soil" epidemics which devastated native peoples. Syphilis, also introduced by the Spanish, assumed epidemic proportions for the entire mission era, contributing to the die-off both directly and indirectly — the latter through overall weakening of the population, thereby enhancing its susceptibility to "virgin soil" epidemics and by reducing fertility. From a contact figure of 310,000 people the overall population dropped 21 percent by 1830, the eve of secularization. In the missions the losses had been far greater. Beginning with 65,000 in the mission zone in 1770 only 17,000 Indians remained in 1830, a decline of 74 percent.[8] The magnitude of these stark losses prompted mission critics, beginning in the mid-twentieth century, to charge the Spanish and the Franciscans with pursuing a policy toward California native peoples equivalent to that which Adolf Hitler implemented against European Jewry during the Holocaust. Had Serra and the Franciscans committed genocide against the California Indians?[9]

Historians strive to write the difference in human affairs between what people intended to do in the past and the results they accomplished. Often great disparity emerges between the two. For California history the question, like the charges themselves, is ahistorical and confuses results with intentions. In the matter of genocide and with a comparison to the Holocaust great care must be taken to accurately reflect the past. Hitler and the Nazis intended to destroy the Jews of Europe and created secret places to achieve that end, ultimately destroying millions of people in a systematic program of labor exploitation and death camps. Spanish authorities and Franciscan missionaries, however, sought to bring Indians into a new Spanish society they intended to build on the California frontier and were distressed to see the very objects of their religious and political desire die in droves. From the standpoint of intention alone, there can be no valid comparison between Franciscans and Nazis.

In the area of results the differences are also striking. Hitler intended to implement a "final solution" to the so-called Jewish problem and was close to accomplishing his goal when the Allies stopped him. In contrast, neither Spanish soldiers nor missionaries knew anything about the germ theory of disease, which was not widely accepted until late in the nineteenth century. They had no knowledge that congregating Indians at the mission, confining them in close quarters, and having them work together at tasks would facilitate the spread of disease and contribute to the deaths of those they sought to save or control. Nor did they have any sense of how devastating venereal disease would be, especially upon women and, consequently, fertility rates. The Spanish in California were ignorant of what they had done in introducing Old World pathogens to native peoples. The Spanish and Franciscan ignorance that resulted in the unintentional diminishment of the California Indian population is not comparable to the deliberate Nazi practice in Europe.

A related question about missionaries and Indian population decline moves away from the Holocaust comparison. Did the Franciscans, watching the Indians die from disease, stay aloof from their plight because the priests were too absorbed in their spiritual mission to worry about the Indians' temporal condition? That is the premise that underlies the observation that "the missionaries would have philosophically preferred dead Christians to live pagans."[10] That insight needs qualification. From Padre Jayme's insistence in San Diego in the early 1780s that he preferred good pagans to bad Christians to Father President Payeras's 1820 use of neophyte mortality to question the first principles of the missionary endeavor, important Franciscans challenged the notion that evangelization justified all behavior. Hence it would be unfair to accuse the Franciscans of automatically placing the goal of Christian salvation above human life.

Did Franciscans succeed in converting California Indians? According to missionary logic in California, belied by Indian behavior, each baptism represented a convert to Christianity. Such a narrow definition has led apologists to argue for mission success by pointing to large numbers of Native American Catholics today as seemingly linked to the historical experience. It has led Indian mission critics to counter that many contemporary California Indians are seeking to practice their old rituals, and to argue that their ancestors rejected Franciscan evangelization. By moving beyond the fallacy that baptism meant conversion and looking at conversion as a historical process it is possible to discern some remarkable patterns.

Consider the Franciscan advantages of success in transforming Indian societies. Franciscans offered the power of Iron Age technology to Stone Age people. The opportunity to learn about that power clearly attracted native peoples to the missions. That power could be and was used coercively once they entered mission life to keep them in place. Franciscans offered a single language, Spanish, as a potential unifier, but believed that their Indian charges did not learn it. Yet through the introduction of European music and the training of musicians and choristers the missionaries found a way to bond with Indians. By creating choirs—new organizations of high-status Indians within the missions independent of Indians with individual status in their aboriginal society — Franciscans created a cadre of mostly loyal followers who accepted Christianity. Many of these Indians persevered after mission secularization, as Stevenson's experience in 1879 at Carmel mission attests. Mission choristers and their families formed the nucleus of converts whom the Franciscans had made and who continued to worship as Catholics well into the twentieth century. This group and their families may have constituted at least 10 percent of the mission population.

Music helped to bond those Indians who were not choristers, although to a lesser degree. By bringing diverse Indian groups together to worship and work, the Franciscans taught Indians the rudiments of "keeping together in time," of cooperative action by many people.[11] Nowhere was this lesson more poignant than in the training of Indian auxiliaries to return runaway neophytes to the missions. This large-scale training reached its apex in the formation of Indian military units to combat the Bouchard invasion in 1818. For these units to function properly their members had to know enough Spanish to communicate with one another and with their European-American military commander. The success of these units gave the Franciscans much pride in what they took to be their successful spiritual and temporal accomplishments.

Such military training, however, had unintended results. Native peoples converted Franciscan assets to their own advantage, with younger Indians using Spanish as a lingua franca to launch pan-Indian revolts against the missions in the 1820s. Indian violence in that decade and the next added pressure from below to demands from above for mission secularization. This violent resistance to the missions was accompanied and preceded by less visible conspiracies — poisonings, work slowdowns, graffiti, and other bits of evidence from the hidden transcript of mission life that belied the Franciscan official transcript of order and tranquility. The official transcript claimed success; the hidden transcript revealed the shortcomings of such claims.

To answer the question of Indian conversion requires consideration of what impact the missions had on Indian tribes and what Indians got from the missions. Some Indian societies were overwhelmed by the mission experience and lost touch with their old culture quickly. With a few significant exceptions, this was the case in the San Francisco Bay Area. In southern California, the home of the Toloache Cults, Indians proved more resilient. Southern California Indians continued as much of their pre-contact religion and culture as they could throughout the life of the missions and beyond, just outside of the view of missionaries and other outsiders.

Although many historians once thought that Indian culture had been eradicated in the missions, anthropologists and other observers have provided evidence to the contrary. Through the vehicle of the Spanish language Indian shamans and ceremonial leaders as well as their followers kept knowledge of their tribal lore alive and transmitted it to succeeding generations through oral tradition. They also preserved what they could of their original Indian language. Late in the nineteenth century the Diegueño continued to cremate their dead who believed in the old ways and yet allowed the Christianized among them to be buried according to that religion's belief. In the mid-twentieth century, more than 120 years after mission San Luis Rey had been secularized, a Luiseño chief and native religious leader explained to an anthropologist what he knew of the ancient stories and beliefs of his people. He also knew Christianity well and probably had attended Christian ceremonies. At one point in their conversation the anthropologist questioned him about what seemed a fundamental contradiction in religious philosophy. The Indian explained, "But that is *another* religion."[12] The religious leader went on to say that each religion must be understood on its own terms and should not be confused with another. The anthropologist concluded that religious syncretism — the worship of one religion behind the façade of practicing another — had not taken place, that the Luiseño had added Christianity to their store of knowledge-power. The same can be said about the Chumash as well.[13] From the standpoint of Christian conversion — meaning to the Franciscan the expulsion of native beliefs and their wholesale replacement by the word of Christ — conversion of the Diegueños, Luiseños, and Chumash had been at best incomplete and perhaps a near failure.

One prescient historian of the Borderlands has observed that the "Franciscans did not succeed unless Indians cooperated, and Indians cooperated only when they believed that they had something to gain from the new religion and the material benefits that accompanied it, or too much to lose from resisting it."[14] From a temporal standpoint Indians practicing "protective ingratiation" needed to provide only minimal cooperation in the missions to produce the surpluses that advertised success. As Father President Lasuén remarked during the pinnacle of mission accomplishment, only about half the mission population worked at any given time and then at workdays only half as long as those required in pueblos or presidios. In religious matters the overall evangelizing effort converted some Indians and not others. It would appear, then, that for Serra and his Franciscans converting California had been only partially successful.

Franciscan partial success in the missions looks much different when compared to the fate of nonmissionized Indians. The historical accidents of American conquest of California in the Mexican War in 1848, followed by the discovery of gold — gold made available to all Americans without governmental restraint or control — had an impact of profound importance on California Indians. The gold country lay inland from San Francisco beyond Sacramento, and the newcomers overran Indian territory that had previously known little or no contact with non-Indians. American rule produced a precipitous decline in the Indian population. At the time of gold discovery, about 150,000 native people were still living in California. That number dropped to 30,000 in 1860, an 80 percent decline in just twelve years.[15] Gold seekers waged a war of extermination against Indians, a race war that received the financial backing of the State of California and the U.S. government to pay the expenses of Indian killers. One historian, after careful consideration of the evidence, has concluded that the only word to describe this episode is genocide.[16] When disappointed gold seekers turned away from the mines and entered other areas of the state the former mission Indians did better in coping with them. For the long-term history of California, former mission Indians adapted and survived the American onslaught occasioned by the gold discovery in 1848, something that gentiles, innocent of European contact, did not.

Junípero Serra would have remained an obscure Franciscan missionary who had labored on New Spain's most remote and isolated frontier had it not been for the historical accidents of American conquest and gold discovery, events that propelled California into the United States in 1850. As the thirty-first state, California was instantly rich and lacking an English background and history. The search for something palatable to say about the Spanish and Mexican past brought observers of various persuasions to write about it. The most persuasive and popular of these observers was Helen Hunt Jackson. Her version of Serra, derived from the hagiography written by Serra's friend and associate Palóu, combined with her understanding of nineteenth-century trade schools, cast Serra and the missions as efficient American-style enterprises. She contrasted English and American policies of exclusion and destruction of native peoples to her notions of Spanish love for the mission Indians. In essays on Serra and especially in her enormously popular novel *Ramona* (1884), Jackson helped to create the mission myth, an idyllic world where, as one scholar phrased it, "grateful Indians, happy as peasants in an Italian opera, knelt dutifully before the Franciscans to receive the baptism of a superior culture, while in the background the angelus tolled from a swallow guarded campanile and a choir of friars intoned the *Te Deum*."[17]

Jackson's impact upon popular culture had its counterpart academically in Bolton, who through his Borderlands school of scholarship made legitimate the study of the Spanish past by American undergraduate and graduate students. As part of the American Catholic community and from a diocese with financial resources to pursue the matter, the campaign within California to make Serra a saint began in 1934. Drawing upon the mission myth and Bolton's romanticism and professional testimony the case has moved slowly forward. As part of its ongoing promotion Serra has been advertised as the first candidate for sainthood for the state. This canonization, ironically, would ignore Padre Jayme, who was murdered for his faith in 1775 by the Diegueño—as a martyr, he would automatically have become a saint, the state's first. Even Serra understood at the time that Jayme's martyrdom meant eventual sainthood. The first of three steps in the long process of advancing a candidate to sainthood was accomplished in 1985 when Serra was declared Venerable by the pope. Three years later and following confirmation of Serra's first miracle, the pope declared him Blessed, meaning that his cause had accomplished the second step. One more confirmed miracle should complete the canonization process and make Serra a saint, a person who is in heaven and capable of interceding for the faithful in this world.[18] At some point the papacy will decide whether Serra becomes a saint, and that decision will become part of California history. Students of that history, however, must confront the historical evidence. Serra had a medieval Franciscan utopian dream that he tried with all his being to institute in Alta California; his dream—along with many other dreams of Indians, Spaniards, Mexicans, and Americans in what became the American West—ended in failure.

Sainthood for Serra, however, has unleashed a firestorm of controversy in California, increasing the growing body of literature of both the Christophilic Triumphalists and the Christophobic Nihilists. When advocates of the Serra cause ask that Serra be judged by eighteenth-century standards, not twenty-first, they strike a resonant note with historians. But their request is disingenuous, given their purpose, which is canonization. Sainthood requires that Serra's experiences, especially those with the California Indian, transcend time and place. Sainthood means that his is a universal example for all Catholics to follow; it means that the eighteenth-century expression of Serra's medieval worldview would judge the twenty-first century and whatever centuries are to come.

From a scholarly perspective, however, Indians and Franciscans *together* created mission culture in a complex interplay in which the identification of heroes and villains is as difficult as it is irrelevant. Yet the sainthood campaign for Junípero Serra continues to galvanize popular outpourings that can distract from more informed inquiry. Regardless of the outcome of canonization for Serra, it is clear that for history the process of converting California has not yet run its course.

Notes

Introduction

1. Weber, "Blood of Martyrs, Blood of Indians," 429–48.

2. Franciscans have been in the forefront of this writing. I list the major authors and a representative publication for each. Palóu, *Relación Histórica de la Vida y Apostólicas Tareas del Venerable Padre Fray Junípero Serra,* hereafter cited as Palóu, *La Vida de Junípero Serra;* Engelhardt, *The Franciscans in California;* Geiger, *Life and Times of Junípero Serra,* 2 vols.; Tibesar, ed., *Writings of Junípero Serra,* 4 vols.; Luzbetak, "If Junípero Serra Were Alive: Missiological-Anthropological Theory Today," 512–519; and Guest, "Junípero Serra and His Approach to the Indians," 223–61.

3. McWilliams, *Southern California Country;* Fogel, *Junípero Serra, the Vatican, and Enslavement Theology;* Costo and Costo, *The Missions of California: A Legacy of Genocide.*

4. Sandos, "Between Crucifix and Lance," 222.

5. This school begins with the work of Sherburne F. Cook, especially "The Indian versus the Spanish Mission," and other essays that appeared in *Ibero Americana,* 21–24 (1943) and reprinted with two other studies as *The Conflict between the California Indian and White Civilization.* All others have been influenced by him. I list major authors and a representative publication. Castillo, "The Impact of Euro-American Exploration and Settlement"; Johnson, "Chumash Social Organization: An Ethnohistoric Perspective"; Milliken, "An Ethnohistory of the Indian People of the San Francisco Bay Area from 1770–1810"; Hackel, "The Staff of Leadership: Indian Authority in the Missions of Alta California"; Jackson and Castillo, *Indians, Franciscans, and Spanish Colonization:*

The Impact of the Mission System on California Indians; Shoup and Milliken, *Inigo of Rancho Posolmi: The Life and Times of a Mission Indian.* Some of these authors, beginning with Cook, could be cast with the Christophobic Nihilists because of negative comments about the religion or accusations that Franciscans committed genocide or charges that they made mission Indians slaves.

6. Guest, *Hispanic California Revisited.* Others who have considered Franciscan theological context for missionary behavior have been Nolan, "Anglo-American Myopia and California Mission Art," and the emerging work of Beebe and Senkewicz as illustrated in note 20 below.

7. Gutiérrez, *When Jesus Came the Corn Mothers Went Away.*

8. Weber, "Bourbons and Bárbaros," 79–103.

9. Junípero Serra to the Superiors of San Fernando College, October 17, 1767, Tibesar, ed., *Writings of Junípero Serra,* I, 79–103.

10. Saranyana, "Métodos de Catequización," 563–64.

11. Junípero Serra to Governor Felipe de Neve, January 5, 1779, in Tibesar, ed., *Writings of Junípero Serra,* III, 280–91.

12. Junípero Serra to Juan Figuer, March 30, 1779, in Tibesar, ed., *Writings of Junípero Serra,* III, 302–9. Serra's exact language was, *"Allá está Santa Clara, allá está San Francisco que quando no tenían qué comer atribuyan a dicha falta, y el no hazer prodigios de conversiones, y bautismos."*

13. Junípero Serra to Viceroy Antonio María de Bucareli, June 30, 1778, in Tibesar, ed., *Writings of Junípero Serra,* II, 427n3; III, 194–201.

14. Junípero Serra and Mathías Antonio Noriega, "Report about the Missions," July 1, 1784, Tibesar, ed., *Writings of Junípero Serra,* IV, 256–79, in reporting on activity in 1776 noted that "seventy-one baptisms were accomplished this year which, added to the years before brought the number of Christians to 439." (*Setenta y un bautismos fueron los de este año con los que añadidos a los de antes fue el número de 439 christianos.*)

15. Palóu, *La Vida de Junípero Serra,* 286, upon Serra's death reports the Franciscan in charge of San Juan Capistrano, "in the last four months we have baptized more pagans than in the last three years and we attribute these conversions to the intercession of our Venerable Padre Junípero." (*en estos quatro meses últimos hemos bautizado más Gentiles que en los tres años últimos, y atribuimos estas conversiones a la intercesion de nuestro V. P. Junípero*). The second father president in a report to the bishop of Sonora wrote, "we are (assigned) to the conversion of these pagans and the education of the converts." Fermín Lasuén to Don Fray Francisco Rouset, April 26, 1797, in Kenneally, ed. and trans., *Writings of Fermín Francisco de Lasuén,* II, 20–24.

16. Some examples include, Bancroft, *History of California,* I, 301, 655; II, 160; Cook, *The Conflict Between the California Indian and White Civilization,* 73–79; Geiger, *Mission Santa Barbara,* 28–31; Guest, "An Examination of the Thesis of S. F. Cook on the Forced Conversion of Indians in the California Missions," 64–67; Cook and Borah, *Essays in Population History,* III, 177–311, where table 3.5 includes "age of convert at baptism"; Jackson, *Indian Population Decline,* 84–116; Jackson and Castillo, *Indians, Franciscans, and Spanish Colonization,* 13, 19, 208.

17. Fermín Lasuén, "Refutation of Charges," June 19, 1801, Kenneally, ed. and trans., *Writings of Fermín Francisco de Lasuén,* II, 200.

18. Sandos, "Christianization among the Chumash," 71–72.

19. One can see such an attempt at describing the Franciscans of colonial New Mexico in Gutiérrez, *When Jesus Came the Corn Mothers Went Away,* 3–142.

20. José María Fernández to Governor Diego Borica, June 29, 1797, cited, translated and annotated by Beebe and Senkewicz, *Tensions among the Missionaries in the 1790s,* 16–18, n24.

21. Palóu, *La Vida de Junípero Serra,* 130. On the priests see Geiger, *Franciscan Missionaries in Hispanic California,* 38–40, 87, and appendix II, folio 11.

22. Heizer, ed. and ann., *The Indians of Los Angeles County,* 52–53.

23. Junípero Serra to Francisco Pangua and the Discretorium [body of counselors of the College of San Fernando, the organization sponsoring Serra's operation], 13 April 1776, in Tibesar, ed., *Writings of Junípero Serra,* II, 427, where Fernández Somera is identified by his first name, Ángel. Serra wrote, "I arranged for the removal of Father Ángel for reasons known to myself, which I will give you if you ask for them." Apparently no one at the college did.

24. According to Geiger, *Franciscan Missionaries in Hispanic California,* appendix II, folios 1–12, the College of San Fernando sent five other priests from New Spain to California, all of them after Serra's death. One of these men, Luís Gil y Taboada, had Spanish parents. Of the other four likely *mestizos* (mixed bloods) or Indians, two were brothers, Antonio and José Jimeno. Romualdo Gutiérrez and Antonio Rodríguez complete the list. Thus three Indian families from New Spain contributed priests to converting California under the auspices of the College of San Fernando. In the 1820s the Mexican government broke San Fernando's monopoly on California by drawing native clergy from the Apostolic College of Our Lady of Guadalupe in Zacatecas and assigning them control of the missions from Carmel north to Sonoma.

25. I capitalize God/s for Indians because the long-standing practice of denigrating non-Christian deities by using a lower case for their creators or primary supernatural beings is Eurocentric. That practice intentionally designates non-Christian religions as mere superstition, relegates them to an inferior status, and simultaneously implies that such deficient beliefs left Indians spiritually hungry for the Christian message.

Chapter 1. California's Missions as Instruments of Social Control

1. Gerhard, *The North Frontier of New Spain,* 304–12; Cook, *The Population of the California Indians, 1769–1970,* 20–43; Cook and Marino, "Roman Catholic Missions in California and the Southwest," 472–79.

2. Arriaga, "Reglamento e Instrucción para los Presidios Que Se Han de Formar en la Línea de Frontera de la Nueva España," 11–67; Weber, *The Spanish Frontier in North America,* 212–16.

3. Fray Francisco Palóu, Mission San Carlos, to Fray Juan Sancho, September 13, 1784, in Bolton, *Historical Memoirs of New California by Fray Francisco Palóu, O.F.M.,* IV, 371.

4. The core of the documentation for this case is found in the trial transcript in AGN, PI, Tomo 120, Expediente 3, "Ynterrogatorio sobre la sublevación de San Gabriel, 10 octubre de 1785," microfilm, 31a–47b, Bancroft Library. Lepowsky, "Indian Revolts

and Cargo Cults," views this within the anthropological literature as a revitalization movement.

5. Mason, *The Census of 1790,* 96 entry #41, wherein Montero is classified as "español."

6. Castillo, "Gender Status Decline, Resistance, and Accommodation among Female Neophytes in the Missions of California," 78–81.

7. Hurtado, *Intimate Frontiers,* 25–26, Table 2.1.

8. Sandos, "Christianization among the Chumash," 65–89.

9. Jones, *Ingratiation,* 47.

10. Geiger, "Instructions Concerning the Occupation of California, 1769," 209–18, quoted at 212. For Fages' new regulations see Mason, "Fages' Code of Conduct Toward Indians, 1787," 90–100.

11. Castañeda, "Sexual Violence in the Politics and Policies of Conquest," 15–33.

12. I disagree with apologists for the Franciscans who claim, as does Francis F. Guest, that "When a neophyte was whipped at a mission, he was, as a general rule, spanked rather than flogged." His reasoning is historically faulty and he tortures the Spanish words "azotes" and the verb "azotear" into absurd meanings. See his "The California Missions Were Far from Faultless," 255–307, quoted at 265. See also Guest, "The Indian Policy Under Fermín Francisco de Lasuén," 202–5. Guest mistranslates the sixteenth- to nineteenth-century Spanish verb "azotear," which meant "to flog," into a twentieth-century Bolivian variant, meaning "to spank," thereby rendering "azotes" not as "lashes" but as "light blows" to exculpate the missionaries from charges of abuse. Such a tortuous misreading of the evidence of flogging contributes to general confusion about historic mission life and contradicts his earlier work.

13. My discussion of Ross is informed by the sources I cite in "Between Crucifix and Lance," 214–15, n56. Seed, *Ceremonies of Possession in Europe's Conquest of the New World.*

14. Kotzebue, *A New Voyage Around the World,* II, 123–24.

15. Geary, *The Secularization of the California Missions,* 18–19.

16. Geary, *The Secularization of the California Missions,* 26–32. Weber, *Spaniards and Their Savages in the Age of Enlightenment,* chapter 3, notes 118–21, has the last word on an extraordinarily complicated issue, one in which he corrects an error by Geary and clarifies that Viceroy Juan Francisco Revillagigedo the elder correctly interpreted the Crown's decree of 1749 as a royal desire to secularize missions after ten years of service. This means that the evangelization of California was conducted under the new law that was not enforced in California.

17. Miller and Hyslop, *California,* 146. Engstrand, "California Ranchos, 281–90.

18. At the time of the California Land Commission in the 1850s, the secularized holdings of the former missions ranged from a low of 6.5 acres at San Rafael to a high of 283 acres at Santa Barbara. Most were less than 35 acres. Perez, *Land Grants in Alta California,* 73–75.

19. Gutiérrez, *When Jesus Came, the Corn Mothers Went Away,* 123–25, 313–15, describes Franciscans fornicating with women and men.

20. Geiger, *Franciscan Missionaries in Hispanic California,* x–xi, Spanish and Mexi-

can era missionaries I calculated from appendix II, 281–93. Nunis, Jr., "The Franciscan Friars of Mission San Fernando, 1797–1847," 217–48.

21. My calculations are from Cook, *The Population of the California Indians*, 107, table 13.

Chapter 2. Indians at Contact

1. Cook, *The Population of the California Indians*, 42–43.

2. Linguistic information comes from Shipley, "Native Languages of California," 80–90; Simmons, "Indian Peoples of California," 48–56; Hinton, *Flutes of Fire*, 75–85; Heizer and Elsasser, *The Natural World of the California Indian*, 1–27. I use the long-standing names for Indian groups, since most general readers are more familiar with them than with the more precise names anthropologists now employ. Where appropriate, however, I will note newer names in parentheses. The term *Gabrielino* used now to designate those called *Gabrieleño* in Spanish seems to be an Anglicized word.

3. Milliken, *A Time of Little Choice*, 24–26, 231–61. At contact Indians spoke Costanoan, sometimes called Ohlone, Bay and Plains Miwok, Wappo, and Patwin. People who spoke Southern Pomo and Northern Yokuts were missionized later.

4. Kenneally, ed. and trans., *Writings of Fermín Francisco de Lasuén*, II, 200–201.

5. Lee, *Freedom and Culture*, 139.

6. Kenneally, ed. and trans., *Writings of Fermín Francisco de Lasuén*, II, 202.

7. Young, "Pagans, Converts, and Backsliders, All," 78.

8. Francis Bacon argued that knowledge is power, but that does not seem to be a uniquely European idea.

9. White, "Luiseño Social Organization," 38–40.

10. Boscana, *Chinigchinich*, 87.

11. Shipek, "California Indian Reactions to the Franciscans," 480–92.

12. Harrington, "A New Original Version of Boscana's Historical Account of the San Juan Capistrano Indians of Southern California," 41–42, hereafter cited as Harrington, "A New Version of Boscana." Both versions complement one another and together give greater insight into Boscana's study.

13. White, "Luiseño Social Organization" 187. The word was *tchelopish*.

14. Milliken, *A Time of Little Choice*, 198–99.

15. King, "Central Ohlone Ethnohistory," 203–28.

16. Harrington, "A New Version of Boscana," 21.

17. Bolton, *Fray Juan Crespi*, 171.

18. Priestly, *A Historical, Political, and Natural Description of California by Pedro Fages*, 33.

19. Geiger, *Palóu's Life of Fray Junípero Serra*, 198–99.

20. Harrington, "A New Version of Boscana," 27–28. Anthropologist Harrington was so embarrassed by this passage that he left it untranslated in the text.

21. Lang, *Men as Women, Women as Men*, xi–xvii. See also Williams, *The Spirit and the Flesh*; Herdt, *Third Sex, Third Gender*; and Trexler, *Sex and Conquest*.

22. Geiger and Meighan, *As the Padres Saw Them*, 71–81.

23. Heizer, ed. and ann., *The Indians of Los Angeles County,* 87.

24. Unless otherwise specified, my discussion of shamanism and Datura use comes from Bean, *California Indian Shamanism;* Applegate, *?Atishwin;* Willoughby, "Division of Labor among the Indians of California"; Gayton, "The Narcotic Plant Datura in Aboriginal American Culture"; and Voght, "Shamans and Padres."

25. Toffelmier and Luomala, "Dreams and Dream Interpretation of the Diegueño Indians of Southern California," 195–225.

26. Applegate, *?Atishwin,* 55.

27. Applegate, "The Datura Cult among the Chumash," 7–17.

28. Toffelmier and Luomala, "Dreams and Dream Interpretation of the Diegueño Indians of Southern California," 199.

29. My reconstruction of the Chinigchinich religion, in addition to Boscana, draws upon the following: Bean and Vane, "California Religious Systems and Their Transformations"; Moriarty, "Cosmogony, Rituals, and Medical Practice among the Diegueño Indians of Southern California"; DuBois, "Mythology of the Mission Indians"; DuBois, "The Mythology of the Diegueños"; DuBois, "San Luiseño Creation Myth"; DuBois, "Religious Ceremonies and Myths of the Mission Indians"; and Moriarty, *Chinigchinix.*

30. Woodward, "Notes on the Indians of San Diego County," 140–50.

31. Jackson, *Indian Population Decline,* 88–90.

32. Geiger and Meighan, ed. and trans., *As the Padres Saw Them,* 72.

33. White, "Luiseño Social Organization," 91–103.

34. Discussion of *?antap* derives from: Bean and Vane, "California Religious Systems and Their Transformations," 44–46; Hudson and Blackburn, "The Integration of Myth and Ritual in South-Central California," 225–50; Librado, *Breath of the Sun,* passim; and Blackburn, *December's Child,* 1–88.

35. Librado, *Breath of the Sun,* passim.

36. Bean and Vane, "California Religious Systems and Their Transformations," 39–43.

37. Milliken, *A Time of Little Choice,* passim.

Chapter 3. Junípero Serra and Franciscan Evangelization

1. Hornbeck, "Early Mission Settlement," 55–66.

2. Noel F. Moholy, O. F. M., then vice postulator of the Serra Cause, the Franciscan advocating Serra's canonization, or sainthood, in "Saint or Sinner: Junípero Serra," on William F. Buckley's *Firing Line,* (# 809) broadcast in southern California, March 20, 1989. Braunstein, *The Chuetas of Majorca,* appendix II, 139–73, shows the name "Serra" appearing frequently in the Inquisition's investigations. See also Forteza, *Els Descendents Dels Jeus Conversos de Mallorca.*

3. Geiger, *Franciscan Missionaries in Hispanic California,* 243.

4. Palóu, *La Vida de Junípero Serra,* 9–10. Geiger, *Palóu's Life of Fray Junípero Serra,* 10–11, 329n14, discusses the origins of the alleged Mallorcan "instability of character."

5. Morgado, *Junípero Serra,* 1–51.

6. Geiger, *Franciscan Missionaries in Hispanic California,* xii.

7. My comments on Francis of Assisi are derived from inter alia: Thurston and

Atwater, *Butler's Lives of the Saints*, IV, 22–32; Clement, *Saints in Art*, 353–82; Martin, *Salvation*, 4–14 and passim. Maiarelli, *Assisi*, 6–9. For the hair shirt (*cilizio*, in Italian) see "The Ashen Habit/Tunic," in *The Relics of St. Francis*, 3. For an invaluable compendium of early sources on his life, translated into English, see Habig, ed., *St. Francis of Assisi: English Omnibus of Sources*.

8. Guest, "Cultural Perspectives on California Mission Life," 6–22, with a photograph of a *disciplina* on 19; Palóu, *La Vida de Junípero Serra*, 44; Geiger, *Life and Times of Junípero Serra*, I, 146–47.

9. Troiano and Pompei, *Illustrated Guide of Assisi*, 82; Maiarelli, *Assisi*, 56; Fresco XIII, "The Crib at Greccio," in Mizzi, *The Message of St. Francis with Frescoes from the Basilica of St. Francis at Assisi*, 42–43; Thurston and Atwater, *Butler's Lives of the Saints*, IV, 29.

10. "Scotism," *New Catholic Encylopedia*, XII, 1226–29.

11. María de Agreda, *Mystica Ciudad de Dios . . .* , 3 vols. A comprehensive English-language translation with commentary is Marison, *City of God*, 4 vols. Kendrick, *Mary of Agreda*, 80–93. Colahan, *The Visions of Sor María de Agreda*, 34–41, argues that her writing was influenced by Jewish mysticism.

12. Serra had a copy of *Mystica Ciudad de Dios* in the Sierra Gorda; see Geiger, *Life and Times of Junípero Serra*, I, 115. In the Santa Clara University Archives the copy of *Mystica Ciudad de Dios* bears the inscription, "For the use of Father Francisco Palóu (Del uso de Fr Francisco Palou [sic])" on Vol. II. Volumes I and III indicate that they belonged to Tomás de la Peña Sarravia [sic] "from the College of San Fernando (del Col de Sn Fernando)," headquarters for the California missions. According to Geiger, *Franciscan Missionaries in Hispanic California*, 189–90, Saravia came to California in 1772 and by 1776 served with Palóu at mission San Carlos Borromeo (Carmel) and later at mission Santa Clara, where these volumes were inventoried as part of the first library in California. See Downie, "California's First Library," Spearman Collection, Santa Clara University Archives; Nolan, "Anglo-American Myopia and California Mission Art," 185–95, 204.

13. Weckman, *The Medieval Heritage of Mexico*, 144–45; Kendrick, *Mary of Agreda*, 35–55; Weber, *The Spanish Frontier in North America*, 99–100. Palóu regarded Mary of Agreda's miraculous visits to the New World so important to the spiritual conquest of California that he included the report of these matters as an appendix to his hagiography of Serra. See Palóu, *La Vida de Junípero Serra*, 331–41, and Geiger, *Palóu's Life of Fray Junípero Serra*, 299–306.

14. Palóu, *La Vida de Junípero Serra*, 8; Geiger, *Palóu's Life of Fray Junípero Serra*, 9–10.

15. Morgado, *Junípero Serra*, 2; O'Brien, "The Life of Padre Serra," xxxviii; Geiger, *Palóu's Life of Fray Junípero Serra*, 329n14.

16. Palóu, *La Vida de Junípero Serra*, 20, and Geiger, *Life and Times of Junípero Serra*, I, 86–89, think it either a penetration of Serra's skin by a chigger or a bite by a particularly poisonous mosquito of the region Palóu calls a *zancudo*.

17. Palóu, *La Vida de Junípero Serra*, 28–29, 261–62; Geiger, *Palóu's Life of Junípero Serra*, 29, 236.

18. Palóu, *La Vida de Junípero Serra*, 44; Geiger, *Palóu's Life of Junípero Serra*, 41–42.

19. Palóu, *La Vida de Junípero Serra*, 29–30. Geiger, *Palóu's Life of Junípero Serra*, 29, 346–47 nn9, 11.

20. Cervantes, *The Devil in the New World*, 112–61; Junípero Serra, "Report to the Inquisition of Mexico City," September 1, 1752, in Tibesar, ed., *Writings of Junípero Serra*, I, 18–21. Geiger, *Life and Times of Junípero Serra*, I, 115, indicates that little documentation from this aspect of Serra's life has been found.

21. Geiger, *Life and Times of Junípero Serra*, I, 22, 58; Geiger, *Palóu's Life of Fray Junípero Serra*, 319n12.

22. Junípero Serra to Juan Andrés, July 3, 1769, in Tibesar, ed., *Writings of Junípero Serra*, I, 132–39. Although Francis of Assisi died 266 years before Columbus encountered the New World, according to María de Agreda, Jesus had told him of the role his followers would play in its conversion.

23. Geiger, *Palóu's Life of Fray Junípero Serra*, 76; Palóu, *La Vida de Junípero Serra*, 82–87.

24. Luomala, "Tipai-Ipai," 601–2.

25. Junípero Serra to Juan Andrés, February 10, 1770, in Tibesar, ed., *Writings of Junípero Serra*, I, 148–55, 416n76.

26. Engstrand, "Founding Father of San Diego," 48.

27. Palóu, *La Vida de Junípero Serra*, 86; Geiger, *Palóu's Life of Fray Junípero Serra*, 77–78. Curiously, Geiger in his two-volume biography of Serra does not mention this incident.

28. Palóu, *La Vida de Junípero Serra*, 94–97; Geiger, *Palóu's Life of Fray Junípero Serra*, 86–88; Engstrand, "Founding Father of San Diego," 49.

29. Junípero Serra to Francisco Palóu, June 13, 1770, in Tibesar, ed., *Writings of Junípero Serra*, I, 176–79; Palóu, *La Vida de Junípero Serra*, 102–3; Geiger, *Palóu's Life of Fray Junípero Serra*, 92–93.

30. Junípero Serra to Juan Andrés, June 12, 1770, in Tibesar, ed., *Writings of Junípero Serra*, I, 166–75.

31. Palóu, *La Vida de Junípero Serra*, 122–23; Geiger, *Palóu's Life of Fran Junípero Serra*, 110–11.

32. Palóu, *La Vida de Junípero Serra*, 124–25; Geiger, *Palóu's Life of Fray Junípero Serra*, 112.

33. Palóu, *Memoirs*, I, 54, cited in Nolan, "Anglo-American Myopia and California Mission Art," 267. The other statue was La Conquistadora. Serra also brought a painting of La Dolorosa. Nolan's lengthy essay, informed by a rich reading of Serra's writings including his lectures in Mallorca on Scotist philosophy and theology, is important for a clearer understanding of Serra's purpose in California.

34. Quoted in Martin, *Salvation*, 187. On the placement of images see Nolan, "Anglo-American Myopia and California Mission Art," 263–331.

35. Weber, comp. and ed., *The Mission in the Valley*, 24, lists the contents of the *doctrina* as follows: "the Sign of the Cross, Lord's Prayer, Hail Mary, Apostles Creed, *Confiteor*, Acts of Faith, Hope and Charity, Ten Commandments, Precepts of the Church, Seven Sacraments, Six Necessary points of Faith and the Four Last things." See also Kenneally, ed. and trans., *Writings of Fermín Francisco de Lasuén*, II, 199–201.

36. Nolan, "Anglo-American Myopia and California Mission Art," 34.

37. Nolan, "Anglo-American Myopia and California Mission Art," 2–11, 20–33. Nolan finds that Zephyrin Engelhardt mistakenly placed the crucifix as the central icon on the altar, following a 1901 papal directive, and then inappropriately projected the new twentieth-century practice back on Serra and the eighteenth century.

38. Junípero Serra to Juan Andrés, July 3, 1769, in Tibesar, ed., *Writings of Junípero Serra*, I, 132–39, quoted on 137 (136). Serra's phrase, often repeated, is "en estos últimos siglos." See also in the same volume 65 (64).

39. Palóu, *La Vida de Junípero Serra*, 290.

40. Palóu, *La Vida de Junípero Serra*, 49. Geiger, *The Life and Times of Junípero Serra*, I, 154–56, gives evidence that Palóu was one of Serra's companions on this trip and that he is recounting his own experience along with Serra's.

41. Guest, "The Indian Policy Under Fermín Francisco de Lasuén, California's Second Father President," 195–206.

42. Junípero Serra to Viceroy Bucareli, August 24, 1774, in Tibesar, ed., *Writings of Junípero Serra*, II, 136–47. A Spanish league of 2.6 miles meant that in Serra's plan the priest would travel about 22 miles each day. Since priests generally had to travel with a military escort and since soldiers never walked, the distances Serra reckoned were based upon travel by horseback. The myth that missions were spaced one day's walk apart is a nineteenth-century American myth. Yet it persists. Ruscin, *Mission Memoirs*, x, writes that "Distances between these outposts (missions) allowed for, roughly, one-day journeys by foot or on the back of burros or horses." Such a romantic view ignores the differences in ground covered in a day by a person walking versus two different modes of animal transport that would have taken the person to his destination in up to half the time.

43. Guest, "Cultural Perspectives on California Mission Life," 31–34.

44. Nirenberg, "Conversion, Sex, and Segregation: Jews and Christians in Medieval Spain," 1067.

45. Junípero Serra to Viceroy Bucareli, July 31, 1775, in Tibesar, ed., *Writings of Junípero Serra*, IV, 425, Serra sent four returned neophytes to the civil authority for punishment since three were repeat deserters and the fourth a potential ringleader of dissent. Serra wrote, "I am sending them to you so that a period of exile, and two or three whippings (*raziones de azotes*) . . . applied to them on different days may serve for them and for the rest as a warning, and may be of spiritual benefit for all." Should the commander need shackles, Serra offered to send them to him from the mission.

46. Mansfield, *The Humiliation of Sinners*, passim.

47. See for example, Edwards, *Encyclopedia of Philosophy*, I, 519–25; and Craig, *Routledge Encyclopedia of Philosophy*, 367–77.

48. Geiger, *Life and Times of Junípero Serra*, I, 340–47.

49. Junípero Serra to Viceroy Bucareli, January 8, 1775, in Tibesar, ed., *Writings of Junípero Serra*, II, 198–99.

50. For example see Palóu, *La Vida de Junípero Serra*, 221–22; Geiger, *Palóu's Life of Fray Junípero Serra*, 198–99.

51. On the problems at San Gabriel and San Diego see, Junípero Serra to Viceroy Bucareli, May 21, 1773, in Tibesar, ed., *Writings of Junípero Serra*, I, 344–73. For the problems at San Antonio and San Luis see, Junípero Serra to Francisco Pangua and the Discretorium, July 18, 1774, in Tibesar, ed., *Writings of Junípero Serra*, II, 94–119.

52. Palóu, *La Vida de Junípero Serra*, 150–51, 49–50, 308; Geiger, *Palóu's Life of Fray Junípero Serra*, 136–37, 46–47, 276.

53. Junípero Serra to Viceroy Bucareli, March 13, 1773, in Tibesar, ed., *Writings of Junípero Serra*, I, 294–327.

54. Geiger, *Life and Times of Junípero Serra*, I, 292, 371–87. De Nevi and Moholy, *Junípero Serra*, 126, describe Serra's *representación* of March 13, 1773, as a "Bill of Rights" for Indians. This is incorrect and can be found in no other biography of Serra. Their wording, except for the falsehood, follows that of Geiger, *Life and Times of Junípero Serra*, I, 371, almost verbatim. Indian rights were already defined in the Laws of the Indies. Such a false comparison doubtless has been prompted by the notion that Serra was an "American Founding Father" in the same vein as George Washington, Thomas Jefferson, John Adams, and others. Gasnick and Tartaglione, *Serra: American Founding Father*, make this point in an English and Spanish-language comic book that intends to portray Serra as a superhero. To compare Serra's attitude on religious orthodoxy to that of Jefferson, who succeeded in passing the Virginia Statute for Establishing Religious Freedom (introduced 1779, passed 1786), is a travesty of both men's beliefs. Serra recognized one religion and all were obliged to obey it. Jefferson's statute sought "freedom *for* religion, but also freedom *from* religion," Gaustad, *Faith of Our Fathers*, 38, text of statute 149–151.

55. Palóu, *La vida de Junípero Serra*, 160; Geiger, *Palóu's Life of Fray Junípero Serra*, 146.

56. Serra's original wording in the *representación* of March 13, 1773, and the subsequent *reglamento* of May 6, 1773, incorporating that wording are quoted by Father President Mariano Payeras to the Guardian and Discretorio of the College of San Fernando, June 18, 1821, in Cutter, *Writings of Mariano Payeras*, 293–294. See also Guest, "The Indian Policy Under Fermín Francisco de Lasuén," 204.

57. Guest, "Junípero Serra and His Approach to the Indians," 238.

58. Osante, "La Colonización Familiar en el Norte de Nueva España"; Weber, *The Spanish Frontier in North America*, 194.

59. Guest, *Hispanic California Revisited*, 91–94; Osante, "La Colonización Familiar en el Norte de Nueva España"; Weber, *Spaniards and Their Savages in the Age of Enlightenment*, chap. 3.

Chapter 4. The Indians of San Diego Say "No!"

1. The background of the assault and its aftermath is drawn from, inter alia: Carrico, "Sociopolitical Aspects of the 1775 Revolt at Mission San Diego de Alcalá," 142–157; Geiger, *Life and Times of Junípero Serra*, II, 58–108; Geiger, *Letter of Luis Jayme, O.F.M., San Diego, October 17, 1772*, for quotations from Jayme's correspondence; Vicente Fuster to Junípero Serra, November 28, 1775, in Tibesar, ed., *Writings of Junípero Serra*, II, 449–458, for a translation of Fuster's eyewitness account of the attack. Unless otherwise specified, the translations from Spanish are mine.

2. Thomas Powers, "The Trouble with the CIA," *New York Review of Books* XLIX (January 17, 2002), 29, writes "At the time of the simultaneous attacks on the US embas-

sies in East Africa in August 1998, the CIA officer Milt Bearden told a reporter, 'Two at once is not twice as hard. Two at once is a hundred times as hard.' "

3. Palóu, *La Vida de Junípero Serra,* 184; Geiger, *Palóu's Life of Fray Junípero Serra,* 167.

4. Weber, "Blood of Martyrs, Blood of Indians," 429–448.

5. Ortega, "Expediente de Investigación," November 30, 1775.

6. Junípero Serra to Viceroy Bucareli, December 15, 1775, in Tibesar, ed., *Writings of Junípero Serra,* II, 400–407.

7. Bolton, *Font's Complete Diary,* 199.

8. Palóu, *Historical Memoirs of New California,* I, 62.

9. Guest, "Junípero Serra and His Approach to the Indians," 229–230.

10. Ortega, "Expediente de Investigación," November 30, 1775; Rivera y Moncada, *Diario del Capitan Comandante Fernando Rivera y Moncada,* 447–453; Ortega, "Complot de Indios Para Fugarse y Destruir Los Blancos," January 13, 1776.

11. Bolton, *Font's Complete Diary,* 205–213.

12. Viceroy Bucareli to Junípero Serra, March 26 and April 3, 1776, cited in Geiger, *Palóu's Life of Fray Junípero Serra,* 169–171; Palóu, *La Vida de Junípero Serra,* 187–190. Ortega, "Insurrección de Indios-Resultados Castigo de Cabecillas," April 16, 1778, records having captured Indian conspirators, tried, convicted, and sentenced them to death only to spare their lives as a result of this clemency from the viceroy.

13. Geiger, *Life and Times of Junípero Serra,* II, 88–98. Twenty years later in July 1794, Governor José Joaquin Arrillaga learned that an Indian named Meve who had abetted his brother Charquin's insurgency against mission Santa Cruz, had sought asylum in the church at mission Santa Clara. Arrillaga instructed the lieutenant he sent after Meve not to accept an asylum plea. "In case the missionaries deny him to us," Arrillaga wrote, "the corporal should enter the church and bring the culprit out, forgetting all the niceties, because this was not a crime that is given ecclesiastical immunity." Apparently the priests did not object and Meve was banished to a year at San Diego presidio, while Charquin was banished to the Santa Barbara presidio for two years. Arrillaga is cited in and translated by Milliken, *Time of Little Choice,* 123. As this incident attests, Franciscan relations with the military after Serra were much improved by Father President Fermín Francisco de Lasuén.

14. Palóu, *La Vida de Junípero Serra,* 87–88; Geiger, *Palóu's Life of Fray Junípero Serra,* 78–79.

15. Geiger, *Life and Times of Junípero Serra,* II, 122.

16. Geiger, *Life and Times of Junípero Serra,* II, 120–132.

17. Geiger, *Franciscan Missionaries in Hispanic California,* 88.

18. Vicente Fuster to Junípero Serra, November 28, 1775, in Tibesar, ed., *Writings of Junípero Serra,* II, 453.

19. On post-traumatic stress disorder, formally recognized by the American Psychiatric Association in 1980, see Dean, *Shook Over Hell,* 14–15, 194–202.

20. Geiger, *Franciscan Missionaries in Hispanic California,* 92.

21. Junípero Serra to Antonio Bucareli, October 7, 1776, in Tibesar, ed., *Writings of Junípero Serra,* III, 72–77.

22. Junípero Serra to Antonio Bucareli, June 1, 1777, in Tibesar, ed., *Writings of Junípero Serra*, III, 138–147, 450–451n96.

23. Junípero Serra to Antonio Bucareli, October 4, 1778, in Tibesar, ed., *Writings of Junípero Serra*, III, 260–265.

24. Beilharz, *Felipe de Neve*, 134; Junípero Serra to Fermín Francisco Lasuén, January 12, 1780, in Tibesar, ed., *Writings of Junípero Serra*, III, 418–427.

25. Geiger, *Life and Times of Junípero Serra*, II, 310.

Chapter 5. Serra Refuses to Turn Back

1. See Guest, "Junípero Serra and His Approach to the Indians," 246–248; Margolin, *Monterey in 1786*, 83–84 presents La Pérouse's view of Neve.

2. Filgueira Alvado, "Capacidad Intelectual y Actitud del Indio Ante El Castellano," 165–185, especially 180n57.

3. Junípero Serra to Fermín Francisco Lasuén, July 10, 1778, in Tibesar, ed., *Writings of Junípero Serra*, III, 202–214.

4. Junípero Serra to Fermín Francisco Lasuén, September 28, 1779, in Tibesar, ed., *Writings of Junípero Serra*, III, 386–391.

5. Phelipe [sic] de Neve to Commandant General Teodoro de Croix, March 26, 1781, translated and cited in Beilharz, *Felipe de Neve*, 153–155.

6. Beilharz, *Felipe de Neve*, 7.

7. Beilharz, *Felipe de Neve*, 97–109; Geiger, *Life and Times of Junípero Serra*, II, 192–202, 267–269. Neve later admitted that he had established the town of San José too close to mission Santa Clara.

8. Neve quoted in Beilharz, *Felipe de Neve*, 52.

9. Geary, *Secularization of the California Missions*, 26–27. This matter is discussed more fully in Chapter 7.

10. Junípero Serra to Rafael Verger, August 15, 1779, in Tibesar, ed., *Writings of Junípero Serra*, III, 334–353.

11. Hackel, "The Staff of Leadership," 355–356; Beilharz, *Felipe de Neve*, 64–66.

12. Hackel, "The Staff of Leadership," 356.

13. Junípero Serra to Fermín Francisco Lasuén, March 29, 1779, in Tibesar, ed., *Writings of Junípero Serra*, III, 292–301.

14. Junípero Serra to Rafael Verger, August 15, 1779, and Junípero Serra to Felipe de Neve, January 7, 1780, in Tibesar, ed., *Writings of Junípero Serra*, III, 334–355, 406–417; Culleton, *Indians and Pioneers of Old Monterey*, 88–89.

15. Junípero Serra to Felipe de Neve, January 7, 1780, in Tibesar, ed., *Writings of Junípero Serra*, III, 406–417.

16. Junípero Serra to Fermín Francisco Lasuén, April 25 & 26, 1780, in Tibesar, ed., *Writings of Junípero Serra*, IV, 2–11.

17. Junípero Serra to Teodor de Croix, April 26, 1782, in Tibesar, ed., *Writings of Junípero Serra*, IV, 116–123.

18. Junípero Serra to Felipe de Neve, January 7, 1780, in Tibesar, ed., *Writings of Junípero Serra*, III, 406–417.

19. Junípero Serra to Fermín Francisco Lasuén, January 8, 1781, in Tibesar, ed., *Writings of Junípero Serra,* IV, 60–67. On pages 62 and 63 the phrase "porque en Roma se permite, y en Madrid se tolera" is translated as "because it is winked at in Rome and tolerated in Madrid." Some have mistaken the "winked at" construction to mean Neve condoned rape, which he certainly did not.

20. Beilharz, *Felipe de Neve,* 157, 172n4.

21. Serra and Neve's other disputes have consumed sufficient ink elsewhere to exempt their coverage here. The most important of these involved Serra's right to administer the sacrament of Confirmation and his refusal to show his letter of appointment to do so to Neve. A view favorable to Serra is in Geiger, *Life and Times of Junípero Serra,* II, 216–233, 293–294. A view favorable to Neve is found in Beilharz, *Felipe de Neve,* 56–61, 153–155.

22. Weber, *The Spanish Frontier in North America,* 256–258; Beilharz, *Felipe de Neve,* 121–129; Geiger, *Franciscan Missionaries in Hispanic California,* 92–95; Tibesar, ed., *Writings of Junípero Serra,* IV, 437nn48, 49. See also Kroeber and Fontana, *Massacre on the Gila,* and Santiago, *Massacre at Yuma Crossing.* For a contemporary Franciscan view see Hammond and Rey, *Apostolic Chronicle of Juan Domingo Arricivita,* 225–267.

23. Junípero Serra to Fermín Francisco Lasuén, December 8, 1781, in Tibesar, ed., *Writings of Junípero Serra,* IV, 98–107.

24. Phelipe de Neve, "Instrucción," September 7, 1782, translated by and cited in Beilharz, *Felipe de Neve,* 156–172.

25. Junípero Serra to Juan Sancho, October 29, 1783, in Tibesar, ed., *Writings of Junípero Serra,* IV, 198–207.

26. Junípero Serra and Mathías Antonio Noriega, Report of the Missions, July 1, 1784, in Tibesar, ed., *Writings of Junípero Serra,* IV, 256–279.

27. Bonaventure quoted in Nolan, "Anglo-American Myopia and California Mission Art," 178 (my emphasis).

28. "The Serra Lectures," *CompendiumScoticum* and Sitjar's drawing from the Bancroft Library, in Nolan, "Anglo-American Myopia and California Mission Art," 174–185.

29. Pedro Fages to Padre Mathías [Noriega], June 11, 1785, cited in Guest, "The Indian Policy Under Fermín Francisco de Lasuén, California's Second Father President," 205, 221n36.

30. Geiger, *Franciscan Missionaries in Hispanic California,* 165–166.

31. Guest, "Cultural Perspectives on California Mission Life," 7. Guest, in addition to referring to Noriega's case here and in the article cited in note 29 above, discussed it in his book *Fermín Francisco de Lasuén,* 203.

Chapter 6. Fermín Francisco Lasuén and Evangelization

1. Francisco Lasuen to José de Jesús María Vélez, October 3, 1782, in Kenneally, ed. and trans., *Writings of Fermín Francisco de Lasuén,* I, 86–87.

2. Junípero Serra to Francisco Lasuén, December 8, 1781, in Tibesar, ed., *Writings of Junípero Serra,* IV, 98–107.

3. Francisco Lasuén to Francisco Pangua, August 3, 1775, and January 30, 1776, in Kenneally, ed. and trans., *Writings of Fermín Francisco de Lasuén*, I, 48–56, 62–63; Geiger, *Life and Times of Junípero Serra*, II, 26–34, 304.

4. Geiger, *Franciscan Missionaries in Hispanic California*, 141; Guest, *Fermin Francisco de Lasuén*, 57–62ff, 320–321. For a nuanced discussion of Lasuén's handling of scandals at missions Santa Cruz and San Francisco in the years 1795–1797, see Beebe and Senkewicz, *Tensions among the Missionaries in the 1790s*, 2–18.

5. Geiger, *Franciscan Missionaries in Hispanic California*, 140.

6. The conventional conversion figure for a *fanega* is 1.6 bushels. See, for example, Archibald, *The Economic Aspects of the California Missions*, 6n12. Donald C. Cutter, however, uses 1.25 bushels, which I rounded up to 1.3. Cutter does so because the fanega was not uniform; even in Spain, it varied in size from province to province, and California missionaries computed fanegas in accordance with the practice of their Spanish province of origin. While the figure is always an approximation, Cutter's is doubtlessly closer to historical fact and he corrects the work of Hubert Howe Bancroft in this matter. See Cutter, *The California Coast*, 126n9. For further discussion and with yet a different value for the fanega see Perissinotto, *Documenting Everyday Life in Early Spanish California*, 24–25.

7. Archibald, *The Economic Aspects of the California Missions*, 154, 169, 179; Geiger, *Franciscan Missionaries in Hispanic California*, 140; and Guest, *Fermín Francisco de Lasuén*, xix — all three sources present figures slightly different from these.

8. Beebe and Senkewicz, "Uncertainty on the Mission Frontier."

9. Buenaventura Sitjar to Francisco Lasuén, January 31, 1799, cited and translated in Beebe and Senkewicz, *Tensions among the Missionaries in the 1790s*, 32–40. At one point Sitjar recorded the following exchange between Concepción Horra and himself: CH: "This afternoon I am going off with a boy (Indian) and I am going to order him to fornicate." S: "Father I do not intend to pardon you for those or similar, serious crimes."

10. Antonio de la Concepción Horra to the Viceroy, July 12, 1798, Archivo General de la Nación (Mexico City), Provincias Internas, Legajo 216, Expediente 14, 7–9, cited and translated by Beebe and Senkewicz, *Tensions among the Missionaries in the 1790s*, 21–27.

11. Geiger, *Franciscan Missionaries in Hispanic California*, 122–124.

12. Lasuén, "Refutation of Charges," June 18, 1801, in Kenneally, ed. and trans., *Writings of Fermín Francisco de Lasuén*, II, 194–234. Subsequent discussion will be drawn from this source.

13. Several sources cover this well. See Bancroft, *History of California*, I, 587–597; Engelhardt, *The Missions and Missionaries of California*, II, 566–615; Guest, *Fermín Francisco de Lasuén*, 223–239; and Beebe and Senkewicz, "Uncertainty on the Mission Frontier."

14. Kenneally, ed. and trans., *Writings of Fermín Francisco de Lasuén*, II, 197.

15. Kenneally, ed. and trans., *Writings of Fermín Francisco de Lasuén*, II, 221, gives the figure of twenty-one, which is a misprint. See Guest, "An Inquiry into the Role of the Discipline in California Mission Life," 7, 61n37.

16. Kenneally, ed. and trans., *Writings of Fermín Francisco de Lasuén*, II, 218.

17. Kenneally, ed. and trans., *Writings of Fermín Francisco de Lasuén*, II, 220.

18. Kenneally, ed. and trans., *Writings of Fermín Francisco de Lasuén,* II, 222–223.

19. Kenneally, ed. and trans., *Writings of Fermín Francisco de Lasuén,* II, 222–223.

20. Kenneally, ed. and trans., *Writings of Fermín Francisco de Lasuén,* II, 208 (Lasuén's emphasis).

21. Kenneally, ed. and trans., *Writings of Fermín Francisco de Lasuén,* II, 207.

22. Kenneally, ed. and trans., *Writings of Fermín Francisco de Lasuén,* II, 212.

23. Kenneally, ed. and trans., *Writings of Fermín Francisco de Lasuén,* II, 213.

24. Kenneally, ed. and trans., *Writings of Fermín Francisco de Lasuén,* II, 212–214.

25. Kenneally, ed. and trans., *Writings of Fermín Francisco de Lasuén,* II, 211.

26. Kenneally, ed. and trans., *Writings of Fermín Francisco de Lasuén,* II, 202.

27. Francisco Lasuén to Antonio Nogueyra, January 21, 1797, in Kenneally, ed. and trans., *Writings of Fermín Francisco de Lasuén,* II, 6.

28. Kenneally, ed. and trans., *Writings of Fermín Francisco de Lasuén,* II, 205.

29. Kenneally, ed. and trans., *Writings of Fermín Francisco de Lasuén,* II, 202.

30. Kenneally, ed. and trans., *Writings of Fermín Francisco de Lasuén,* II, 200–201.

31. The exact number of weeks of leave each year is unclear. Lasuén indicated that one-fifth of the neophyte population at mission Santa Barbara was permitted to go to the *monte* every Sunday for a week or two, and that a similar system was adopted elsewhere. Bancroft, *History of California,* I, 592. By this formula, then, if one-fifth left every week for just one week, each Indian would have ten weeks' furlough annually. Geiger, *Mission Santa Barbara,* 66–67, clarified the formula by noting that during the monthlong harvest no one could leave and that at other times those whose *rancherías* were close to the mission had one-week passes; those whose families lived at greater remove had two weeks. Nevertheless multiple visits seemed the norm. Guest concluded that a total of five to six weeks constituted the normal annual leave for Indians. See the following, all by Guest, "Cultural Perspectives on California Mission Life," 45; "The California Missions Were Far from Faultless," 275; "Junípero Serra and His Approach to the Indians," 230; and "New Look at the California's Missions [sic]," 84. In "An Examination of the Thesis of S. F. Cook on the Forced Conversion of Indians in the California Missions," he used the phrase "a few weeks each year."

32. Francisco Lasuén to Diego de Borica, June 15, 1795, Kenneally, ed. and trans., *Writings of Fermín Francisco de Lasuén,* I, 338–340. Other examples of Lasuén's concern for a sufficient number of soldiers to permit missionaries to perform their duties and return runaways can be found in Kenneally, ed. and trans., *Writings of Fermín Francisco de Lasuén,* I, 131–132, 135, 167, 179, 375, 398; II, 116, 122.

33. This story comes from the report of an Italian navigator in the employ of Spain, Alejandro Malaspina, who visited Monterey in 1791. See Cutter, *Malaspina in California,* 50; Guest," An Inquiry into the Role of the Discipline in California Mission Life," 4–5.

34. Francisco Lasuén to José Gasol, June 16, 1802, Kenneally, ed. and trans., *Writings of Fermín Francisco de Lasuén,* II, 276–279.

35. A fascinating study of the consumption of imported goods by the Santa Barbara presidio from 1779 to 1810 with detailed listings of sundry items is Perissinotto, *Documenting Everyday Life in Early Spanish California.* See also Thurman, *The Naval Department of San Blas.*

36. McGarry, "Educational Methods of the Franciscans in Spanish California," 342–345; Scheutz-Miller, *Building and Builders in Hispanic California*, 51–105.

37. Barth, *Franciscan Education and the Social Order in Spanish North America*, 150–157; McGarry, "Educational Methods of the Franciscans in Spanish California," 339–340.

38. Engelhardt, *The Missions and Missionaries of California*, II, 288.

39. Lasuén, "Catechism at Mission San Carlos," undated but taken with the Malaspina expedition and archived with their documents, cited in Cutter, *California in 1792*, 151–155. This citation will cover subsequent quotations in the text.

40. Mariano Payeras to Estevan Tapis, January 13, 1810, in Cutter, trans. and ed., *Writings of Mariano Payeras*, 49–53.

41. Sandos, "Levantamiento!" 115–116; Alva, *A Guide to Confession Large and Small in the Mexican Language*, 53–158; Kelsey, *The Doctrina and Confesionario of Juan Cortes*; Beeler, *The Ventureño Confesionario of José Señán, O.F.M.*

42. Sandos, "Levantamiento!" 118–120.

Chapter 7. Evangelization in Serra's Shadow

1. Mariano Payeras to Estevan Tapis, January 13, 1810, in Cutter, trans. and ed., *Writings of Mariano Payeras*, 49.

2. Margolin, *Monterey in 1786*, 86.

3. Langsdorff, *Langsdorff's Narrative of the Rezanov Voyage to Nueva California in 1806*, 64.

4. Webb, *Indian Life at the Old Missions*, illustrations opposite 30, 47, 182, 183. Webb also indicates that grist mills were developed at six missions, four of them after 1800, but the reliance on women grinding by hand continued (*Indian Life at the Old Missions*, 154–164). See also Archibald, *Economic Aspects of the California Missions*, 182–183. George Vancouver in his visit in 1792 suggested the use of mills for fulling wool, removing the grease and dirt and binding the fibers to make a commercially acceptable fabric. California wool did not reach commercial standards because human effort alone—through Indian foot-stomping of fiber in water—could not properly clean and soften the fiber. Under the direction of Father President Mariano Payeras in the 1820s attempts to construct and implement such mills were made at missions Santa Inés and La Purísima but failed due to the turmoil accompanying Mexican Independence and subsequent Mexican hostility toward the missions. See Hoover, "An Early Attempt at Industrial Revolution in California," 12–19, and Vancouver, *A Voyage of Discovery to the North Pacific Ocean and Around the World, 1791–1795*, II, 712–713.

5. Castillo, "Gender Status Decline, Resistance, and Accommodation among Female Neophytes in the Missions of California," 77. George Vancouver thought the missionaries kept large numbers of women and children around them at the missions to prevent the men from rising against them. Vancouver, *A Voyage of Discovery to the North Pacific Ocean and Around the World, 1791–1795*, II, 713.

6. Kenneally, ed. and trans., *Writings of Fermín Francisco de Lasuén*, II, 217.

7. Margolin, *Monterey in 1786*, 89.

8. Sandos, "Between Crucifix and Lance," 201, 224n17. For a vivid description of the

practice at San Gabriel mission see Reid, "New Era in Mission Affairs," 87. Lasuén in his "Refutation of Charges" specifically accused Chumash women of having abortions and committing infanticide, noting that "we employ for their correction all the care and vigilance, all the expedients, and all the diligence which a matter of such importance demands." Kenneally, ed. and trans., *Writings of Fermín Francisco de Lasuén,* II, 210. Vallejo, "Ranch and Mission Days in Alta California," 186, described the punishment for women at mission San José.

9. Guest, "Junípero Serra and His Approach to the Indians," 234–235.

10. In 1979 Francis F. Guest considered all the historical charges against the Franciscans for "forced conversion" and found them all to be unproven. Guest, "An Examination of the Thesis of S. F. Cook on the Forced Conversion of Indians in the California Missions," 1–77.

11. For a superb account of the incident in detail, see Uhrowczik, *The Burning of Monterey.*

12. Bancroft, *History of California,* II, 210–249, 264; Geiger, *Mission Santa Barbara,* 80–84; Sandos, "Levantamiento!" 119–120. The 1824 Chumash uprising is treated in the chapter on resistance.

13. Mariano Payeras to José de la Guerra y Noriega, October 24, 1818, in Cutter, trans. and ed., *Writings of Mariano Payeras,* 159.

14. Mariano Payeras to Governor Pablo Vicente de Solá, December 21, 1818, in Cutter, trans. and ed., *Writings of Mariano Payeras,* 164.

15. Mariano Payeras to the Reverend Father Guardian and the Discretorio, June 18, 1821, in Cutter, trans. and ed., *Writings of Mariano Payeras,* 292–303.

16. Bolton, *The Spanish Borderlands,* 283.

17. Mariano Payeras to Governor Pablo Vicente de Solá, July 7, 1821, in Cutter, trans. and ed., *Writings of Mariano Payeras,* 303–304.

18. Mariano Payeras to Father Guardian, May 31, 1822, in Cutter, trans. and ed., *Writings of Mariano Payeras,* 320–322.

19. Mariano Payeras, mission La Purísima, to Reverend Father Guardian and Venerable *Discretorio* [body of counselors] of Our Apostolic College of San Fernando de México, February 2, 1820, in Cutter, trans. and ed., *Writings of Mariano Payeras,* 225–228.

20. Weber, *The Mexican Frontier, 1821–1846,* 103.

21. Mariano Payeras to the Reverend Father Apostolic Preachers and Ministers of the Missions from San Carlos to San Diego, October 9, 1822, in Cutter, trans. and ed., *Writings of Mariano Payeras,* 327–328.

22. Neve quoted in Beilharz, *Felipe de Neve,* 52.

23. Margolin, *Monterey in 1786,* 70.

24. Archibald, "Indian Labor at the California Missions: Slavery or Salvation," 181.

25. Neely, *The Abraham Lincoln Encyclopedia,* 152.

26. Magliari, "Free Soil, Unfree Labor," details the binding of former San Luis Rey neophytes to American rancho owner Cave J. Couts in northern San Diego County. Magliari thinks Lincoln's "either or" generalization missed the mark.

27. Borah, *New Spain's Century of Depression,* 37.

28. See Chapter 6, note 31, for the sources.

29. See "Indulgences," and "Purgatory," in *New Catholic Encyclopedia,* 7, 11, 482–484, 1034–1039.

30. Neri, *Hispanic Catholicism in Transitional California,* 20–23. Geiger, *Franciscan Missionaries in Hispanic California,* x, has the Zacatecans take control at Soledad, as do other sources, apparently because Durán had wanted to cede ten missions but the Zacatecans could staff only eight.

31. Robinson, *Land in California,* 33–34, note 1, gives four square leagues as the standard grant to presidio and pueblo.

32. Calculations based on Cleland, *The Cattle on a Thousand Hills,* 21–22, with 1 league equal to 2.6 miles and 640 acres in a square mile.

33. Engelhardt, *San Juan Capistrano Mission,* 112–125, 141–142.

34. Hutchinson, *Frontier Settlement in Mexican California,* passim.

35. Hansen, *The Search for Authority in California,* 20–29.

36. Neri, "Narciso Durán and the Secularization of the California Missions," 411–429. See also Neri, *Hispanic Catholicism in Transitional California,* 27–28; Servín, "The Secularization of the California Missions," 133–149.

37. Cook, *The Conflict Between the California Indian and White Civilization,* 12; Hansen, *The Search for Authority in California,* 32.

38. Jackson and Castillo, *Indians, Franciscans, and Spanish Colonization,* 98–99.

Chapter 8. Syphilis, Gonorrhea, and Other Diseases

1. Geiger and Meighan, ed. and trans., *As the Padres Saw Them,* 74.

2. Crosby, "Virgin Soil Epidemics as a Factor in the Aboriginal Depopulation in America," 289–299.

3. Cook, *The Conflict between the California Indian and White Civilization,* 23–34, first considered in some detail the impact of syphilis on the Indians. That study, originally published in 1943, needs to be extended by additional medical information gathered since then. When a review of the health literature appeared in 1989, however, Walker, Lambert, and DeNiro, "The Effects of European Contact on the Health of the California Indians," 535–539, gave only one sentence to syphilis. Three years later Walker and Johnson devoted about a page to it. See "Effects of Contact on the Chumash Indians," 132–133.

4. For example, *The Columbia University College of Physicians and Surgeons Complete Home Medical Guide,* 444–445; *The New Complete Medical and Health Encyclopedia,* 2, 553–555; *The American Medical Association Family Medical Guide,* 612–613; McFalls and McFalls, *Disease and Fertility,* 247–255.

5. Employing the term STD, avers French historian Claude Quétel, isolates the role of sex to an "innocent vector" and conceals it hypocritically within an abbreviation. In this approach the disease, he writes, "is transmitted by sex, just as malaria is transmitted by mosquitoes. One does not become infected through carelessness, or ignorance of elementary preventive measures, and certainly not as a just punishment for having sinned, but by a trick of fate." See, Quétel, *History of Syphilis,* 3.

6. Foucault, *The History of Sexuality,* 53–78.

7. Cited in Cook, *The Conflict between the California Indian and White Civilization*, 23.

8. Cook, *The Conflict between the California Indian and White Civilization*, 23.

9. For examples from Junípero Serra's letters from 1777 and 1779 see Tibesar, ed., *Writings of Junípero Serra*, III, 159, 305, 349.

10. Cook, *The Conflict between the California Indian and White Civilization*, 25.

11. Jackson, "Epidemic Disease and Population Decline in the Baja California Missions, 1697–1834," 336–337; Rudkin, *Observations on California 1772–1790 by Father Luis Sales, O.P.*, 55.

12. Milliken, "An Ethnohistory of the Indian People of the San Francisco Bay Area from 1770 to 1810," 251.

13. Unless otherwise specified, my discussion of the origins of syphilis and its early history in Europe are from Crosby, "The Early History of Syphilis: A Reappraisal," in *The Columbian Exchange*, 122–164. The text and notes following from pp. 147–160 are materials added to his earlier essay of the same name that appeared in the *American Anthropologist*.

14. Baker and Armelagos, "The Origin and Antiquity of Syphilis," 703–738, quoted at 719, followed by individual comments from 720–729, their reply 729–733, and their sources. My discussion of skeletal evidence, unless otherwise cited, derives from this essay and its accompanying discussion by scholars from around the world.

15. Rudd, "Depopulation in Polynesia," 589. Smith, "The Introduction of Venereal Disease into Tahiti: A Re-examination," 4; McFalls and McFalls, *Disease and Fertility*, 328–329.

16. Quétel, *History of Syphilis*, 10.

17. Sandos, "Prostitution and Drugs," 622. But salvarsan had drawbacks. The regimen of injections required more than a year to succeed and side effects from arsenic poisoning, like the earlier consequences of mercury poisoning from quicksilver-based "medications," proved common. No genuine medical treatment, then, existed to combat syphilis until nearly four centuries after it appeared, and only penicillin, used in treatment during and after World War II, could bring the disease under a genuinely effective, albeit temporary, control.

18. Thayer and Moore, "Gonorrhea," 755.

19. Zimmermann, "Extragenital Syphilis as Described in the Early Literature (1497–1624)," Part 1, 758; Part 2, 72–73, and 121–122, for indirect transmission. There is no evidence that California Indians practiced circumcision or that Franciscans introduced such a practice.

20. My general discussion of syphilis is taken from the sources cited in note 4 above, supplemented by Jones, *Bad Blood*, 2–4.

21. Ingall and Musher, "Syphilis," 338–339.

22. Unless otherwise specified, my discussion of the European medical and sociocultural practices comes from Zimmermann, "Extragenital Syphilis as Described in the Early Literature (1497–1624)," 72, 757–780, 73, 104–122. "Wet cupping," a technique used since the ancient Greek physician Galen, involved scarifying the skin at the site of suspected discomfort until blood or pus issued, then creating a vacuum by sucking,

followed by the application of a cup to contain the liquid released. When the desired amount of fluid had been drawn—the appropriate number of cups—the treatment ended. Cupping was done routinely at public baths. Self-administered cupping sufficed for disorders readily reached, but a barber or attendant would be needed for hard-to-reach sites. Employing this practice when a sufferer experienced the lesions or rash of primary or secondary syphilis—moments of spirochetemia—would make the uninfected practitioner highly vulnerable to contracting the disease. Of course, as the disease progressed through its natural stages, unaffected by treatments, successive treatments involving cupping merely increased others' exposure to *T. pallidum*.

23. Geiger and Meighan, ed. and trans., *As the Padres Saw Them*, 71.

24. Zimmermann, "Extragenital Syphilis as Described in the Early Literature (1497–1624)," 72, 758; Pusey, *The History and Epidemiology of Syphilis*, 91.

25. Geiger and Meighan, ed. and trans., *As the Padres Saw Them*, 72–75.

26. Geiger and Meighan, ed. and trans., *As the Padres Saw Them*, 75–76.

27. Geiger and Meighan, ed. and trans., *As the Padres Saw Them*, 76–77.

28. Geiger and Meighan, ed. and trans., *As the Padres Saw Them*, 78–79.

29. Fermín Lasuén, "Refutation of Charges," June 19, 1801, in Kenneally, ed. and trans., *Writings of Fermín Francisco Lasuén*, II, 212.

30. Geiger and Meighan, ed. and trans., *As the Padres Saw Them*, 105–106. Of the three missions not referring to sex, Soledad cited "laziness," San Juan Capistrano disingenuously remarked "we cannot say," and Santa Inés did not answer the question.

31. These were San Diego, San Gabriel, San Fernando, San Buenaventura, Santa Barbara, San Luis Obispo, San Miguel, Soledad, San Juan Bautista, Santa Cruz, Santa Clara, San José, and San Francisco. Of the remaining five missions, two, San Juan Capistrano and Santa Inés, made no comment regarding venereal infection. The remaining three, San Luis Rey, San Antonio, and San Carlos, mentioned the importance to the Indians of their sweathouses, available only to men, in curing skin diseases which may have been symptomatic of primary or secondary syphilis. See Geiger and Meighan, ed. and trans., *As the Padres Saw Them*, 71–80.

32. Dr. [no first name given] Rollin, physician with the La Pérouse expedition, Rudkin, *The First French Expedition to California*, 98–113.

33. Vancouver, *A Voyage of Discovery to the North Pacific Ocean and Round the World, 1791–1795*, 2, 714; 3, 1092.

34. Ingall and Musher, "Syphilis," 335–374.

35. Cook, "California's First Medical Survey," 353.

36. George von Langsdorff in, *Langsdorff's Narrative of the Rezanov Voyage to Nueva California in 1806*, 60, 127.

37. Louis Choris cited in Mahr, *The Visit of the "Rurik" to San Francisco in 1816*, 99.

38. Mariano Payeras to Pedro Martínez, April 13, 1812, in Cutter, trans. and ed., *Writings of Mariano Payeras*, 60–61.

39. Engelhardt, *San Juan Capistrano*, 15–16, says only Indian boys and men, never women, were allowed to attend priests.

40. Archibald Menzies, accompanying George Vancouver's voyage, thought Peña a "very corpulent man." See Vancouver, *A Voyage of Discovery to the North Pacific Ocean*

and Round the World, 1791–1795, 2, 718n2. Geiger, *Franciscan Missionaries in Hispanic California,* 208–210, on Rodríguez. Vallejo, *Historical and Personal Memoirs,* 3, 405, considered Durán "as fat as an Easter bull." Payeras described Ripoll as "my fat companion" in Mariano Payeras to Juan Norberto, September 21, 1813, in Cutter, trans. and ed., *Writings of Mariano Payeras,* 70. Lasuén acknowledged his heaviness in a letter to Francisco Pangua, July 19, 1775, in Kenneally, ed. and trans., *Writings of Fermín Francisco de Lasuén,* I, 45–48.

41. Guest, "Cultural Perspectives on California Mission Life," 115–182.

42. Dumke, "The Masters of San Gabriel Mission's Old Mill, 261–262; Geiger, *Franciscan Missionaries in Hispanic California,* 104–106, 266–269.

43. Nunis, "The Franciscan Friars of Mission San Fernando, 1797–1847," 241–243; Geiger, *Franciscan Missionaries in Hispanic California,* 210–212. Indians had an oral tradition of priestly dalliances with Indian women. Fernando Librado claimed that priests entered the *monjerío* at night and had the adult woman in charge begin singing. The girls would join in, and, with the sound as muffler, the priests had sex with whomever they chose. See Librado, *Breath of the Sun,* 53. At Mission Santa Cruz, Lorenzo Asisara claimed that the priest mentioned in the text in connection with his practice of cesarian section, Padre Taboada, was known to Indians as being "very amorous. He hugged and kissed the Indian women, and he had contact with them until he had syphilis and skin eruptions broke out." See Castillo, "An Indian Account of the Decline and Collapse of Mexico's Hegemony Over the Missionized Indians of California," 399.

44. Baker and Peppercorn, "Enteric Diseases of Homosexual Men," 33.

45. Williams, *The Spirit and the Flesh,* 110–151; Harris, *California's Medical Story,* 16–18.

46. Palóu, *La Vida de Junípero Serra,* 221–222; Geiger, *Palóu's Life of Fray Junípero Serra,* 198–199; Priestly, *A Historical, Political, and Natural Description of California by Pedro Fages, Soldier of Spain,* 33; Bolton, *Fray Juan Crespi,* 171.

47. McFalls and McFalls, *Disease and Fertility,* xix.

48. McFalls and McFalls, *Disease and Fertility,* 51–60.

49. McFalls and McFalls, *Disease and Fertility,* 267–270, 335.

50. Voluntary abortion will be considered under the topics of Indian resistance to Franciscan social control.

51. Castillo, "An Indian Account of the Decline and Collapse of Mexico's Hegemony over the Missionized Indians of California," 397–398. Lorenzo Asisara, who told this story that happened before his birth, undoubtedly heard it from his father.

52. Dr. Rollin noted miscarriages, in Rudkin, *The First French Expedition to California,* 113; Langsdorff, *Langsdorff's Narrative of the Rezanov Voyage to Nueva California in 1806,* 127, wrote about Indian women, "Miscarriages, usually from the third to the seventh month, are by no means an infrequent occurrence among them."

53. In addition to the descriptions in the text given earlier, see Remington and Klein, ed., *Infectious Diseases of the Fetus and Newborn Infant,* 342–353.

54. McFalls and McFalls, *Disease and Fertility,* 331.

55. On the limitations of the mission records see, Cook and Borah, "Mission Registers as Sources of Vital Statistics: Eight Missions of Northern California," 177–192; Johnson,

"Mission Registers as Anthropological Questionnaires: Understanding the Limitations of the Data," 9–30. For the basic contents of the mission registers see Engelhardt, *Mission San Carlos Borromeo* (Carmelo), 224, and *San Miguel Arcángel*, 40–41.

56. Definitions are from Wilson, *The Dictionary of Demography*, passim.

57. Jackson, *Indian Population Decline*, 83–116. One must approach Jackson's work cautiously, as his definition of NRR differs from that of demographers. He writes that a "ratio of 1.0 (NRR) indicates the doubling of a population over a generation, and a figure of 0.5 of halving of the population" (p. 11).

58. Brown et al., *Syphilis and Other Venereal Diseases*, 101.

59. Gjestland, *The Oslo Study of Untreated Syphilis*, 134–146; Brown et al., *Syphilis and Other Venereal Diseases*, 103–105.

60. Cook and Marino, "Roman Catholic Missions in California and the Southwest," 477.

61. Jackson and Castillo, *Indians, Franciscans, and Spanish Colonization*, 40. Jackson has done the demographic calculations. He provides greater refinement with figures for each mission in *Indian Population Decline*, 83–135.

62. Jackson and Castillo, *Indians, Franciscans and Spanish Colonization*, 56, 58.

63. Fiumara, "A Legacy of Syphilis," 676.

64. The term is from Gilberto Freyre's discussion in *The Masters and the Slaves*, 70–74, cited on 72.

Chapter 9. Music and Conversion

Epigraph: James A. Sandos wrote this epigraph from recollections of personal experience. "Salve Regina," or "Hail Holy Queen," was a popular hymn in my youth and one that has a long history in Alta California. Junípero Serra sang it at the founding of Mission San Carlos on June 3, 1770, right after saying Mass. Serra originally established the mission at Monterey, and later moved it to the banks of the Carmel River. Geiger, *Palóu's Life of Serra*, 92, 390; Culleton, *Indians and Pioneers of Old Monterey*, 48–52.

1. Da Silva, *Mission Music of California*, 19.

2. *The New Grove Dictionary of Music and Musicians*, I, 189.

3. Geiger, *Palóu's Life of Serra*, 29, 116.

4. See the *retablo* (altar screen) at the cathedral in Santa Fe, New Mexico, where both Serra and Solano are depicted, the latter with a violin. On Serra's devotion to Solano see Geiger, *Palóu's Life of Serra*, 41, 280.

5. Palóu, *Noticias de la Nueva California*, I, 266. Engelhardt, *Missions and Missionaries*, second edition, II, 150–151.

6. Geiger, *Palóu's Life of Serra*, 243–245, 473nn7, 8.

7. Bossy, "The Mass as a Social Institution," 29–61.

8. The discussion of the Mass and music is drawn, inter alia, from: Harman et al., *Man and His Music*, 1–10; Seay, *Music in the Medieval World*, 25–29; Thompson, *Music Through the Renaissance*, 26–35; *The Norton/Grove Concise Encyclopedia of Music*, 470, 585; *The New Grove Dictionary of Music and Musicians*, 1, 470–482; 11, 770–781; 15, 320–338, 739–764.

9. Some other examples of the Mass follow. The Gloria, derived from the words of the

Christmas angel, "Gloria in excelsis Deo" (Glory be to God on high), is usually called the Greater Doxology. The celebrant (priest) intones the first four words, then the choir and or congregation joins in. A similar pattern is observed for the Credo, where the celebrant alone intones, "Credo in unum Deum" (I believe in one God), with the choir or congregation joining at "Patrem omnipotentem" (Father almighty) and continuing to the end. Similar patterns apply as well to the Sanctus, the Agnus Dei, and the closing Ite missa est (go, the Mass is over).

10. Geiger and Meighan, ed. and trans., *As the Padres Saw Them,* 133–137.

11. Keeling, "Music and Culture Areas of California," 146–148. See also Keeling, "Sources for Research Concerning Music among Indians of the California Region," 79–85; and Stevenson, "Written Sources for Indian Music until 1882," 1–40.

12. Keeling, "Music and Culture Areas of California," 149–158.

13. Stevens, *Words and Music in the Middle Ages,* 385.

14. Father Luke Dysinger quoted in Mary Rourke, "A Higher Power?" *Los Angeles Times,* August 15, 1995, E 1, 5. Greenberg, "The Middle Ages," lecture 3, in *How to Understand and Listen to Great Music — Part I, Sources,* describes plainchant as creating a mantra state the goal of which is to lose personal identity as the listener merges with the cosmos.

15. He had similar ideas about the function of the music of the Gradual, the Alleluia, and the Offertory. Stevens, *Words and Music in the Middle Ages,* 390.

16. While taking for granted that chant, first and foremost, is prayer and praise, he also believed that the right music could have profound secondary effects upon the congregation. To him, the Alleluia "is fittingly sung before the Gospel, so that by this chant the minds of the faithful may in some way begin to be purified for hearing the word of salvation." Stevens, *Words and Music in the Middle Ages,* 389.

17. Lasuén observed that "there are some [neophytes] who receive these sacraments [penance and the eucharist] two or three times in the course of the year." Francisco Lasuén, Memoranda, July 8, 1789, and February 28, 1791, in Kenneally, ed. and trans., *Writings of Fermín Francisco de Lasuén,* I, 193–194, 216–217. See also Hackel, *Children of Coyote, Missionaries of St. Francis.*

18. This discussion of Guido's system is derived, inter alia, from: Hughes, *Early Medieval Music,* vol. 2, 290–295; *Grove's Dictionary of Music and Musicians,* vol. 7, 879–881, vol. 7, 803–807; *The Norton/Grove Concise Encyclopedia of Music,* 662; Harman et al., *Man and His Music,* 35–37; Seay, *Music in the Medieval World,* 34–37.

19. On the Guidonian Hand see Thompson, *Music Through the Renaissance,* 34–37; *The New Grove Dictionary of Music and Musicians,* vol. 17, 458–462; *Grove's Dictionary of Music and Musicians,* vol. 3, 842–843; Palmer, "Mission San Antonio de Padua: A Tour of Its Music Room," 1–5.

20. Guido D'Arezzo quoted in Strunk, *Source Reading in Music History,* 124.

21. Elson, *Curiosities of Music,* 319.

22. Landon, "Seventeenth and Eighteenth Century English and Colonial American Music Texts," 36–47, 209–218.

23. Engelhardt, *Mission San Juan Bautista,* 131–132.

24. Da Silva, *Mission Music of California,* 6–7.

25. Material on Durán and the experiences at mission San José are from Narciso

Durán, "Prólogo ad Lectorem," Catholic Church, Liturgy, Ritual, MS C-C 59, Bancroft Library (BL). All subsequent Durán quotations on music in this chapter, unless otherwise specified, are from this source. While Da Silva's translation in *Mission Music of California*, 28–33, is generally fine, he chose to translate Durán's *responder* as "answer," but I think in this musical context "respond" is more accurate.

26. Ray and Engbeck, *Gloria Dei*, 11. On the diffusion of polyphony in Spanish California, see Summers, "Recently Recovered Manuscript Sources of Sacred Polyphonic Music from Spanish California," 13–30. For other examples of work attributed to Durán, see Catholic Church, Liturgy, Ritual, CC-59, BL, containing over 125 pieces including a "Misa pro infirmis," and other, unattributed, pieces in California Mission Music, CC-68, BL.

27. Da Silva, *Mission Music of California*, 117–118, is responsible for attributing the works to Durán and reproduces the Misa Viscaina, 35–53. See Summers, "The Misa Viscaína: An 18th Century Musical Odyssey to Alta California," 1–7, contains an extensive listing of his work and that of others. He also notes that de Jerusalem's polychoral Mass has been recorded in Mexico and is available through Urtext Digital Classics, Compact Disc #UMA2001.

28. Ray and Engbeck, *Gloria Dei*, 9.

29. Durán, "Prólogo."

30. Robinson, *Life in California*, 124.

31. José González Rubio to Joachim Adam, September 1864, cited in Neri, *Hispanic Catholicism in Transitional California*, 33–34, 35. McCarthy, *The History of Mission San Jose California*, 1797–1835, 228–234.

32. Engelhardt, *Mission Santa Bárbara*, 242.

33. Some of the important new works aimed at recovering the Spanish and Mexican music of California's past are: Summers, "The Spanish Origins of California Mission Music," 109–126; Summers, "Spanish Music in California, 1769–1840: A Reassessment," 360–380; Summers, "New and Little Known Sources of Hispanic Music from California," 13–24; Summers, "Letter to the Editor," *Latin American Music Review*, III (1981), 131–135; and Russell, "Newly Discovered Treasures from Colonial California: The Masses at the San Fernando Mission," 5–9.

34. Mariano Payeras to Estevan Tapis, January 13, 1810, in Cutter, trans. and ed., *Writings of Mariano Payeras*, 50

35. Engelhardt, *Mission Santa Inés*, 186.

36. Ray and Engbeck, *Gloria Dei*, 17; Da Silva, *Mission Music of California*, 21; Engelhardt, *Mission San Juan Bautista*, 41, 105–106, passim.

37. Da Silva, *Mission Music of California*, 21; Geiger, *Franciscan Missionaries in Hispanic California*, 19–24. Ray and Engbeck, *Gloria Dei*, 17, give an example of Arroyo de la Cuesta's setting of Mitsun to liturgical music.

38. Da Silva, *Mission Music of California*, 21; Vancouver, *A Voyage of Discovery*, III, 1110 and note 1. In 1819, Durán petitioned his superiors in Mexico for an organ to aid him in musical instruction at mission San José, but the threat of mission secularization prevented his being sent one. See Geiger, "Harmonious Notes in Spanish California," 243–248.

39. Ahlborn, "The Mission San Antonio Prayer and Songboard," 1–17. The artifact is in the Smithsonian Museum and is reproduced in a dark photograph in Ahlborn's essay.

40. Neuerburg, *The Decoration of the California Missions,* reproduces the artwork drawn by Father Estevan Tapis to embellish a prayerboard at mission San Juan Bautista; Webb, *Indian Life at the Old Missions,* page facing 239, depicts songbooks used at missions San Juan Bautista and Santa Inés; Ahlborn, "The Mission San Antonio Prayer and Songboard," 17.

41. No one discovered that they had been heard in California until 1992, when musicologist John Koegel found some of them in the archives of San Fernando mission. "It was beautiful music," Koegel said. "I heard the music in my mind as I turned the pages and here were all the parts of the instruments and the singers." As Koegel read the sheets, "he imagined the sounds of the 'Mass in D,' with trumpets, horns, oboes and all the fanfare of a battle Mass; the lyrical 'Mass in F,' which emphasizes woodwinds and gentle, heavenly tones." And he imagined the two-choir echoes of the joyful "Polychoral 'Mass in D,' which at times exults in combined voice and then breathlessly splits into light, complex lines that rush through chord progressions like a river rushes through rapids." John Koegel quoted in Abagail Goldman, "New Song from Old California," *Los Angeles Times,* February 25, 1995, A 1, 20. Selections from de Jerusalem's "Polychoral" Mass in D, including the Kyrie, Gloria, Credo, and Sanctus, can be heard on the compact disc entitled "Mexican Baroque" (TELDEK, 4509-96353-2, 1993) by Chanticleer, a San Francisco–based vocal group.

42. Da Silva, *Mission Music of California,* 22; Geiger, *Franciscan Missionaries in Hispanic California,* 124–125; Halpin, "Musical Activities and Ceremonies at Mission Santa Clara de Asís," 35–42. A similar Pastorela has been revived by the Santa Barbara Trust for Historic Preservation, which has sponsored its performance during the holiday season at the restored Santa Barbara presidio since the mid-1980s; personal communication with Jerald Jackman, director of the Santa Barbara Trust for Historic Preservation, October 17, 1987. I have used the term "choir organizer" instead of "choirmaster" because the Spanish used the latter to refer to the Indian leader of the choir.

43. Ray and Engbeck, *Gloria Dei,* 15; Da Silva, *Mission Music of California,* 6–10.

44. Ray and Engbeck, *Gloria Dei,* 15. A copy of the photograph is presented in Da Silva, *Mission Music of California,* plate 2, page facing 11.

45. Duflot de Mofras, *Travels on the Pacific Coast,* I, 221, indicates that the priest had purchased the uniforms from a French whaler. Halpin, "Musical Activities and Ceremonies at Mission Santa Clara de Asís," 36, 43n4, disputes "whaler" as the source and implies some other merchant vessel. Regardless, the same Frenchman may have sold the same uniform to other missions. See Ray and Engbeck, *Gloria Dei,* 18.

46. Geiger, *Mission Santa Barbara,* 98; Ray and Engbeck, *Gloria Dei,* 18.

47. Beilharz, *Felipe de Neve,* 64–65; Engelhardt, *San Gabriel Mission,* 43. Beginning in 1779, Governor Felipe de Neve created the posts of *alcalde* and *regidor,* two each, to be filled by mission Indians in preparation for the eventual secularization of the institutions. Both posts combined counted four men, annually elected, or about 10 percent of a full choir. See Hackel, "The Staff of Leadership: Indian Authority in the Missions of Alta California."

48. Durán, "Prólogo," 33.

49. Similarities with Kuksu secret societies among the Indians of the San Francisco Bay Area and the ?Antap cult among the Chumash from San Luis Obispo to Malibu are striking. See Bean, ed., *California Indian Shamanism,* and Bean and King, *?Antap: California Indian Political and Economic Organization.*

50. Vallejo, "Ranch and Mission Days in Alta California," 186. According to Sanchez, *Spanish Arcadia,* 398–399, Charles Howard Shinn wrote this essay from notes he obtained from Guadalupe Vallejo, daughter of Jesús and niece of Mariano.

51. Juan B. Alvarado quoted in Ray and Engbeck, *Gloria Dei,* 19.

52. Dale, *The Ashley-Smith Explorations,* 209–210; Engelhardt, *San Gabriel Mission,* 149–151, replicates the quoted passage but excludes Rogers's racist comment without ellipse. I have included it for its comparative value in assessing Indian performance of secular music.

53. Beechey, *An Account of a Visit to California,* 27.

54. Duhaut-Cilly, *A Voyage to California . . . by Auguste Duhaut-Cilly,* 86–87.

55. Le Netrel, *Voyage of the "Héros,"* 22–23. That women were singing suggests a congregational response to choir or priest-led intonation. Le Netrel's comments should be compared to those of Otto von Kotzebue, who visited the same mission a decade earlier and wrote: "The orchestra consisted of a violincello, a violin, and two flutes; these instruments were played by little half-naked Indians and they were very often out of tune." Von Kotzebue, *A Voyage of Discovery into the South Sea,* I, 280–281. Church music performance at San Francisco, and at the other missions, had improved in the intervening decade.

56. Botta, *Observations on the Inhabitants of California,* 8–9.

57. Basso, "Amusia," 391–409.

58. A discussion of music might fruitfully begin with the way the brain perceives pitches. If middle A is sounded on a piano, a complex set of oscillations or waves is transmitted through air to the ear, the frequencies of which consist of the lowest, or "fundamental," in this case 440 Hertz (Hz) and related higher frequencies, or "harmonics," such as 880, 1320, 1760 Hz, etc. The sound receptors in the ear break down musical and other complex audio stimuli into their component frequencies and forward them separately into the auditory system. The brain then makes a "map" of these frequencies and constructs the perception of pitch from this information. This process has been demonstrated experimentally by deleting the fundamental frequency while retaining the harmonics. Test subjects perceived the missing fundamental frequency. Pitch, then, is "constructed" by the brain; it is the psychological perception elicited when a note is sung or sounded on a musical instrument. The frequency map, and thus pitch itself, has been found to lie in the auditory cortex of the brain. See "A Few Notes on Pitch," *Musica,* I (Spring 1994), 3. See also Janata et al., "The Cortical Topography of Tonal Structures Underlying Western Music," 2167–2170.

59. Trehub and Thorpe, "Infants' Perception of Rhythm," 217–229; "The Musical Infant," *Musica,* I (Spring 1994), 1, 6. Zatorre and Krumhansl, "Mental Models and Musical Minds," 2138–2139.

60. Peretz and Morais, "Specificity for Music," 373–390; Petsche et al., "EEG Co-

herence and Musical Thinking," 117–151; Peretz, "Processing of Local and Global Musical Information by Unilateral Brain-Damaged Patients," 1185–1205.

61. Peery and Peery, "The Role of Music in Child Development," 5.

62. Peery and Peery, "The Role of Music in Child Development," 8.

63. Polk and Kertesz, "Music and Language in Degenerative Disease of the Brain," 99; Peery and Peery, "The Role of Music in Child Development," 5.

64. The more a person knows about a particular kind of music or a particular musical piece, the more that person can play that music mentally in his or her head. This facility is called imagining music or inner hearing; in it the musician hears the tones, rhythms, beat, and contour in the brain, increasing coherent transfer of information between hemispheres. See Petsche et al., "EEG Coherence and Musical Thinking," 117–151.

65. Peery and Peery, "The Role of Music in Child Development," 12–13.

66. Rauscher, Shaw, and Ky, "Music and Spatial Task Performance," 611. For a summary of the controversy see "On the Importance of Being Accurate," *Musica* V (Spring 1998), 6. The primary issue is the length of exposure to music over time in its ability to change spatial reasoning. Not surprisingly, the greater the temporal exposure, the more reliable the transfer.

67. Hackel, "Land, Labor, and Production," 124.

68. The same approach today is called using music as a "structural prompt" for teaching and learning nonmusic information. The "ABC" song, set to the melody of "Twinkle Twinkle Little Star," used to teach the alphabet in schools and on television, is a familiar example of the "structural prompt." So also is teaching children to learn their telephone number, or even a series of telephone numbers, by setting them to music. See Wolfe and Hom, "Use of Melodies as Structural Prompts for Learning and Retention of Sequential Verbal Information by Preschool Students," 100–118. Another example, related to the advice columnist Ann Landers, described teaching a three-year-old to sing her address as an aid to finding her parents if lost. See the column in *Redlands Daily Facts*, August 23, 1995.

69. Geiger and Meighan, ed. and trans., *As the Padres Saw Them*, 53–55; Kenneally, ed. and trans., *Writings of Fermín Francisco de Lasuén*, I, 193, 195, 216–217.

70. Graham, "Music and the Learning of Language in Early Childhood," 177–183. See also, "Can Music Really Improve the Mind? The Question of Transfer Effects," *Musica* VI (Spring 1999), 3–4, 7.

71. Geiger and Meighan, ed. and trans., *As the Padres Saw Them*, 20, 35–37, 39–41, 133–137. Barth, "Franciscan Education and the Social Order in Spanish North America, 1502–1821," 152. Barth sees the absence of secular education in the missions of Upper California as an exception to normal Franciscan practice. He notes further that "Engelhardt seem[ed] to rationalize the absence of formal reading and writing schools by declaring that the friars came as missionaries."

72. Eades, "Dimensions of Meaning," 196.

73. Monelle, *Linguistics and Semiotics in Music*, 17.

74. A principle inherent in mission music instruction and the subject of much discussion is the semiotics of music circles. The overall applicability of semiotics to a study of plainchant is limited, however, since most semioticians prefer to begin with the piano and

Mozart but will allow the keyboard and Bach, none of which is directly relevant to Alta California. See,Tarasti, *A Theory of Musical Semiotics,* 3–111; and Monelle, *Linguistics and Semiotics in Music.* Historian turned semiotician William Pencak, in an intriguing article of the same name, poses the question "Of What Is Music a Sign?" Pencak seeks to answer that question by studying three modern composers/conductors/listeners: Arturo Toscanini (1867–1957), Wilhelm Fürtwangler (1886–1954), and Bruno Walter (1876–1962). Pencak concludes with a mixed answer. See Pencak, *History, Signing In,* 289–306.

75. Hurwitz et al., "Nonmusical Effects of the Kodaly Music Curriculum in Primary Grade Children," 45–51.

76. Lasuén, Memorandum, February 28, 1791, in Kenneally, ed. and trans., *Writings of Fermín Francisco de Lasuén,* I, 217. See also, Sanchez, *Spanish Arcadia,* 205–206.

77. Sandos, "Levantamiento!" 109–134. Beebe and Senkewicz, "The End of the 1824 Chumash Revolt in Alta California," 273–283, contains the quote about Jaime from the father president of the California missions who accompanied the military pursuit of the runaways and who negotiated their surrender. Chumash oral tradition also identifies Jaime as "a doctor, singer, and teacher." See Hudson, "The Chumash Revolt of 1824," 124.

78. Abbot, *Santa Ines Hermosa,* 72–79.

79. University of Redlands choirmaster, Jeffrey Rickard, has noted that choirs take on distinct personalities and that workshops on church music invariably produce vulgar or profane versions of what has been taught. One that seems to recur in his experience is the song about five constipated men in the Bible. A sample lyric goes: "The first constipated man in the Bible was Cain, because he was not Abel (able)."

80. Duflot de Mofras, *Travels on the Pacific Coast,* I, 221. When recalling the incident later in his account (II, 14), Duflot de Mofras claims that the choir sang "La Marseillaise" during Mass at Mission Santa Clara, a different version from the first, and probably inaccurate, because the first is detailed and precise, the second a mention in passing while describing the enthusiasm of a Russian for the song, prompting the Frenchman to write "*Marseillaise,* why do you haunt me so?"

81. Ray and Engbeck, *Gloria Dei,* 17–18.

82. *The California Missions: A Pictorial History,* 87. The photograph was taken in 1903.

83. Stevenson, *Across the Plains,* 106.

84. Tac, "Indian Life and Customs at Mission San Luis Rey," 95; César, "Recollections of My Youth at San Luis Rey Mission," 42; Castillo, "An Indian Account of the Decline and Collapse of Mexico's Hegemony Over the Missionized Indians of California," 394; Librado, *Breath of the Sun,* 48, 49, 53, 55, 65, 74; Johnson, "The Indians of Mission San Fernando," 50; Jackson, "Notes on Rujero Rocha," HEHL; and Saunders and O'Sullivan, *Capistrano Nights,* 50–52. For an example of an Indian chorister who left no recorded story, and there must be many of them, see the account of "Old Silvestre" of Mission San José in McCarthy, *The History of Mission San Jose, California, 1797–1835,* 323–324. According to oral tradition at the mission, Silvestre possessed a "sweet voice" and "played excellently on both the violin and guitar."

85. My calculations are as follows. Indian choristers number 30–40. Those whom they directly affect are from the family consisting of: parents (1–2), siblings (1–2), and cousins

(1–2). Fictive kinship relations would include godparent (1) and confirmation sponsor (1). These total 5–8. Using the lower figure to correct for population loss from disease (5) then 30 choristers influenced 150, and if the higher extended family figure is used (8) then those choristers influenced 240. Since the choristers must be included in any final figure, the total numbers ranged from 180 to 270 for a choir of 30 men and boys. For a 40-member choir, the influence range would have been from 200 (40 × 5) to 320 (40 × 8). Again the choristers must be added to these numbers to yield a final figure of 240–360. If I use the lowest total figure for the 30- and 40-member choirs, that is, 180 and 240, and compare it to peak neophyte population at an individual mission, then we find that 180 represents 21 percent of San Carlos's 868 peak, 36 percent of Santa Cruz's 507 peak, and 16 percent of San Juan Bautista's 1,112 peak. When I apply 240, we find that represents 12 percent of San José's 1,886 peak, 8 percent of San Luis Rey's 2,848 peak, and 14 percent of San Gabriel's 1,707 peak. The average of the percentages is 18, so that my figure of 10 percent is conservative and 15 percent more likely. Also note that this estimate is for choristers and their families only and makes no attempt to calculate the impact these choirs doubtless had on others who observed and heard them. On size of the mission choirs see Ray and Engbeck, *Gloria Dei,* 15; Da Silva, *Mission Music of California,* 6–10. Guadalupe Vallejo, "Ranch and Mission Days in Alta California," 186, claimed that every Indian family sought to have a member in the choir. Geiger, *Mission Santa Barbara,* 32, gives the figure of one godparent per child. Peak mission populations are from Bowman, "The Resident Neophytes (*Existentes*) of the California Missions, 1769–1834," 145–148.

Chapter 10. Indian Resistance to Missionization

1. Tac, "Studio garammaticali sulla lingua della California, ca. 1835," mss. HL. Tac titled his study "Conversión de los San Luiseños de la Alta California," but it is not accessioned under that title, so I will use the Italian short title "Studio garammaticali." Hewes and Hewes, eds., "Indian Life and Customs at Mission San Luis Rey," 87–106, is a generally fine and accessible English translation of a published Italian version. Where I differ from their translation, I cite the Italian title at the Huntington Library. The Heweses also discuss briefly Agapito Amamix, another Luiseño youth who accompanied Tac to Rome but died in 1837, four years earlier than Tac. The term "Fernandino" refers to Spanish Franciscans from the Missionary College of San Fernando in Mexico City who staffed the Alta California missions exclusively from 1769 to 1827. See Neri, *Hispanic Catholicism in Transitional California,* 20–21.

2. Hewes and Hewes, "Indian Life and Customs," 94, 106.

3. Basso, *Portraits of "the Whiteman,"* 8–12.

4. Tac, "Studio garammaticali," 863, in which Tac uses "cuervo," and it is more accurate within Luiseño folklore to translate this as "raven" rather than as "crow."

5. Boscana, *Chinigchinich,* 80.

6. Osio, *The History of Alta California: A Memoir of Mexican California,* 68. This is, in general, an excellently translated and superbly annotated edition of an important early California manuscript by Rose Marie Beebe and Robert M. Senkewicz. My translation follows theirs, but with differences. The copy of the original version of Osio's account

that I used, entitled "Crónica de los acontecimientos ocurridos en California desde 1815 hasta 1846," p. 78, copiado por Gulielmo B. Chase, 1876, and called the Doyle Version after John Doyle for whom it was made, is at the Huntington Library. Although the Doyle copy is corrupt in spots, this account is not and accurately reflects the *tu* rather than the *usted* usage first provided in the original.

7. No one has done more over the past two decades to bring forward data on Indian resistance than Edward D. Castillo, a descendant of missionized Indians (Cahuilla-Luiseño). See his "The Impact of Euro-American Exploration and Settlement," 99–127; *Native American Perspectives on the Hispanic Colonization of Alta California;* "Neophyte Resistance and Accommodation in the Missions of California," 60–75. Additional works by Castillo are cited in other notes. An early work by George Harwood Phillips, "Indians and the Breakdown of the Spanish Mission System in California," 291–302, contributed significantly to understanding subtle patterns of resistance. Phillips, *Indians and Intruders in Central California, 1769–1849,* argues that Indians in the interior after 1810 engaged in "defensive resistance" to the Spanish and after 1830 initiated "active resistance." Philips does not clearly define these concepts nor does he apply them to mission Indians. See the review of Phillips's book by James A. Sandos in *American Indian Quarterly* 18 (Spring 1994): 266–267. Jackson and Castillo, *Indians, Franciscans, and Spanish Colonization: The Impact of the Mission System on California Indians,* 73–86, try to distinguish among primary and secondary, passive and active resistance, but, as they indicate on page 73 in discussing primary and secondary, "There was no clear discontinuity between the two forms of resistance." On the conceptual problems plaguing analysis of mission Indian resistance see Sandos, "Neophyte Resistance in the Alta California Missions," 170–178. Study of Indian resistance to European colonization has been more sophisticated in other parts of the Spanish Borderlands, as a perusal of David Hurst Thomas's three volumes of invited essays in *Columbian Consequences* reveals.

8. Bolton, "The Mission as a Frontier Institution in the Spanish American Colonies," 44–45.

9. Scott, *Domination and the Arts of Resistance: Hidden Transcripts,* xi and passim.

10. On Indian assaults against Spanish animals see, for example, Serra's January 12, 1780, comment that "about three days ago, in full light of day, and inside the mission compound, a number of gentiles shot some cattle with arrows," in Tibesar, ed., *Writings of Junípero Serra,* III, 421. See also Mason, "Fages' Code of Conduct Toward Indians, 1787," 97. On animals being released in Indian cultivated fields see Shipek, "California Indian Reactions to the Franciscans," 482–484.

11. Bancroft, *History of California,* II, 387–389. For an example of agreement with the public transcript see Engelhardt, *Missions and Missionaries of California,* III, 12–16.

12. Castillo, "The Assassination of Padre Andrés Quintana by the Indians of Mission Santa Cruz in 1812: The Narrative of Lorenzo Asisara," 117–125, 150–152. For a dissenting view see Nunis, "California Mission Indians: Two Perspectives," 207–212, 236–238, and Castillo's reply, 212–215, 238. For another Spanish view see Chapman, "Early Days at Mission Santa Clara: Recollections of Nasario Galindo," 101–111.

13. Milliken, "An Ethnohistory of the Indian People of the San Francisco Bay Area from 1770 to 1810," 2, 23. Milliken's dissertation has been published as *A Time of Little Choice.*

14. Bancroft, *History of California*, I, 590 ff.

15. Starr, *Inventing the Dream*, 58.

16. Bancroft, *History of California*, I, 711n33. A slightly different version of this document, including the depositions of eleven additional Indians along with tribal affiliation and mission register data for all, can be found in Milliken, *Time of Little Choice*, 299–303.

17. Bancroft, *History of California*, I, 711–712. Father President Lasuén publicly defended Danti against charges of cruelty toward Indians, but then he rarely found any substance to such Indian complaints. See Geiger, *Franciscan Missionaries in Hispanic California*, 61–63. For Lasuén's private views and actions to remove Danti see Beebe and Senkewicz, *Tensions among the Missionaries in the 1790s*, 2–13.

18. Tibesar, ed., *Writings of Junípero Serra*, III, 409.

19. Cook, *The Conflict Between the California Indian and White Civilization*, 61.

20. Bancroft, *History of California*, II, 34–35; Geiger, *Franciscan Missionaries in Hispanic California*, 57–61; Milliken, *Time of Little Choice*, 186–189, 313–314.

21. Bancroft, *History of California*, I, 208–209; Engelhardt, *Mission San Luis Obispo in the Valley of the Bears*, 18–19. On the sequencing of the fires see Geiger, *Palóu's Life of Fray Junípero Serra*, 410n20. Also on 410n21 Geiger argues that the use of roof tiles began slightly earlier at mission San Antonio.

22. Bancroft, *History of California*, II, 150–151.

23. For an example of a rumored Indian conspiracy against Mission San Carlos instigated by an unhappy neophyte see Bancroft, *History of California*, II, 146–147. For suspected poisoning episodes at missions San Miguel and San Diego see Bancroft, *History of California*, II, 149–150, 344–345. For a discussion of these episodes see Nunis, "California Mission Indians: Two Perspectives," 207–208, 236–237.

24. Beechey, *An Account of a Visit to California, 1826–1827*, 32.

25. Kenneally, ed. and trans., *Writings of Fermín Francisco de Lasuén*, II, 207, 212–213. Hackel, "Land, Labor, and Production," 126–127, calls this activity "covert informal labor."

26. Tibesar, ed., *Writings of Junípero Serra*, III, 67, 75, 143, 253.

27. In 1786 a mission Santa Clara Indian named Plácido Ortiz, originally from Baja California and part of the initial occupation accompanying the Franciscans, accused Fray Tomás de la Peña of having killed neophyte Sixto Antonio, an irrigation worker, by striking him in the head with the very hoe Sixto used to clean the irrigation ditches. The charges against Peña eventually amounted to four Indians he allegedly had murdered. Ten years of investigation revealed that Sixto had died of disease, Peña had not touched him except to administer sacraments, and Plácido had become disgruntled with Peña because the priest had relieved him of the keys to the storeroom because the priest found that Plácido had abused his trust by engaging in graft. Plácido used his position to bribe witnesses against the priest. Peña suffered physically from the ongoing legal struggle against the charges and left California in August 1794. A year later he was cleared of all charges. See Kenneally, ed. and trans., *Writings of Fermín Francisco de Lasuén*, I, 109–137, 148–149, 184, 306–311, 348–349. See also Guest, *Fermín Francisco de Lasuén*, 159–172.

28. On the Franciscan opinion of Indians as lazy and intellectually limited, see Rudkin,

The First French Expedition to California, 96–97; Vancouver, *A Voyage of Discovery to the North Pacific and Around the World,* II, 714; Langsdorff, *Langsdorff's Narrative of the Rezanov Voyage to Nueva California in 1806,* 62; Choris, *San Francisco One Hundred Years Ago,* 11; Rudkin, *Camille de Roquefeuil in San Francisco, 1817–1818,* 71; and Bandini, *A Description of California in 1828,* 7. Failure to learn a new language, or feigning such ignorance, is an old trick of resistance and caused Eric Hobsbawm to claim that "the refusal to understand is a form of class struggle." Hobsbawm quoted in Scott, *Domination and the Arts of Resistance,* 133n46.

29. Sandos, "Christianization among the Chumash," 65–89.

30. Sandos, "Neophyte Resistance," 173.

31. Neuerburg, "Indians as Artists in California before and after Contact with the Europeans," 43–60, quoted at 47. This is a "much revised version" of Georgia Lee and Norman Neuerburg, "The Alta California Indians as Artists before and after Contact," 467–480. See also Neuerburg, "Indian Pictographs at Mission San Juan Capistrano," 55–58.

32. Neuerburg, "Indians as Artists," 47. For the image see Boscana, *Chinigchinich,* page facing 58.

33. Neuerburg, "Indians as Artists," 48. On the choirloft at mission San Miguel see Baer, *Architecture of the California Missions,* 60.

34. As has been presented in Chapters 3–6, although customary Franciscan practice was to baptize no more gentiles than they could feed, Serra disagreed and encouraged more baptizing. Much of the fuel for the argument that Franciscans carefully balanced baptisms against food resources can be found in the work of anthropologists Gary Coombs and Fred Plog. See their "Chumash Baptism: An Ecological Perspective," 137–53; and "The Conversion of the Chumash Indians: An Ecological Interpretation," 309–328. The evidence does not support their thesis. See Sandos, "Christianization among the Chumash," 68–70. See also Jackson and Castillo, *Indians, Franciscans, and Spanish Colonization,* 172n22. Coombs and Plog's flawed arguments have influenced others as evidenced in Larson, Johnson, and Michaelson, "Missionization among the Coastal Chumash of Central California," 263–299.

35. Milliken, "An Ethnohistory of the Indian People," 202–206.

36. Calculation derived from Johnson, "Chumash Social Organization: An Ethnohistoric Perspective," 88.

37. Castañeda, "Sexual Violence in the Politics and Policies of Conquest," 15–33.

38. Castillo, "Gender Status Decline, Resistance, and Accommodation among Female Neophytes in the Missions of California," 67–93, especially 78–81. Lepowsky, "Indian Revolts and Cargo Cults."

39. Sandos, "Christianization among the Chumash," 73–74; Heizer, "A California Messianic Movement of 1801 among the Chumash," 128–129.

40. See Reid, "New Era in Mission Affairs," 87, for San Gabriel; Geiger, *Letter of Luís Jayme, O.F.M., San Diego, October, 17, 1772,* 42–44, for San Diego. Kenneally, ed. and trans., *Writings of Fermín Francisco de Lasuén,* II, 378; Sandos, "Neophyte Resistance," 174–175.

41. Mason, "Fages' Code of Conduct Toward Indians, 1787," 94. See also Engstrand, "The Role of the *Comisionado* in Spanish California," 13–18. On female witchcraft, the

Toypurina uprising, and the Chumash 1801 revitalization movement see Castañeda, "Engendering the History of Alta California, 1769–1848," 235–237, and Lepowsky, "Indian Revolts and Cargo Cults."

42. In revenge, the Gabrielino capitan joined with the Catalina capitan to murder the two sorcerers (*hechiceros*). See Hudson, "A Rare Account of Gabrielino Shamanism from the Notes of John P. Harrington," 356–362.

43. Blackburn, "The Chumash Revolt of 1824," 223–227.

44. Harrington, "A New Original Version of Boscana," 41–42.

45. Hudson et al., *The Eye of the Flute,* 85–87.

46. Tac, "Studio garammaticali," 64–65. The Heweses divided this long enumeration into two sentences and omitted Tac's original capitalization, which I have retained here because it more forcefully conveys the Indian's sense of mission hierarchy. The rest of the list enumerates mission landholdings and the size of the herds.

47. Hewes and Hewes, "Indian Life and Customs," 99.

48. Tibesar, ed., *Writings of Junípero Serra,* III, 408–409, 420–421, 462n256. See also Hackel, "The Staff of Leadership," 364–366. The alcalde's whip at mission San Gabriel was braided as thick as a man's wrist, see Phillips, "The Alcaldes," 85.

49. Hackel, "Indian-Spanish Relations in Alta California," 202 and passim.

50. The best account remains Brown, "Pomponio's World," 1–20. He was apparently a Coast Miwok from Bolinas whose Indian name was Lúppuh-éyum. Vallejo, "Historical and Personal Memoirs," I, 106–112. See also, Alvarado, *Vignettes of Early California,* 33–39. When Duhaut-Cilly heard the story he thought that Pomponio had cut off both his heels to escape; see *A Voyage to California, the Sandwich Islands and Around the World in the Years 1826–1829,* 93.

51. Dmytryshyn and Crownhart-Vaughan, *Colonial Russian America,* 130.

52. In addition to the fight the Chumash waged at La Purísima and the flight to the *tulares,* other Chumash took Mission Santa Barbara's two oceangoing plank canoes (*tomols*) and fled to the Channel Islands. Yet others among those who fled initially to the tulares went farther inland into what is now Kern County in the area later called Walker Pass, where they fused Spanish and traditional ways to form a new culture. See Sandos, "Levantamiento!" 109–133. See also Sandos, "Christianization among the Chumash," 76–86.

53. My reconstruction of Estanislao's revolt is derived from Cook, "Expeditions to the Interior of California: Central Valley, 1820–1840," 168–180, 205–206; Osio, *The History of Alta California,* 89–94; Orsi, "Estanislao's Rebellion, 1829," 53–68; Rosenus, *General M. G. Vallejo,* 11–12. See also McCarthy, *The History of Mission San José California, 1797–1835,* 201–217, 260–262. Mexicans later called "Estanislao" the branch of the river where they had fought the rebel. With Americanization the river became known as the Stanislaus, and later, when the county was created, it was named for the river.

54. Phillips, *Indians and Intruders,* 65–106, which also incorporates his earlier work on Indians and secularization; Hutchinson, "The Mexican Government and the Missions of Upper California, 1821–1835," 335–362; Servin, "The Secularization of the California Missions," 133–149.

Chapter 11. Assessing California's Missions

1. Bolton, "The Mission as a Frontier Institution in the Spanish American Colonies," 42–61.

2. Sandos, "Junípero Serra's Canonization and the Historical Record," 1253–1262.

3. See note 5 in the Introduction.

4. Margolin, *Monterey in 1786*, 77–80n9. La Pérouse gave the population figure of 701, whereas Bowman, "The Resident Neophytes of the California Missions," 145, calculated 694.

5. Petit-Thouars, *Voyage of the* Venus, 5.

6. Stevenson, *Across the Plains*, 106–107. Stevenson is perhaps best known as the author of *Treasure Island*.

7. Francisco García Diego y Moreno to José Figueroa, June 30, 1833, cited and translated in Cook, *The Conflict Between the California Indian and White Civilization*, 129–130. Bancroft, *History of California*, III, 322, cites July 4, 1833, "Carta Pastoral a los padres Zacatecanos contra la costumbre de azotar a los indios," in which García Diego y Moreno tells his fellow Franciscans, "Mi genio, mis ideas, mi sensibilidad, todo junto se opone a esta costumbre que jamás aprobaré." On García Diego y Moreno, who became California's first bishop, see Geiger, *Franciscan Missionaries in Hispanic California*, 98–103.

8. Calculations are based on the figures cited in Chapter 1.

9. Sandos, "Junípero Serra's Canonization and the Historical Record," 1258–1259; Sandos, "Junípero Serra, Canonization, and the California Indian Controversy," 321–329.

10. Archibald, "Indian Labor at the California Missions Slavery or Salvation," 180.

11. See McNeill, *Keeping Together in Time*, passim.

12. White, "Luiseño Social Organization," 136–137, emphasis in the original.

13. See my discussion of the work of anthropologist John Peabody Harrington in Sandos, "Levantamiento!" 109–110, 130nn4–7. See also Sandos, "Christianization among the Chumash," 65–89.

14. Weber, *The Spanish Frontier in North America*, 115.

15. Hurtado, *Indian Survival on the California Frontier*, 1, summarizes the figures derived by Sherburne F. Cook. Sandos, " 'Because He Is a Liar and a Thief,' " 96, cites them also.

16. Hauptman, *Tribes and Tribulations*, 3–14, 123–127.

17. Starr, *Inventing the Dream*, 58.

18. Sandos, "Junípero Serra's Canonization and the Historical Record," 1253; Sandos, "Junípero Serra, Canonization, and the California Indian Controversy," 313–315. Serra's was not the first cause for sainthood advanced from California. Magín Catalá, Franciscan missionary at Santa Clara renowned for his holiness, was first advocated in 1882 by the Jesuits who had taken over Santa Clara. Engelhardt, *The Holy Man of Santa Clara or Life, Virtues, and Miracles of Fr. Magín Catalá, O.F.M.*, is the published version of the hagiography for sainthood that Engelhardt had prepared. The case has quietly dropped from view since the advent of the Serra cause. See Engelhardt's diary for 1909 in *Provincial Annals of Santa Barbara* (April, July 1941). Geiger, *Franciscan Missionaries in Hispanic California*, 42–46.

Bibliography

The American Medical Association Encyclopedia of Medicine. New York: Random House, 1989.

The American Medical Association Family Medical Guide. New York: Random House, 1982.

The Columbia University College of Physicians and Surgeons Complete Home Medical Guide. New York: Crown, 1985.

The Modern Medical Encyclopedia. New York: Golden Press, 1965.

New Catholic Encyclopedia. New York: McGraw-Hill, 1967.

The New Complete Medical and Health Encyclopedia. Chicago: J. G. Ferguson, 1990.

The New Grove Dictionary of Music and Musicians. New York: Macmillan, 1993.

The Norton/Grove Concise Encyclopedia of Music. New York: Norton, 1988.

Abbot, Marie Goulet. *Santa Ines Hermosa: The Journal of a Padre's Niece.* Montecito, Calif.: Sunwise Press, 1951.

Agreda, María de, *City of God*, 4 vols., trans. Fiscar Marison (George J. Blatter). Washington, N.J.: Ave Maria Institute, 1971.

———. *Mystica Ciudad de Dios . . . , 3 Tomos.* Madrid: Imprenta de la Casus de la V. Madre, 1744.

Ahlborn, Richard E. "The Mission San Antonio Prayer and Song Board." *Southern California Quarterly* 74 (1992): 1–17.

Allen, Rebecca. *Native Americans at Mission Santa Cruz, 1791–1834: Interpreting the Archaeological Record.* Los Angeles: Institute of Archaeology, University of California, Los Angeles, 1998.

Alva, Bartolomé de. *A Guide to Confession Large and Small in the Mexican Language, 1634*, ed. Barry D. Sell and John Frederick Schwaller. Norman: University of Oklahoma Press, 1999.

Alvarado, Juan Bautista. *Vignettes of Early California: Childhood Reminiscences of Juan Bautista Alvarado*, trans. John H. R. Polt. San Francisco: Book Club of California, 1982.

Anderson, M., Kat Michael, J. Barbour, and Valerie Whitworth. "A World of Balance and Plenty: Land, Plants, Animals, and Humans, in a Pre-Conquest California," in *Contested Eden: California Before the Gold Rush*, eds. Ramón Gutiérrez and Richard J. Orsi, 12–47. Berkeley: University of California Press, 1998.

Applegate, Richard B. *?Atishwin: The Dream Helper in South-Central California*. Socorro, N.M.: Ballena Press, 1978.

——. "The Datura Cult among the Chumash." *Journal of California Anthropology* 2 (1975): 7–17.

Archibald, Robert. *The Economic Aspects of the California Missions*. Washington, D.C.: Academy of American Franciscan History, 1978.

——. "Indian Labor at the California Missions: Slavery or Salvation?" *Journal of San Diego History* 24 (1979): 172–182.

Arriaga, Julián de. "Reglamento e Instrucción para los Presidios Que Se Han de Formar en la Línea de Frontera de la Nueva España, 10 Septiembre 1772," in *Lancers for the King: A Study of the Frontier Military System of Northern New Spain, with a Translation of the Royal Regulations of 1772*, trans. Sidney B. Brinkerhoff and Odie B. Faulk, 11–67. Phoenix: Arizona Historical Foundation, 1965.

Baer, Kurt. *Architecture of the California Missions*. Berkeley: University of California Press, 1958.

——. "California Indian Art." *The Americas* 16 (July 1959): 23–44.

Baker, Brenda J., and George J. Armelagos. "The Origin and Antiquity of Syphilis: Paleopathological Diagnosis and Interpretation." *Current Anthropology* 29 (1988): 703–738.

Baker, Robert W., and Mark A. Peppercorn. "Enteric Diseases of Homosexual Men." *Pharmacotherapy* 2 (1982): 32–42.

Bancroft, Hubert Howe. *History of California*, 4 vols. San Francisco: Various Publishers, 1884–1886.

Bandini, José. *A Description of California in 1828 by José Bandini*, trans. Doris Marion Wright. Berkeley, Calif.: Friends of the Bancroft Library, 1951.

Bankmann, Ulf. "A Prussian in Mexican California: Ferdinand Deppe, Horticulturist, Collector for European Museums, Trader and Artist." *Southern California Quarterly* 84 (2002): 1–32.

Barth, Joseph Pius. "Franciscan Education and the Social Order in Spanish North America, 1502–1821." PhD diss., University of Chicago, 1945.

Basso, Anna. "Amusia," in *Handbook of Neuropsychology*, eds. H. Spindler and F. Boller, 391–409, vol. 8. Amsterdam: Elsevier Science Publishers, 1993.

Basso, Keith. *Portraits of "the Whiteman": Linguistic Play and Cultural Symbols among the Western Apache*. Cambridge: Cambridge University Press, 1979.

Bean, Lowell John, ed. *California Indian Shamanism*. Menlo Park, Calif.: Ballena Press, 1992.

Bean, Lowell, and Thomas Blackburn, eds. *Native Californians: A Theoretical Perspective*. Socorro, N.M.: Ballena Press, 1976.

———. "Social Organization," in *California*, ed. Robert F. Heizer, 673–682. *Handbook of North American Indians*, gen. ed. William Sturtevant, vol. 8. Washington, D.C.: Smithsonian Institution, 1978.

Bean, Lowell John, and Thomas F. King, eds. *?Antap: California Indian Political and Economic Organization*. Ramona: Ballena Press, 1974.

Bean, Lowell John, and Sylvia Brakke Vane. "California Religious Systems and Their Transformation," in *California Indian Shamanism*, ed. Lowell John Bean, 33–51. Menlo Park, Calif.: Ballena Press, 1992.

Beebe, Rose Marie, and Robert M. Senkewicz. "The End of the 1824 Chumash Revolt in Alta California: Father Vicente Sarría's Account." *The Americas* 53 (1996): 273–283.

———. *Tensions among the Missionaries in the 1790s*. Bakersfield, Calif.: California Mission Studies Association, 1996.

———. "Uncertainty on the Mission Frontier: Missionary Recruitment and Institutional Stability in Alta California in the 1790s," in *The Franciscan Experience in the Americas*, ed. Fritz Schwaller. Berkeley: Academy of American Franciscan History, 2004.

Beechey, Frederick W. *An Account of a Visit to California, 1826–1827*, introduction by Edith M. Coulter. San Francisco: Grabhorn Press, 1941.

Beeler, Madison S., ed. *The Ventureño Confesionario of José Señán, O.F.M.* Berkeley: University of California Press, 1967.

Beilharz, Edwin A. *Felipe de Neve: First Governor of California*. San Francisco: California Historical Society, 1971.

Bell, Horace. *Reminiscences of a Ranger: Of Early Times in Southern California*. Los Angeles: Yarnell, Caystile & Mathes Printer, 1881.

Black, Francis L. "Infectious Diseases in Primitive Societies." *Science* 187 (1975): 515–518.

Blackburn, Thomas. "The Chumash Revolt of 1824: A Native Account." *Journal of California Anthropology* 2 (1975): 223–227.

———. *December's Child: A Book of Chumash Oral Narratives*. Berkeley: University of California Press, 1975.

Blackburn, Thomas, and M. Kat Anderson, eds. *Before the Wilderness: Environmental Management by Native Californians*. Menlo Park, Calif.: Ballena Press, 1993.

Blom, Eric, ed. *Grove's Dictionary of Music and Musicians*, 5th edition. London: Macmillan, 1954.

Blanco S., Antonio. *La Lengua Española en la Historia de California*. Madrid: Ediciones Cultura Hispanoamérica, 1971.

Bolton, Herbert E. "The Mission as a Frontier Institution in the Spanish American Colonies." *American Historical Review* 22 (1917): 42–61.

———. *The Spanish Borderlands: A Chronicle of Old Florida and the Southwest*. New Haven: Yale University Press, 1921.

———, trans. and ed. *Font's Complete Diary: A Chronicle of the Founding of San Francisco*. Berkeley: University of California Press, 1931.

———, trans. and ed. *Fray Juan Crespi: Missionary Explorer on the Pacific Coast*. Berkeley: University of California Press, 1927.

——, trans. and ed., *Historical Memoires of New California by Fray Francisco Palóu,* O.F.M. 4 vols. Berkeley: University of California Press, 1926.

Borah, Woodrow W. "The California Mission," in *Ethnic Conflict in California History,* ed. Charles Wallenberg, 3–16. Los Angeles: Tinnon-Brown, 1970.

——. *New Spain's Century of Depression.* Berkeley: University of California Press, 1951.

Boscana, Gerónimo. *Chinigchinich: Historical Account of the Belief, Usage, Customs and Extravagancies of the Indians of This Mission of San Juan Capistrano Called the Acagchemem Tribe,* trans. Alfred Robinson, ann. John P. Harrington. Banning, Calif.: Malki Museum Press, 1978.

Bossy, John. "The Mass as a Social Institution, 1200–1700." *Past and Present* 100 (1983): 29–61.

——. "The Social History of Confession in the Age of Reformation." *Transactions of the Royal Historical Society,* fifth series 25 (1975): 21–38.

Botta, Paolo Emilio. *Observations on the Inhabitants of California, 1827–1828,* trans. John Francis Bricca. Los Angeles: Glen Dawson, 1952.

Bowman, J. N. "The Resident Neophytes (Existentes) of the California Missions, 1769–1834." *Historical Society of Southern California Quarterly* 40 (1958): 138–148.

Bowman, Mary M. "Christmas in Old Los Angeles, and Los Pastores a Miracle Play." *Bowman Scrapbook,* vol. 3, Santa Barbara Mission Archive Library.

Braunstein, Baruch. *The Chuetas of Majorca: Conversos and the Inquisition of Majorca.* New York: KTAV Publishing House, 1972.

Brinckerhoff, Sidney B., and Odie B. Faulk. *Lancers for the King: A Study of the Frontier Military System of Northern New Spain, with a Translation of the Royal Regulations of 1772.* Phoenix: Arizona Historical Foundation, 1965.

Brown, Alan K. "Pomponio's World." *Argonaut* 6, San Francisco Corral of Westerners (May 1975): 1–20.

Brown, William J., James F. Donohue, Norman W. Axnick, Joseph H. Blount, Neal H. Ewen, and Oscar G. Jones. *Syphilis and Other Venereal Diseases.* Cambridge: Harvard University Press, 1970.

Burrus, Ernest J. "The Author of the Mexican Council Catechisms." *The Americas* 15 (October 1958): 171–178.

California Missions: A Pictorial History. Menlo Park, Calif.: Sunset, 1979.

Carrico, Richard L. "Sociopolitical Aspects of the 1775 Revolt at Mission San Diego De Alcalá: An Ethnohistorical Approach." *The Journal of San Diego History* 43 (Summer 1997): 142–157.

Castañeda, Antonia I. "Engendering the History of Alta California, 1769–1848," in *Contested Eden: California Before the Gold Rush,* ed. Ramón Gutiérrez and Richard J. Orsi, 230–259. Berkeley: University of California Press, 1998.

——. "Sexual Violence in the Politics and Policies of Conquest: Amerindian Women and the Spanish Conquest of Alta California," in *Building with Our Hands: New Directions in Chicana Studies,* ed. Adela de la Torre and Beatríz M. Pesquera, 15–33. Berkeley: University of California Press, 1993.

Castillo, Edward D., ed. and trans. "The Assassination of Padre Andrés Quintana by the Indians of Mission Santa Cruz in 1812: The Narrative of Lorenzo Asisara." *California History* 68 (Fall 1989): 117–125.

———. "California Mission Indians: Two Perspectives." *California History* 70 (Summer 1991): 212–215, 238.

———. "Gender Status Decline, Resistance, and Accommodation among Female Neophytes in the Missions of California: A San Gabriel Case Study." *American Indian Culture and Research Journal* 18 (1994): 67–93.

———. "The Impact of Euro-American Exploration and Settlement," in *California,* ed. Robert F. Heizer, 99–127. *Handbook of North American Indians,* gen. ed. William Sturtevant, vol. 8. Washington, D.C.: Smithsonian Institution, 1978.

———, ed. and trans. "An Indian Account of the Decline and Collapse of Mexico's Hegemony Over the Missionized Indians of California." *American Indian Quarterly* 13 (1989): 391–408.

———, ed. *Native American Perspectives on the Hispanic Colonization of Alta California.* New York: Garland Publishing, 1991.

———. "Neophyte Resistance and Accommodation in the Missions of California," in *The Spanish Missionary Heritage of the United States,* 60–75. San Antonio: National Park Service, 1993.

———. "The Other Side of the 'Christian Curtain': California Indians and the Missionaries." *The Californians* 10 (1992): 8–17.

Cervantes, Fernando. *The Devil in the New World: The Impact of Diabloism in New Spain.* New Haven: Yale University Press, 1994.

César, Julio. "Recollections of My Youth at San Luis Rey Mission," trans. Nellie Van de Grift Sanchez. *Touring Topics* 22 (1930): 42–43.

Chapman, Cristina Alviso. "Early Days at Mission Santa Clara: Recollections of Nasario Galindo." *California Historical Quarterly* 38 (June 1959): 101–111.

Choris, Louis. *San Francisco One Hundred Years Ago,* trans. Porter Garnett. San Francisco: A. M. Robertson, 1913.

Clark, E. Gurney, and Niels Danbolt. "The Oslo Study of the Natural Course of Untreated Syphilis: An Epidemiologic Investigation Based on a Re-Study of the Boeck-Bruusgaard Material." *The Medical Clinics of North America* 48 (1964): 613–623.

Cleland, Robert Glass. *The Cattle on a Thousand Hills: Southern California, 1850–1880.* San Marino, Calif: Huntington Library, 1967.

Clement, Clara Erskine. *Saints in Art.* Boston: L.C. Page, 1899.

Colahan, Clark. "María de Jesús de Agreda: The Sweetheart of the Holy Office," in *Women in the Inquisition: Spain and the New World,* ed. Mary E. Giles, 155–170. Baltimore: Johns Hopkins University Press, 1999.

———. *The Visions of Sor María de Agreda: Writing Knowledge and Power.* Tucson: University of Arizona Press, 1994.

Cook, Sherburne F. "California's First Medical Survey: Report of Surgeon-General José Benites." *California and Western Medicine* 45 (1936): 532–554.

———. *The Conflict Between the California Indian and White Civilization.* Berkeley: University of California Press, 1976.

———. "Expeditions to the Interior of California: Central Valley, 1821–1835." *Anthropological Records* 20 (1962): 168–180, 205–206.

———. "Historical Demography," in *California,* ed. Robert F. Heizer, 91–98. *Handbook of North American Indians,* gen. ed. William Sturtevant, vol. 8. Washington, D.C.: Smithsonian Institution, 1978.

——. "The Monterey Surgeons during the Spanish Period in California." *Bulletin of the Institute of the History of Medicine* 5 (1937): 43–72.

——. *The Population of the California Indians, 1769–1970.* Berkeley: University of California Press, 1976.

——. "Population Trends among the California Mission Indians." *Ibero-Americana* 17 (1940): 1–48.

Cook, Sherburne F., and Woodrow Borah. *Essays in Population History: California and Mexico,* vol. 3. Berkeley: University of California Press, 1979.

——. "Mission Registers as Sources of Vital Statistics: Eight Missions of Northern California," in *Essays in Population History: Mexico and California,* vol. 3. Berkeley: University of California Press, 1979.

——. "On the Credibility of Contemporary Testimony on the Population of Mexico in the Sixteenth Century," in *Homenaje a Roberto Weitlaner,* 229–239. Mexico, D.F.: Instituto Nacional Antropológico de México, 1966.

Cook, Sherburne F., and Cesare Marino. "Roman Catholic Missions in California and the Southwest," in *History of Indian-White Relations,* ed. Wilcomb E. Washburn, 472–80. *Handbook of North American Indians,* gen. ed. William Sturtevant, vol. 4. Washington, D.C.: Smithsonian Institution, 1988.

Coombs, Gary. "With What God Will Provide: A Reexamination of the Chumash Revolt of 1824." *Noticias* 26 (1980): 21–28.

Coombs, Gary, and Fred Plog. "Chumash Baptism: An Ecological Perspective," in *?Antap: California Indian Political and Economic Organization,* eds. Lowell John Bean and Thomas F. King, 137–153. Ramona, Calif.: Ballena Press, 1974.

——. "The Conversion of the Chumash Indians: An Ecological Interpretation." *Human Ecology* 5 (1977): 309–328.

Costo, Rupert, and Jeannette Henry Costo, eds. *The Missions of California: A Legacy of Genocide.* San Francisco: Indian Historian Press, 1987.

Craig, Edward, gen. ed. *Routledge Encyclopedia of Philosophy.* London: Routledge, 1998.

Crawford, Michael H. *The Origins of Native Americans: Evidence from Anthropological Genetics.* Cambridge: Cambridge University Press, 1998.

Crosby, Alfred. "The Early History of Syphilis: A Reappraisal." *American Anthropologist* 71 (1969): 218–227.

——. "The Early History of Syphilis: A Reappraisal," in *The Columbian Exchange: Biological and Cultural Consequences of 1492,* 122–164. Westport, Conn.: Greenwood Press, 1972.

——. *Ecological Imperialism: The Biological Expansion of Europe.* New York: Cambridge University Press, 1988.

——. "Virgin Soil Epidemics as a Factor in the Aboriginal Depopulation in America." *William and Mary Quarterly* 3d series, 33 (1976): 289–299.

Culleton, James. *Indians and Pioneers of Old Monterey.* Fresno: Academy of California Church History, 1950.

Curletti, Rosario. "Christmas in Old Santa Barbara." *Noticias* 33 (Winter 1989): 86–90.

Cutter, Donald C. *The California Coast: Documents From the Sutro Collection.* Norman: University of Oklahoma Press, 1969.

——. *California in 1792: A Spanish Naval Visit.* Norman: University of Oklahoma Press, 1990.

——. *Malaspina in California.* San Francisco: J. Howell, 1960.

——, trans. and ed. *Writings of Mariano Payeras.* Santa Barbara, Calif.: Bellerophon Press, 1995.

Da Silva, Owen. *Mission Music of California.* Los Angeles: Warren F. Lewis, 1941.

Dale, Harrison Clifford, ed. *The Ashley-Smith Explorations and the Discovery of a Central Route to the Pacific, 1822–1829.* Cleveland, Ohio: Arthur H. Clark, 1918.

De Nevi, Don, and Noel F. Moholy. *Junípero Serra: The Illustrated Story of the Franciscan Founder of California's Missions.* San Francisco: Harper & Row, 1985.

Dean, Eric T. Jr. *Shook Over Hell: Post-Traumatic Stress, Vietnam, and the Civil War.* Cambridge, Mass.: Harvard University Press, 1997.

Dmytryshyn, Basil, and E. A. P. Crownhart-Vaughan, trans. and anns. *Colonial Russian America: Kyrill T. Khlebnikov's Reports, 1817–1832.* Portland: Oregon Historical Society, 1976.

Downie, Harry J. "California's First Library." Arthur D. Spearman Collection, Santa Clara University Archives.

DuBois, Constance Goddard. "The Mythology of the Diegueños." *Journal of American Folklore* 14 (1901): 181–85.

——. "Mythology of the Mission Indians." *Journal of American Folklore* 17 (1904): 185–88.

——. "Mythology of the Mission Indians: San Luiseño Creation Myth." *Journal of American Folklore, NS* 19 (1906): 52–54.

——. "Religions, Ceremonies, and Myths of the Mission Indians." *American Anthropologist* 7 (1905): 620–29.

Duflot de Mofras, Eugene. *Travels on the Pacific Coast,* ed. and trans. Marguerite Eyer Wilbur, 2 vols. Santa Anna, Calif.: Fine Arts Press, 1937.

Duhaut-Cilly, Auguste. *A Voyage to California, the Sandwich Islands and Around the World in the Years 1826–1829,* trans. and ann. August Frugé and Neal Harlow. San Francisco: Book Club of California, 1997.

Dumke, Glenn S. "The Masters of San Gabriel Mission's Old Mill." *California Historical Society Quarterly* 45 (1966): 259–265.

Durán, Narciso. "Prólogo," in *Mission Music of California,* trans. Owen Da Silva, 28–33. Los Angeles: Warren F. Lewis, 1941.

——. "Prólogo Ad Lectorem." Catholic Church, Liturgy, Ritual, 1812. Bancroft Library, Berkeley, California.

Dutton, Davis, ed. *Missions of California.* New York: Ballantine Books, 1972.

Eades, J. S. "Dimensions of Meaning: Western Music and the Anthropological Study of Symbolism," in *Religious Organization and Religious Experience,* ed. J. Davis, 195–207. London: Academic Press, 1982.

Editorial Staff of Sunset Books. *The California Missions: A Pictorial History.* Menlo Park, Calif.: Lane Book Company, 1964.

Edwards, Paul, ed. *The Encyclopedia of Philosophy.* New York: Macmillan, 1967.

El-Najjar, My. "Human Treponematosis and Tuberculosis: Evidence from the New World." *American Journal of Physical Anthropology* 51 (1979): 599–618.

Elson, Louis. *Curiosities of Music*. Boston: Oliver Detson, 1880.

Engelhardt, Zephyrin. *The Franciscans in California*. Harbor Springs, Mich.: Holy Childhood Indian School, 1897.

——. *The Holy Man of Santa Clara or Life, Virtues, and Miracles of Father Magin Catalá, O.F.M.* San Francisco: James H. Barry, 1909.

——. *Mission Nuestra Señora de la Soledad*. Santa Barbara: Schauer Printing Studio, 1929.

——. *Mission San Carlos Borromeo (Carmelo): Father of the Missions*. Santa Barbara: Schauer Printing Studio, 1934.

——. *Mission San Juan Bautista: A School of Church Music*. Santa Barbara: Schauer Printing Studio, 1931.

——. *Mission San Luis Obispo in the Valley of the Bears*. Santa Barbara: Schauer Printing Studio, 1933.

——. *Missions and Missionaries of California*, 2d, revised edition. Santa Barbara, Calif.: Santa Barbara Mission, 1930.

——. *San Antonio De Padua: The Mission in the Sierras*. Santa Barbara: Schauer Printing Studio, 1929.

——. *San Diego Mission*. San Francisco: James H. Barry, 1920.

——. *San Francisco or Mission Dolores*. Chicago: Franciscan Herald Press, 1924.

——. *San Gabriel Mission and the Beginnings of Los Angeles*. Chicago: Franciscan Herald, 1927.

——. *San Juan Capistrano: The Jewel of the Missions*. Los Angeles: Standard Printing, 1922.

——. *San Luis Rey Mission*. San Francisco: James H. Barry, 1921.

——. *San Miguel Arcángel: The Mission on the Highway*. Santa Barbara, Calif.: Schauer Printing Studio, 1929.

——. *Santa Barbara Mission*. San Francisco: James H. Barry, 1923.

Engstrand, Iris H. "California Ranchos: Their Hispanic Heritage." *Southern California Quarterly* 67 (1985): 281–290.

——. "Founding Father of San Diego," in *Some Reminiscences about Fray Junípero Serra*, ed. Francis J. Weber, 47–54. Santa Barbara, Calif.: Kimberly Press, 1985.

——. "The Role of the Comisionado in Spanish California." *California Mission Studies Association Boletín* 19 (2002): 13–18.

Filgueira Alvado, Alejandro. "Capacidad Intelectual y Actitud del Indio ante el Castellano." *Revista de Indias* 7 (1979): 163–186.

Fiumara, Nicholas J. "A Legacy of Syphilis." *Archives of Dermatology* 92 (1965): 676–678.

Flemming, William L. "Syphilis Through the Ages." *The Medical Clinics of North America* 48 (1964): 587–612.

Fogel, Daniel. *Junípero Serra, the Vatican, and Enslavement Theology*. San Francisco: ISM Press, 1988.

Forteza, Miquel. *Els Descendents dels Jueus Conversos de Mallorca*. Mallorca: Grafiques Miramar, 1966.

Foucault, Michel. *The History of Sexuality: Volume I: An Introduction*, trans. Robert Hurley. New York: Pantheon Books, 1978.

Frati Minori Conventuali. *The Relics of St. Francis.* Assis: Basilica of St. Francis, nd.

Freyre, Gilberto. *The Masters and the Slaves: A Study in the Development of Brazilian Civilization,* trans. from the fourth and definitive Brazilian edition by Samuel Putnam. New York: Knopf, 1946.

Gasnick, Roy, and John Tartaglione. *Serra: American Founding Father.* Los Angeles: Franciscan Communications, 1987.

Gaustad, Edwin S. *Faith of Our Fathers: Religion and the New Nation.* Cambridge: Harper & Row, 1987.

Gayton, Anna H. "The Narcotic Plant Datura in Aboriginal American Culture." PhD diss., University of California at Berkeley, 1928.

Geary, Gerald J. *The Secularization of the California Missions.* Washington, D.C.: Catholic University of America, 1934.

Geiger, Maynard. *The Franciscan Conquest of Florida, 1573–1618.* Washington, D.C.: Catholic University of America, 1937.

———. *Franciscan Missionaries in Hispanic California, 1769–1848: A Biographical Dictionary.* San Marino, Calif.: Huntington Library, 1969.

———. "Fray Antonio Ripoll's Description of the Chumash Revolt at Santa Barbara in 1824." *Southern California Quarterly* 52 (1970): 345–364.

———. "Fray Rafael Verger, O.F.M., and the California Mission Enterprise." *Southern California Quarterly* 49 (June 1967): 205–231.

———. "Harmonious Notes in Spanish California." *Southern California Quarterly* 57 (1975): 243–250.

———. "Instructions Concerning the Occupation of California, 1769." *Southern California Quarterly* 47 (1965): 209–218.

———, trans. *Letter of Luis Jayme, O.F.M., San Diego, October 17, 1772.* Los Angeles: Dawson's Book Shop, 1970.

———. *The Life and Times of Junípero Serra,* 2 vols. Washington, D.C.: Academy of American Franciscan History, 1959.

———. *Mission Santa Barbara, 1782–1965.* Santa Barbara, Calif.: Kimberly Litho, 1965.

———. "Our Lady in Franciscan California." *Franciscan Studies* 23 (New Series, 2) June 1942): 99–112.

———. *Palóu's Life of Fray Junípero Serra.* Washington, D.C.: American Academy of Franciscan History, 1955.

Geiger, Maynard, and Clement Meighan, ed. and trans. *As the Padres Saw Them: California Indian Life and Customs as Reported by the Franciscan Missionaries, 1813–1815.* Santa Barbara, Calif.: Santa Barbara Mission Archives Library, 1976.

Gerhard, Peter. *The North Frontier of New Spain.* Princeton: Princeton University Press, 1982.

Gjestland, Trygve. "The Oslo Study of Untreated Syphilis." *Acta Venereologica* 35 Supplementum 34 (1955).

González, Michael J. " 'The Child of the Wilderness Weeps for the Father of Our Country': The Indian and the Politics of Church and State in Provincial California," in *Contested Eden: California Before the Gold Rush,* ed. Ramón Gutiérrez and Richard J. Orsi, 147–172. Berkeley: University of California Press, 1998.

Graham, C. Ray. "Music and the Learning of Language in Early Childhood," in *Music and Child Development,* ed. Irene Weiss Peery, Thomas W. Draper, and J. Craig Peery, 177–183. New York: Springer-Verlag, 1987.

Greenberg, Robert. "Sources: The Ancient World Through the Early Baroque," in *How to Understand and Listen to Great Music.* 2 VHS tapes. New York: The Teaching Company, 1993.

Grove's Dictionary of Music and Musicians. 5th edition. London: Macmillan, 1954.

Guest, Francis F. "The California Missions Were Far from Faultless." *Southern California Quarterly* 76 (1994): 255–307.

———. "Cultural Perspectives on California Mission Life," in *Hispanic California Revisited: Essays by Francis F. Guest, O.F.M.,* ed. Doyce B. Nunis. Santa Barbara, Calif.: Santa Barbara Mission Archive Library, 1996.

———. "An Examination of the Thesis of S. F. Cook on the Forced Conversion of Indians in the California Missions." *Southern California Quarterly* 61 (1979): 1–77.

———. *Fermín Francisco de Lasuén: A Biography.* Washington, D.C.: Academy of American Franciscan History, 1973.

———. *Hispanic California Revisited: Essays by Francis F. Guest, O.F.M.,* ed. Doyce B. Nunis. Santa Barbara, Calif.: Santa Barbara Mission Archive Library, 1996.

———. "The Indian Policy Under Fermín Francisco de Lasuén, California's Second Father President." *California Historical Society Quarterly* 45 (1966): 195–224.

———. "An Inquiry into the Role of the Discipline in California Mission Life." *Southern California Quarterly* 71 (1989): 1–68.

———. "Junípero Serra and His Approach to the Indians." *Southern California Quarterly* 67 (1985): 223–261.

———. "New Look at the California's Missions [Sic]." *Some Reminiscences about Fray Junípero Serra,* ed., Francis J. Weber, 77–87. Santa Barbara, Calif.: Kimberly Press, 1985.

Gutiérrez, Ramón A. *When Jesus Came the Corn Mothers Went Away: Marriage, Sexuality, and Power in New Mexico, 1500–1846.* Stanford, Calif.: Stanford University Press, 1991.

Habig, Marion, ed. *St. Francis of Assisi: Writings and Early Biographies: English Omnibus of Sources for the Life of St. Francis.* 4th revised edition. Chicago: Franciscan Herald Press, 1983.

Hackel, Steven. *Children of Coyote, Missionaries of St. Francis: Indian-Spanish Relations in Colonial California, 1769–1850.* Durham, N.C.: Omohundro Institute of Early American History and Culture and University of North Carolina Press, 2005.

———. "Land, Labor, and Production: The Colonial Economy of Spanish and Mexican California," in *Contested Eden: California Before the Gold Rush,* ed. Ramón Gutiérrez and Richard J. Orsi, 111–146. Berkeley: University of California Press, 1998.

———. "The Staff of Leadership: Indian Authority in the Missions of California." *The William and Mary Quarterly,* 3d series, vol. 54 (1997): 347–376.

Halpin, Joseph. "Musical Activities and Ceremonies at Mission Santa Clara De Asís." *California Historical Quarterly* 50 (1971): 35–42.

Hammond, George P., and Agapito Rey, trans. *Apostolic Chronicles of Juan Domingo Arricivita: The Franciscan Mission Frontier in the Eighteenth Century in Arizona, Texas and California,* 2 vols. Berkeley, Calif.: Academy of American Franciscan History, 1995.

Hansen, Woodrow James. *The Search for Authority in California.* Oakland, Calif.: Biobooks, 1960.

Harman, Alec, Anthony Milner, and Wilfrid Mellers. *Man and His Music: The Story of Musical Experience in the West.* London: Barrie and Jenkins, 1988.

Harrington, John P., trans. "A New Original Version of Boscana's Historical Account of the San Juan Capistrano Indians of Southern California." *Smithsonian Miscellaneous Collections* 92 (June 27, 1934): 1–62.

Harris, Henry. *California's Medical Story.* San Francisco: Grabhorn Press, 1932.

Hauptman, Lawrence M. *Tribes and Tribulations: Misconceptions about American Indians and Their Histories.* Albuquerque: University of New Mexico Press, 1995.

Heizer, Robert F. "A California Messianic Movement of 1801 among the Chumash." *American Anthropologist* new series 43 (1941): 128–129.

——. "Indian Servitude in California," in *History of Indian-White Relations,* ed. Wilcomb E. Washburn, 414–417. *Handbook of North American Indians,* gen. ed. William Sturtevant, vol 4. Washington, D.C.: Smithsonian Institution, 1988.

——. ed. and ann. *The Indians of Los Angeles County: Hugo Reid's Letters of 1852.* Los Angeles: Southwest Museum, Southwest Museum Paper no. 21, 1968.

Heizer, Robert F., and Albert B. Elsasser. *The Natural World of the California Indians.* Berkeley: University of California Press, 1980.

Henige, David. *Numbers from Nowhere: The American Indian Contact Population Debate.* Norman: University of Oklahoma Press, 1998.

Herdt, Gilbert, ed. *Third Sex, Third Gender: Beyond Sexual Dimorphism in Culture and History.* New York: Zone, 1994.

Hinton, Leanne. *Flutes of Fire: Essays on California Indian Languages.* Berkeley, Calif.: Heyday Books, 1994.

Holmes, King K. "Gonococcal Infection," in *Infectious Diseases of the Fetus and Newborn Infant,* 2d edition, ed. Jack S. Remington and Jerome O. Klein, 619–635. Philadelphia: W.B. Saunders, 1983.

Homza, Lu Ann. "The European Link to Mexican Penance: The Literary Antecedents to Alva's Confessionario," in *A Guide to Confession Large and Small in the Mexican Language, 1634,* ed. Barry D. Sell and John Frederick Schwaller, 33–48. Norman: University of Oklahoma Press, 1999.

Hoover, Robert L. "An Early Attempt at Industrial Revolution in California." *La Gazeta Del Archivo* (2001–2002): 13–19.

Hornbeck, David. "Early Mission Settlement," in *Some Reminiscences about Fray Junípero Serra,* ed. Francis J. Weber, 55–66. Santa Barbara, Calif.: Kimberly Press, 1985.

Hudson, Travis. "The Chumash Revolt of 1824: Another Native Account from the Notes of John P. Harrington." *Journal of California and Great Basin Anthropology* 2 (1980): 123–126.

Hudson, Travis, and Thomas Blackburn. "The Integration of Myth and Ritual in South-Central California: The Northern Complex." *Journal of California Anthropology* 5 (Winter 1978): 225–50.

Hughes, Don Anselm, ed. *Early Medieval Music Up to 1300,* 2 vols. London: Oxford University Press, 1955.

Hughes, Rupert, ed. *Music Lovers' Cyclopedia.* Garden City, N.J.: Doubleday & Doran, 1929.

Hultkrantz, Ake. *The Religions of the American Indians,* trans. Monica Setterwall. Berkeley: University of California Press, 1979.

Hurst-Thomas, David, ed. *Columbian Consequences,* 3 vols. Washington, D.C.: Smithsonian Institution, 1989–1991.

Hurtado, Albert L. *Intimate Frontiers: Sex, Gender, and Culture in Old California.* Albuquerque: University of New Mexico Press, 1999.

Hurwitz, I., P. H. Wolff, B. D. Bortnick, and K. Kokas. "Nonmusical Effects of Kodaly Music Curriculum in Primary Grade Children." *Journal of Learning Disabilities* 8 (1975): 45–51.

Hutchinson, C. Alan. *Frontier Settlement in Mexican California: The Hijar-Padrés Colony, and Its Origins, 1769–1835.* New Haven: Yale University Press, 1969.

———. "The Mexican Government and the Missions of Upper California, 1821–1835." *The Americas* 21 (April 1965): 335–362.

Ingall, David, and Daniel Musher. "Syphilis," in *Infectious Diseases of the Fetus and Newborn Infant,* second edition, ed. Jack S. Remington and Jerome O. Klein, 335–374. Philadelphia: W.B. Saunders, 1983.

Jackson, Robert H. "Epidemic Disease and Population Decline in the Baja California Missions, 1697–1834." *Southern California Quarterly* 63 (1981): 138–143.

———. *From Savages to Subjects: Missions in the History of the American Southwest.* Armonk, N.Y.: M.E. Sharpe, 2000.

———. *Indian Population Decline: The Missions of Northwestern New Spain.* Albuquerque: University of New Mexico Press, 1994.

———. "The Population of the Santa Barbara Channel Missions (Alta California), 1813–1832." *Journal of California and Great Basin Anthropology* 12 (1990): 268–274.

Jackson, Robert H., and Edward Castillo. *Indians, Franciscans, and Spanish Colonization: The Impact of the Mission System on California Indians.* Albuquerque: University of New Mexico Press, 1995.

Janata, Petr, et al. "The Cortical Topography of Tonal Structures Underlying Western Music." *Science* 298 (2002): 2167–2170.

Johnson, John R. "Chumash Social Organization: An Ethnohistoric Perspective." Ph.D. dissertation, University of California at Santa Barbara, 1988.

———. "Indians of Mission San Fernando," in *Mission San Fernando Rey De España, 1797–1997: A Bicentennial Tribute,* ed. Doyce B. Nunis, Jr. Los Angeles: Historical Society of Southern California, 1997.

———. "Mission Registers as Anthropological Questionnaires: Understanding the Limitations of the Data." *American Indian Culture and Research Journal* 12 (1988): 9–30.

Jones, Edward. *Ingratiation: A Social Psychological Analysis.* New York: Appleton-Century-Crofts, 1964.

Jones, James H. *Bad Blood: The Tuskegee Syphilis Experiment.* New York: Free Press, 1981.

Keeling, Richard. "Music and Culture Areas of Native California." *Journal of California and Great Basin Anthropology* 14 (1992): 146–158.

———. "Sources for Research Concerning Music among Indians of the California Region," in *California's Musical Wealth: Sources for the Study of Music in California,* ed. Stephen M. Fry. Np.: Southern California Chapter of the Music Library Association, 1988.

Kelsey, Harry. *The Doctrina and Confesionario of Juan Cortés.* Altadena, Calif.: Howling Coyote Press, 1979.

Kendrick, T. D. *Mary of Agreda: The Life and Legend of a Spanish Nun.* London: Routledge and Kegan Paul, 1967.

Kenneally, Finbar, Editor and Translator. *Writings of Fermín Francisco de Lasuén,* 2 vols. Washington, D.C.: Academy of American Franciscan History, 1965.

King, Chester. "Central Ohlone Ethnohistory," in *The Ohlone: Past and Present,* comp. and ed. Lowell John Bean, 203–247. Menlo Park, Calif.: Ballena Press, 1994.

Kirkby, Dianna. "Colonial Policy and Native Depopulation in California and New South Wales, 1770–1840." *Ethnohistory* 31 (1984): 1–16.

——. "Frontier Violence: Ethnohistory and Aboriginal Resistance in California and New South Wales, 1770–1840." *Journal of Australian Studies* (1980): 36–48.

Kotzebue, Otto von. *A New Voyage Around the World in the Years 1823, 1824, 1825, and 1826.* 2 vols. London: Henry Colburn and Richard Bentley, 1830.

——. *A Voyage of Discovery into the South Sea and Bering Straits,* 3 vols. London: Langman, Hurst, Rees, Orme, and Brown, 1822.

Kroeber, Clifton, and Bernard Fontana. *Massacre on the Gila: An Account of the Last Major Battle between American Indians with Reflections on The Origins of the War.* Tucson: University of Arizona Press, 1986.

Landon, Esther Abrams. "Seventeenth and Eighteenth Century English and Colonial American Music Texts: An Analysis of Instructional Content." Ph.D dissertation, University of California, Los Angeles, 1977.

Lang, Sabine. *Men as Women, Women as Men: Changing Gender in Native American Cultures,* trans. John L. Vantine. Austin: University of Texas Press, 1998.

Langellier, John Phillip, and Daniel B. Rosen. *El Presidio de San Francisco: A History Under Spain and Mexico, 1776–1846.* Spokane, Wash.: Arthur H. Clark Company, 1996.

Langsdorff, George H. von. *Langsdorff's Narrative of the Rezanov Voyage to Nueva California in 1806,* trans. Thomas C. Russell. San Francisco: Thomas C. Russell, 1927.

Larson, Daniel O., John R. Johnson, and Joel C. Michaelson. "Missionization among the Coastal Chumash of Central California: A Study of Risk Minimization Strategies." *American Anthropologist* 96 (June 1994): 263–299.

Le Netrel, Edmond. *Voyage of the Héros Around the World with Duhaut-Cilly in the Years 1826, 1827, 1828, & 1829,* trans. Blanche Collet Wagner. Los Angeles: Glen Dawson, 1951.

Lee, Dorothy. *Freedom and Culture.* New York: Prentice-Hall, 1959.

Lee, Georgia, and Norman Neuerburg. "The Alta California Indians as Artists Before and After Contact," in *Columbian Consequences,* ed. David Hurst Thomas, 467–480, vol. 1. Washington, D.C.: Smithsonian Institution, 1989.

Lepowsky, Maria. "Indian Revolts and Cargo Cults: Ritual Violence and Revitalization in California and New Guinea," in *Reassessing Revitalization: Cases from North America and Oceania,* ed. Michael Harkin. Lincoln: University of Nebraska Press, 2004.

Librado, Fernando. *Breath of the Sun: Life in Early California as Told by a Chumash Indian, Fernando Librado to John P. Harrington,* ed. and ann. Travis Hudson. Banning, Calif.: Malki Museum Press, 1979.

Luomala, Katharine. "Tipai-Ipai," in *California,* ed. Robert F. Heizer, 592–609, *Handbook of North American Indians,* gen. ed. William Sturtevant, vol. 8. Washington, D.C.: Smithsonian Institution, 1978.

Luzbetak, Louis J. "If Junípero Serra Were Alive: Missiological-Anthropological Theory Today." *The Americas* 42 (1985): 512–519.

Magliari. "Free Soil, Unfree Labor: Cave Johnson Couts and the Binding of Indian Workers in California, 1850–1867," paper given at The Annual Meeting of the Western History Association, San Diego, Calif, Oct. 11, 2001.

Mahr, August C. *The Visit of the "Rurik" to San Francisco in 1816.* Stanford: Stanford University Press, 1932.

Maiarelli, Paolo Stanislao. *Assisi, Franciscan Itinerary.* Portiuncula Sanctuary, Assisi: St. Mary of the Angels, nd.

Mansfield, Mary C. *The Humiliation of Sinners: Public Penance in Thirteenth-Century France.* Ithaca, N.Y.: Cornell University Press, 1995.

Margolin, Malcolm, ed. and commentary. *Monterey in 1786: The Journals of Jean François de la Pérouse.* Berkeley, Calif.: Heyday Press, 1989.

Marison, Fiscar (George J. Blatter). *City of God.* 4 vols. Washington, N.J.: Ave Maria Institute, 1971.

Martin, Valerie. *Salvation: Scenes from the Life of St. Francis.* New York: Knopf, 2001.

Mason, J. Alden. "The Ethnology of the Salinan Indians." *University of California Publications in American Archaeology and Ethnology* 10, no. 4 (1912): 97–240.

———. "The Language of the Salinan Indians." *University of California Publications in American Archaeology and Ethnology* 14, no. 1 (1918): 1–154.

Mason, William Marvin. *The Census of 1790: A Demographic History of Colonial California.* Menlo Park, Calif.: Ballena Press, 1998.

———. "Fages' Code of Conduct Toward Indians, 1787." *Journal of California Anthropology* 2 (1975): 90–100.

McCarthy, Francis Florence. *The History of Mission San José California, 1797–1835.* Fresno, Calif.: Academy Library Guild, 1958.

McCarty, Kieran. "Apostolic Colleges of the Propagation of the Faith: Old and New World Background." *The Americas* 19 (July 1962): 50–58.

McFalls, Joseph A., and Marguerite Harvey McFalls. *Disease and Fertility.* Orlando, Fla.: Academic Press, 1984.

McGary, Daniel D. "Educational Methods of the Franciscans in Spanish California." *The Americas* 6 (1950): 335–358.

McNeill, William H. *Keeping Together in Time: Dance and Drill in Human History.* Cambridge: Harvard University Press, 1995.

McWilliams, Carey. *Southern California Country: An Island on the Land.* New York: Duell, Sloan & Pearce, 1946.

Merriam, C. Hart. "The Indian Population of California." *American Anthropologist* new series 7: 594–606.

Miller, Crane S., and Richard S. Hyslop. *California: The Geography of Diversity.* Mountain View, Calif.: Mayfield Publishing, 1983.

Miller, Robert Ryal. *Juan Alvarado: Governor of California, 1836–1842.* Norman: University of Oklahoma Press, 1998.

Milliken, Randall. "An Ethnohistory of the Indian People of the San Francisco Bay Area from 1770–1810." Ph.D. dissertation, University of California at Berkeley, 1991.

——. *A Time of Little Choice: The Disintegration of Tribal Culture in the San Francisco Bay Area, 1769–1810.* Menlo Park, Calif.: Ballena Press, 1995.

Mitzman, Arthur. "The Civilizing Offensive: Mentalities, High Culture and Individual Psyches." *Journal of Social History* (1987): 663–687.

Mizzi, Maximilian. *The Message of St. Francis with Frescoes from the Basilica of St. Francis of Assisi,* extracts selected by Sister Nan. New York: Penguin Putnam, 1999.

Monelle, Raymond. *Linguistics and Semiotics in Music.* Switzerland: Harwood Academic Publishers, 1992.

Morgado, Martin Jay, *Junípero Serra: A Pictorial Biography.* Monterey, Calif.: Siempre Adelante Publishing, 1991.

Moriarty, James Robert. *Chinigchinix.* Los Angeles: Southwest Museum, 1969.

——. "Cosmogony, Rituals, and Medical Practice among the Diegueño Indians of Southern California." *Anthropological Journal of Canada* 3 (1965): 2–16.

Nag, Moni. *Factors Affecting Human Fertility in Nonindustrial Societies: A Cross-Cultural Study.* New Haven: Yale University Publications in Anthropology no. 66, 1962.

Neely, Mark. *The Abraham Lincoln Encyclopedia.* New York: McGraw-Hill, 1982.

Neri, Michael C. "González Rubio and California Catholicism, 1846–1850." *Southern California Quarterly* 58 (1976): 441–457.

——. *Hispanic Catholicism in Transitional California: The Life of José González Rubio, O.F.M. (1804–1875).* Berkeley, Calif.: Academy of American Franciscan History, 1997.

——. "Narciso Durán and the Secularization of the California Missions." *The Americas* 33 (January 1977): 411–429.

Neuerburg, Norman. *The Decoration of the California Missions.* Santa Barbara, Calif.: Bellerophon Books, 1989.

——. "Indian Pictographs at Mission San Juan Capistrano." *The Masterkey* 56 (1982): 55–58.

——. "The Indian Via Crucis from Mission San Fernando: An Historical Exposition," in *Mission San Fernando Rey De España, 1797–1997: A Bicentennial Tribute,* ed. Doyce B. Nunis, 329–382. Los Angeles: Historical Society of Southern California, 1997.

——. "Indians as Artists in California Before and After Contact with the Europeans," in *Les Illes Belears i Amèrica,* ed. Román Piña Homs, 43–60. Palma, Majorca: Congrés Internacional d'Estudis Històrics, 1992.

——. *Saints of the California Missions.* Santa Barbara, Calif.: Bellerophon Books, 1990.

Nirenberg, David. "Conversion, Sex, and Segregation: Jews and Christians in Medieval Spain." *The American Historical Review* 107 (2002): 1065–1093.

Nolan, James L. "Anglo-American Myopia and California Mission Art." *Southern California Quarterly* 58 (1976): 1–44, 143–204, 261–331.

Nunis, Doyce B. "California Mission Indians: Two Perspectives." *California History* 70 (Summer 1991): 206–212, 236–238.

——. "The Franciscan Friars of Mission San Fernando, 1797–1847," in *Mission San Fernando Rey de España, 1797–1997: A Bicentennial Tribute,* ed. Doyce B. Nunis, 217–248. Los Angeles: Historical Society of Southern California, 1997.

Nuttall, Donald A. "The Fages Marital Crisis of 1785: Elaboration and Explanation." *Southern California Quarterly* 83 (2001): 1–22.

O'Brien, Eric. "The Life of Padre Serra," in *Writings of Junípero Serra*, vol. I, ed. Antonine Tibesar, xxiii–xlv. Washington, D.C.: Academy of American Franciscan History, 1955.

Ogden, Adele. *The California Sea Otter Trade.* Berkeley: University of California Press, 1941.

Ord, Angustias de la Guerra. *Occurrences in Hispanic California.* Washington, D.C.: Academy of American Franciscan History, 1956.

Orsi, Richard J. "Estanislao's Rebellion, 1829," in *The Elusive Eden: A New History of California,* second edition, ed. William A. Burrough, Richard J. Orsi, and Richard B. Rice, 53–68. New York: Knopf, 1996.

Ortega, Francisco. Enero 13, 1776. "Complot de Indios para Fugarse y Destruir los Blancos." Archives of California, Provincial State Papers, Tomo I, Bancroft Library.

———. Noviembre 30, 1775. "Expediente de Investigación." Archives of California, Provincial State Papers, Benicia, Military, Tomo I, Bancroft Library.

———. Abril 6, 1778. "Insurrección de Indios-Resultados Castigo de Cabecillas." Archives of California, Provincial State Papers, Benicia, Military, Tomo I, Bancroft Library.

Osante, Patricia. "La Colonización Familiar en el Norte de Nueva España: El Caso del Nuevo Santander," in *Social Control on Spain's North American Frontiers: Choice, Persuasion, and Coercion,* ed. Ross Frank and Frank de la Teja. Albuquerque: University of New Mexico Press, 2005.

Osio, Antonio Maria. "Crónica de los acontecimientos ocurridos en California desde 1845 hasta 1846." Huntington Library.

———. *The History of Alta California: A Memoir of Mexican California,* trans. and ann. Rose Marie Beebe and Robert M. Senkewicz. Madison: University of Wisconsin Press, 1996.

Palmer, A. Dean. "Mission San Antonio de Padua: A Tour of Its Music Room and Notes on California Mission Music." Copy in author's possession. Permission to cite from A. Dean Palmer, 1993.

Palóu, Francisco. *Noticias de la Nueva California,* 4 vols. San Francisco: Eduardo Bosqui y Cia, 1874.

———. *Relación Histórica de la Vida y Apostólicas Tareas del Venerable Padre Fray Junípero Serra.* Mexico: Imprenta Zuñiga y Ontiveros, 1787.

Peery, J. Craig, and Irene Weiss Peery. "The Role of Music in Child Development," in *Music and Child Development,* ed. Irene Weiss Peery, Thomas W. Draper, and J. Craig Peery, 3–34. New York: Springer-Verlag, 1987.

Pencak, William. *History, Signing In: Essays in History and Semiotics.* New York: Peter Lang, 1993.

Peretz, Isabelle. "Processing of Local and Global Music Information by Unilateral Brain-Damaged Patients." *Brain* 113 (1990): 1185–1205.

Peretz, Isabelle, and José Morais. "Specificity for Music," in *Handbook of Neuropsychology,* ed. H. Spinnler and F. Boller, 373–390, vol. 8. Amsterdam: Elsevier Science Publishers, 1993.

Perez, Crisostomo N. *Land Grants in Alta California*. Rancho Cordova, Calif.: Landmark Enterprises, 1996.

Perissinotto, Giorgio, ed. *Documenting Everyday Life in Early Spanish California: The Santa Barbara Presidio Memorias y Facturas, 1779–1810*. Santa Barbara, Calif.: Santa Barbara Trust for Historic Preservation, 1998.

Petsche, Helmuth, Peter Rochter, Astrid von Stein, Susan Etlinger, and Oliver Filz. "EEG Coherence and Musical Thinking." *Music Perspectives* 11 (1993): 117–151.

Phillips, George Harwood. "The Alcaldes: Indian Leadership in the Spanish Missions of California." The D'Arcy McNickle Center, Newberry Library Occasional Papers in Curriculum Series No. 11, 83–89. Chicago: Newberry Library, 1989.

——. "Indian Paintings for Mission San Fernando: An Historical Interpretation." *Journal of California Anthropology* 3 (1976): 96–114.

——. "Indians and the Breakdown of the Spanish Mission System in California." *Ethnohistory* 21 (1974): 291–301.

——. *Indians and Intruders in Central California, 1769–1849*. Norman: University of Oklahoma Press, 1993.

Polk, Marsha, and Andrew Kertesz. "Music and Language in Degenerative Disease of the Brain." *Brain and Cognition* 22 (1993): 98–117.

Pressat, Roland. *The Dictionary of Demography*, ed. Christopher Wilson. Oxford: Blackwell, 1985.

Preston, William L. "Portents of Plague from California's Protohistoric Period." *Ethnohistory* 49 (2002): 69–121.

Priestley, Herbert Ingram, trans. and ed. *A Historical, Political, and Natural Description of California by Pedro Fages, Soldier of Spain*. Berkeley: University of California Press, 1937.

Pusey, William Allen. *The History and Epidemiology of Syphilis*. Springfield, Mass.: Charles C. Thomas, 1933.

Quétel, Claude. *History of Syphilis*, trans. Judith Braddock and Brian Pike. Baltimore, Md.: Johns Hopkins University Press, 1990.

Quinn, Thomas C. "Gay Bowel Syndrome: The Broadened Spectrum of Nongenital Infection." *Postgraduate Medicine* 76 (1984): 197–210.

Rauscher, Frances H., Gordon L. Shaw, and Katherine N. Ky. "Music and Spatial Task Performance." *Nature* 365 (1993): 611.

Ray, Sister Mary Dominic, and Joseph H. Engback Jr. *Gloria Dei: The Story of California Mission Music*. State of California, Department of Parks and Recreation, 1974.

Reid, Hugo. "New Era in Mission Affairs," in *The Indians of Los Angeles County: Hugo Reid's Letters of 1852*, ed. Robert F. Heizer, 87. Los Angeles: Southwest Museum Papers, no. 21, 1968.

Remington, Jack S., and Jerome O. Klein, eds. *Infectious Diseases of the Fetus and the Newborn*, second edition. Philadelphia: W. B. Saunders, 1983.

Rivera y Moncada, Fernando. *Diario del Capitán Comandante Fernando Rivera y Moncada*, comp. Ernest J. Burrus. Madrid: Colección Chimalistac de Libros Documentos Acerca de la Nueva España, Ediciones Porrua, 1976.

Robinson, Alfred. *Life in California before the Conquest*. San Francisco: Thomas C. Russell, 1925.

Robinson, William W. *Land in California.* Berkeley: University of California Press, 1948.

Rogers, David Banks. *Prehistoric Man of the Santa Barbara Coast.* Santa Barbara, Calif.: Santa Barbara Museum of Natural History, 1929.

Rosenus, Alan. *General M. G. Vallejo and the Advent of the Americans: A Biography.* Albuquerque: University of New Mexico Press, 1995.

Rudd, Charles, Jr. "Depopulation in Polynesia." *Bulletin of the History of Medicine* 51 (1977): 585–593.

Rudkin, Charles N., trans. and ed. *Camille de Roquefeuil in San Francisco, 1817–1818.* Los Angeles: Glen Dawson, 1954.

———, trans. and ed. *The First French Expedition to California: Lapérouse in 1786.* Los Angeles: Glen Dawson, 1959.

———, trans. and ed. *Observations on California, 1772–1790 by Father Luis Sales, O.P.* Los Angeles: Glen Dawson, 1956.

Russell, Craig H. "Newly Discovered Treasures from Colonial California: The Masses at San Fernando Mission." *Inter-American Music Review* 13 (1992): 5–9.

Sadie, Stanley, ed. *The New Grove Dictionary of Music and Musicians.* London: Macmillan, 1980.

———, ed. *The New Grove Dictionary of Music and Musicians.* New York: Macmillan, 1993.

———, ed. *The Norton/Grove Concise Encyclopedia of Music.* New York: Norton, 1988.

Sánchez, Joseph P. *Spanish Bluecoats: The Catalonian Volunteers in Northwestern New Spain, 1767–1810.* Albuquerque: University of New Mexico Press, 1990.

Sanchez, Nellie Van de Grift. *Spanish Arcadia.* Los Angeles: Powell Publishing, 1929.

Sandos, James A. " 'Because He Is a Liar and a Thief': Conquering the Residents of 'Old' California, 1850–1880," in *Rooted in Barbarous Soil: People, Culture, and Community in Gold Rush California,* ed. Kevin Starr and Richard Orsi, 86–112. Berkeley: University of California Press, 2000.

———. "Between Crucifix and Lance: Indian-White Relations in California, 1769–1848," in *Contested Eden: California Before the Gold Rush,* ed. Ramón Gutiérrez and Richard J. Orsi, 196–229. Berkeley: University of California Press, 1998.

———. "Christianization among the Chumash: An Ethnohistoric Perspective." *American Indian Quarterly* 15 (1991): 65–89.

———. "Junípero Serra, Canonization, and the California Indian Controversy." *The Journal of Religious History* 15 (June 1989): 311–329.

———. "Junípero Serra's Canonization and the Historical Record." *The American Historical Review* 93 (December 1988): 1253–1269.

———. "Levantamiento!: The 1824 Chumash Uprising Reconsidered." *Southern California Quarterly* 67 (Summer 1985): 109–133.

———. "Neophyte Resistance in the Alta California Missions," in *Columbus, Confrontation, Christianity: The European-American Encounter Revisited,* ed. Timothy J. O'Keefe, 170–178. Palo Alto, Calif.: Forbes Mill Press, 1994.

———. "Prostitution and Drugs: The United States Army on the Mexican-American Border." *Pacific Historical Review* 49 (1980): 621–645.

Santiago, Mark. *Massacre at Yuma Crossing: Spanish Relations with the Quechans, 1779–1782.* Tucson: University of Arizona Press, 1998.

Saranyana, Josep-Ignasi. "Métodos de Catequización," in *Historia de la Iglesia en Hispanoamérica y Filipinas,* 2 vols., ed. Pedro Borges, 549–68, vol. I. Madrid: Biblioteca de Autores Cristianos, 1992.

Saunders, Charles Francis, and Father Saint John O'Sullivan. *Capistrano Nights: Tales of a California Mission Town.* New York: Robert McBride, 1930.

Scheutz-Miller, Mardith K. *Building and Builders in Hispanic California, 1769–1850.* Tucson and Santa Barbara: Southwest Mission Research Center and Santa Barbara Trust for Historical Preservation, 1994.

Scott, James C. *Domination and the Arts of Resistance: Hidden Transcripts.* New Haven: Yale University Press, 1990.

Seay, Albert. *Music in the Medieval World,* second edition. Englewood Cliffs, N.J., Prentice Hall, 1975.

Seed, Patricia. *Ceremonies of Possession in Europe's Conquest of the New World, 1492–1640.* Cambridge: Cambridge University Press, 1995.

Servin, Manuel. "The Secularization of the California Missions: A Reappraisal." *Southern California Quarterly* 47 (June 1965): 133–149.

Shipek, Florence C. "California Indian Reactions to the Franciscans." *The Americas* 41 (April 1985): 480–492.

Shipley, William F. "Native Languages of California," in *California,* ed. Robert F. Heizer, 80–90. *Handbook of North American Indians,* gen. ed. William Sturtevant, vol. 8. Washington, D.C.: Smithsonian Institution, 1978.

Shoup, Laurence H., and Randall T. Milliken. *Inigo of Rancho Posolmi: The Life and Times of a Mission Indian.* Np.: Ballena Press, 1999.

Simmons, William S. "Indian Peoples of California," in *Contested Eden: California Before the Gold Rush,* ed. Ramón Gutiérrez and Richard J. Orsi, 48–77. Berkeley: University of California Press, 1998.

Smith, Howard M. "The Introduction of Venereal Disease into Tahiti: A Re-Examination." *The Journal of Pacific History* 10 (1975): 38–45.

Snaer, Dorothea S. "Diary of a Priest, 1856." *Annales de la Propagation de la Foi* 30 (1858): 57–68.

Spearman, Arthur D. "The First Stage in California." *The Call Board* 4, no. 7 (1935): 5–6.

Stannard, David E. "Disease and Infertility: A New Look at the Demographic Collapse of Native Populations in the Wake of Western Contact." *Journal of American Studies* 24 (1990): 325–350.

Starr, Kevin. *Inventing the Dream: California Through the Progressive Era.* New York: Oxford University Press, 1985.

Stevens, John. *Words and Music in the Middle Ages: Song, Narrative, Dance and Drama.* Cambridge: Cambridge University Press, 1986.

Stevenson, Robert. "Written Sources for Indian Music Until 1882." *Ethnomusicology* 17 (1973): 1–40.

Stevenson, Robert Louis. *Across the Plains, with Other Memories and Essays.* New York: Scribner's, 1907.

Stokes, John H., Herman Beerman, and Norman R. Ingraham. *Modern Clinical Syphilology: Diagnosis, Treatment, Case Study,* third ed. Philadelphia: W.B. Saunders, 1944.

Strunk, Oliver. *Source Readings in Music History: From Classical Antiquity Through the Romantic Era.* New York: Norton, 1950.

Summers, William J. "Letter to the Editor." *Latin American Music Review* 3 (1981): 130–135.

——. "The Misa Viscaína: An 18th Century Musical Odyssey to Alta California." *California Mission Studies Association* 15 (1998): 1–7.

——. "New and Little Known Sources of Music from California." *Inter-American Music Review* 11 (1991): 13–24.

——. "Spanish Music in California, 1769–1840: A Reassessment," in *International Musicological Society, Report of the Twelfth Congress, Berkeley, 1977,* ed. Daniel Heartz and Bonnie Wade, 360–380. Basel: Bärenreiter Kasse, 1981.

——. "The Spanish Origins of California Mission Music." *Miscellanea Musicologica: Adelaide Studies in Musicology* 12 (1987): 109–126.

Tac, Pablo. "Indian Life and Customs at Mission San Luis Rey," trans. and ed. Minna and Gordon Hewes. *The Americas* 9 (1952): 87–106.

——. "Studio Garammaticali Sulla Lingua Della California, Ca. 1835." Mezzofanti, Caps. III, I, Biblioteca Comunale dell'Archiginnasio. Bologna, Italy: Huntington Library.

Tarasti, Eero. *A Theory of Musical Semiotics.* Bloomington: Indiana University Press, 1994.

Temple, Thomas Workman. "Toypurina the Witch and the Indian Uprising at San Gabriel." *The Masterkey* 32 (1958): 136–152.

Thayer, James D., and M. Brittain Moore Jr. "Gonorrhea: Present Knowledge, Research and Control Efforts." *The Medical Clinics of North America* 48 (1964): 755–765.

Thomas, David Hurst. *Columbian Consequences.* 3 vols. Washington, D.C.: Smithsonian, 1989–1991.

Thompson, James C. *Music Through the Renaissance.* Dubuque, Iowa: William C. Brown, 1968.

Thornton, Russell. *American Indian Holocaust and Survival: A Population History Since 1492.* Norman: University of Oklahoma Press, 1987.

Thurman, Michael E. *The Naval Department of San Blas, New Spain's Bastion for Alta California and Nootka, 1767 to 1798.* Glendale, Calif.: Dawson's Books, 1976.

Thurston, Herbert. *The Stations of the Cross: An Account of Their History and Devotional Purpose.* New York: Benziger Brothers, 1906.

Tibesar, Antonine, ed. *Writings of Junípero Serra,* 4 vols. Washington, D.C.: Academy of American Franciscan History, 1956–1966.

Toffelmeier, Gertrude, and Katharine Luomala. "Dreams and Dream Interpretation of the Diegueño Indians of Southern California." *Psychoanalytic Quarterly* 5 (1936): 195–225.

Trehub, Sandra E., and Leigh A. Thorpe. "Infants' Perception of Rhythm: Categorization of Auditory Sequences by Temporal Structure." *Canadian Journal of Psychology* 43 (1989): 217–229.

Trexler, Richard C. *Sex and Conquest: Gendered Violence, Political Order, and the European Conquest of the Americas.* Ithaca, N.Y.: Cornell University Press, 1995.

Troiano, Costantino, and Alfonso Pompei. *Illustrated Guide of Assisi,* trans. Benedict Fagone. Assisi: Casa Editrice Francescana, nd.

Ubelaker, Douglas H. "North American Indian Population Size: Changing Perspectives," in *Disease and Demography in the Americas,* ed. John W. Verano and Douglas H. Ubelaker, 169–176. Washington, D.C.: Smithsonian Institution Press, 1992.

Uhrowczik, Peter. *The Burning of Monterey: The 1818 Attack on California by the Privateer Bouchard.* Los Gatos: CYRIL Books, 2001.

Vallejo, Guadalupe. "Ranch and Mission Days in Alta California." *The Century Magazine* 41 (1890): 183–192.

Vallejo, Mariano G. "Historical and Personal Memoirs." 4 vols. CD-20, Bancroft Library.

Vancouver, George A. *A Voyage of Discovery to the North Pacific Ocean and Around the World, 1791–1795,* ed. W. Kaye Lamb. London: The Haklyut Society, 1984.

Voght, Martha. "Shamans and Padres: The Religion of the Southern California Mission Indians." *Pacific Historical Review* 36 (1967): 363–373.

Walker, Philip L., and John R. Johnson. "Effects of Contact on the Chumash Indians," in *Disease and Demography in the Americas,* ed. John W. Verano and Douglas H. Ubelaker, 127–139. Washington, D.C.: Smithsonian Institution Press, 1992.

Walker, Phillip L., Patricia Lambert, and Michael DeNiro. "The Effects of European Contact on the Health of the California Indians," in *Columbian Consequences,* ed. David Hurst Thomas, 349–364, vol. 1. Washington, D.C.: Smithsonian Institution Press, 1989.

Wallace, Edith. "Sexual Status and Role Differences," in *California,* ed. Robert F. Heizer, 683–689. *Handbook of North American Indians,* gen. ed. William Sturtevant, vol. 8. Washington, D.C.: Smithsonian Institution, 1978.

Wallace, William J. "Music and Musical Instruments," in ed. Robert F. Heizer, 642–648. *Handbook of North American Indians,* gen. ed. William Sturtevant, vol. 8. Washington, D.C.: Smithsonian Institution, 1978.

Webb, Edith Buckland. *Indian Life at the Old Missions.* Lincoln: University of Nebraska Press, 1982.

Weber, David J. "Blood of Martyrs, Blood of Indians: Toward a More Balanced View of Spanish Missions in Seventeenth Century North America," in *Columbian Consequences,* ed. David Hurst Thomas, 429–448, vol. 2. Washington, D.C.: Smithsonian Institution, 1990.

——. "Bourbons and Bárbaros: Center and Periphery in the Reshaping of Spanish Indian Policy," in *Negotiated Empires: Centers and Peripheries in the Americas, 1500–1820,* ed. Christine Daniels and Michael V. Kennedy. New York: Routledge, 2002.

——. *The Mexican Frontier, 1821–1846: The American Southwest Under Mexico.* Albuquerque: University of New Mexico Press, 1982.

——. *Myth and the History of the Hispanic Southwest.* Albuquerque: University of New Mexico Press, 1988.

——, ed. *New Spain's Far Northern Frontier.* Albuquerque: University of New Mexico Press, 1979.

——. *Spaniards and Their Savages in the Age of Enlightenment.* New Haven: Yale University Press, 2005.

——. *The Spanish Frontier in North America.* New Haven: Yale University Press, 1992.

Weber, Francis J. *The California Missions as Others Saw Them, 1786–1842.* Los Angeles: Dawson's Book Shop, 1972.

——, comp. and ed. *The Mission in the Valley: A Documentary History of San Fernando Rey de España*. Los Angeles: Weber, 1975.

Weckman, Luis. *The Medieval Heritage of Mexico,* trans. Frances M. López-Morillas. New York: Fordham University Press, 1992.

White, Raymond C. "Luiseño Social Organization," *University of California Publications in American Archaeology and Ethnology* 48, no. 2 (1963): 91–194.

Whitehead, Richard S. *Citadel on the Channel: The Royal Presidio of Santa Barbara, Its Founding and Construction, 1782–1798*. Santa Barbara and Spokane: Santa Barbara Trust for Historic Preservation and Arthur H. Clark Company, 1996.

Williams, Walter L. *The Spirit and the Flesh: Sexual Diversity in American Indian Culture*. Boston: Beacon Press, 1986.

Willoughby, Nona C. "Division of Labor among the Indians of California." MA thesis, University of California, 1948.

Wilson, Christopher, ed. *The Dictionary of Demography*. Oxford: Blackwell, 1985.

Wolfe, David E., and Candice Hom. "Use of Melodies as Structural Prompts for Learning and Retention of Sequential Verbal Information by Preschool Students." *Journal of Music Therapy* 30 (1993): 100–118.

Woodward, Arthur. "Notes on the Indians of San Diego County: From the Manuscripts of Judge Benjamin Hayes." *The Masterkey* 5 (1934): 140–150.

Young, Mary. "Pagans, Converts, and Backsliders, All: A Secular View of the Metaphysics of Indian-White Relations," in *The American Indian and the Problem of History*, ed. Calvin Martin, 75–83. New York: Oxford University Press, 1987.

Zatorre, Robert J., and Carol L. Krumhansl. "Mental Models and Musical Minds." *Science* 298 (2002): 2138–2139.

Zimmermann, Ernest L. "Extragenital Syphilis as Described in the Early Literature (1497–1624) with Special Reference to Focal Epidemics, Part 1." *American Journal of Syphilis, Gonorrhea, and Venereal Diseases* 72 (1938): 757–780.

——. "Extragenital Syphilis as Described in the Early Literature (1497–1624) with Special Reference to Focal Epidemics, Part 2." *American Journal of Syphilis, Gonorrhea, and Venereal Diseases* 73 (1939): 104–122.

Index